THE PHILOSOPHY
OF SPIRIT

By

JOHN SNAITH

MCMXIV

CONTENTS

v .

CONTENTS

CONTENTS

CHAPTER I

WHAT IS TRUTH ?

A N exposition of the real nature of Truth must necessarily be based on a logical exposition of the nature of Thought, as expressed in its various forms of love, reason, self-consciousness (ego) and personality. Such an exposition will give us what we may call the science of God, nature and man. Science must be truth, and as such must be fixed, certain and unchangeable. Just as in the eighteenth century the term reason was used in a totally false sense, so now the name science has obtained a universal, though false, vogue. If, as ought to be the case, 'science' stands for established or discovered truth, then the present so-called science is as false and unsatisfactory as was the much-vaunted ' reason ' of the Age of Enlightenment. Present day science excludes from its realm all knowledge of God, declaring that scientific knowledge is based only on experience, a term which is interpreted to apply only to sense experience. Nothing, however, can exist independently of God ; the absolutely un-conditioned Being must be God, as the absolute condition of the sciences of psychology, cosmology and theology. At the same time God, without love, thought, reason and personality, could not be God, but would be merely an empty name. Love, thought, reason and personality when fully expounded are found to be

1   2

mutually necessary; love and personality cannot exist without thought; therefore without a science of Thought we cannot have the science of Truth. But this science exists in logic; i.e. the science of the nature of thought—the science of all sciences—embracing psychology, cosmology and theology. Psychology is the science of thought as manifested in the self-consciousness of man—it is the logical exposition of the soul as ego; cosmology is the logical exposition of the science of thought as manifested in nature. The old theologians defined theology as the science of God and divine things, but did not see that fundamentally this meant the science of the nature of thought, for God without thought is impossible. In the same way there can be no science of nature or of man that is not the science of thought. Thought is the fundamental element of logic, science and philosophy. Without thought I could not say I think I am I; the knowledge or experience gained by sense-experience alone, can never give any certainty, therefore science or truth can never be built upon such experience; in reality, however, the absolutely à priori element of knowledge is found in all sense-experience. Experience may be said to have two aspects or phases—the sensuous and the intellectual; thus a tree is on one side sensuous, but its essential nature is not really known until we recognize that it is living, and we only know what life is when we know that its essential nature is thought. When Christ said, 'the words that I speak unto you they are spirit and they are life,' the words are sensuously perceived, that is the letters may be seen or the sounds heard, but the meaning, which is the spirit or life, can only be intellectually perceived. The one aspect or phase could not exist without the other; the external and the internal are both essential to the apprehension of truth. All nature would be to us a perfect blank apart from thought; sense-experience alone gives no knowledge. A problem in square-root, though worked out fully and correctly on a blackboard, would be a mere mass of marks to an untaught eye; that is to say, without a knowledge of the thought involved in the explanation of the problem, such a problem would for ever remain a blank; sense-perception alone would give no explanation—only reason-thought can do that. Equally, God and nature would be nothing but a blank to a person possessed only of sense-perception; as Hegel says, ' the laws of the heavenly bodies are not written on the sky.' In the expression ' I think I am I ' we have the triple unity of being, thought and ego, as the living concrete totality of all that is. Being is all that is. Thought is all that is and the ego contains in itself all that is as the Absolute Personality of the universe. Ego without thought and being is nothing, just as God is not God without these. God of necessity is Absolute Being, Absolute Thought and Absolute Personality. When emptied of all particularity, being, thought and ego are mere names meaning neither more nor less than nothing means. Since, however, as a matter of fact, we do think such abstractions, and such abstractions are thoughts, we are at once back again to ego, thought and concrete being. Thought is being, and I is being, therefore being is thought, which is the Triple Syllogism—the absolute reason-thought of the totality of Being; that is of God and His universe. This Being is the absolute thought of all that is, and thought is the absolute being of all that is; Man as ego, as thinker, contains in himself the absolute unity of thought and being. This, then, is the proper qualification, definition, vocation and destination of man. The thought of absolute being is the absolute relativity of being, and this is the infinite and includes all that is finite. Since man in his thought thinks the infinite and absolute, the finite and relative, he is in his thought necessarily infinite, and this thought alone makes him to be in the image of God, as the Bible declares.

All human knowledge begins with and contains the triple experience of self, the world and God in the unity of thought. This triple unity in thought begins in its simplest or most meagre form in abstract being, which means neither more nor less than nothing means. It is very significant that in all our dictionaries ' nothing ' is defined as a noun or substantive.

Again, thought takes the three forms of Intuition, Reflection and the Logical Idea. Intuition is thought seeing and thinking itself in its own light ; reflection is thought seeing its own particularity as the universal ; while the logical idea is thought in the process of expressing the necessary relation of the soul, the world and God ; in other words, the particular and the universal are united in the ego as absolute self-consciousness. How, then, do we know that our logical reasoning is true ? It is because intuition accompanies all processes of reflexion and of logical reason ; only through intuition are we sure that the processes are valid or possess universal validity. It is only in the light of intuition that we are sure of the facts of reason-thought and of their relation to sense-facts. This is so because reason-thought is intuition, and shines and sees itself in its own light ; reason-thought is true faith, ' the substance of things hoped for, the evidence of things not seen.'

The term experience, since Kant, has played a most important part in science, philosophy and religion.

In the beginning of his *Critique of Pure Reason* he makes the statement that all our knowledge begins with experience, but he limited the term too much merely to the world of sense, and he declared it to be impossible to have an experience of, or to know the thing-in-itself, by which he means that we cannot have a direct experience of God and spiritual realities. He limited the term 'being' to what he held to be a mere logical copula, and thought that such copula possessed no reality. With him the notion of God does not involve the necessity of the being of God, which is absurd, for absolute being necessarily contains the being of God. In this way he abolished our logical knowledge of God and all reality, but being unable to rid himself of the thought of God, he fell back upon mere blind faith. His theoretical system of Pure Reason seemed to destroy the moral element of experience, therefore to remedy this defect he introduced the moral principles of his Practical Reason. Arguing that the moral element implied the existence of God as the moral governor of the universe, he abolished, as he states, our theoretical (logical) knowledge of God and all spiritual realities only to make way for faith. In these modern times experience has come to be regarded as the supreme test of truth, whereas experience is entirely unsatisfactory as the basis of true knowledge if not based on true reason or the logical idea, since we have now an almost infinite variety of religious and even of Christian experiences. As a consequence, such experiences are mere vagaries, reducing religion to a chaos of fancies and imaginations. Kant's *Critique of Pure Reason* rested ultimately on this subjective experience, which has no objective reality, and consequently gives no true knowledge of God. The modern science of Biblical criticism resembles in this respect Kant's criticism of reason. Kant's pure reason was merely abstract, not concrete, and gives no logical or philosophical exposition of the facts of existence ; thus it issued in a kind of agnosticism wherein reason was made to contradict itself, giving as result a mass of contradictions. Similarly the vaunted 'scientific' criticism of the Bible, dealing with what it calls the facts of the Bible in a superficial manner and not giving a real philosophical explanation of the great truths it contains, must equally lead to the questioning of the Divine authority of the Bible, and to agnosticism. Kant never imagined that his criticism would end in the overthrow of Christian faith, and the modern critics, equally illogical, claim by their results to be demonstrating the permanent value of the Bible, while in reality they only produce a mass of contradictions. The one objective reality pervading the Bible is the objective reality of God—the same reality which pervades the universe. It is this objective reality which gives permanent value to the Scriptures ; 'scientific' criticism, with its analytical methods, will never discover this objective reality, just as scientific dissection can never discover the operation of the spirit, life and being of God in nature. Experience is simply that through which a person passes in life, and may be either true or false ; experience alone is thus no guide to the discovery of truth. The old struggle between faith and reason seemed to culminate with Kant showing the futility of reason itself with regard to moral and spiritual questions— especially the question of the existence of God ; reason was helpless in trying to prove the reality of God's existence, so Kant called in the aid of faith and his practical reason. Hegel shows, however, that Kant had not attained to the true conception of reason, though he had attained to the true conception of the concrete notion. Kant's dialectic is mere sophistical reasoning; when his reason transcends sense-perception, it results only in what he calls dialectical illusions; while Hegel's dialectic is the innate activity of the ego developing itself in man to a knowledge of the Absolute Concrete Spirit. On one side the categories are sensuous, on the other intellectual. The logical dialectical evolution of the categories is that movement of thought in the ego which Hegel speaks of when he says, ' Only so is philosophy capable of being objective demonstrated science, and that is truth.' Hegel's dialectic is the essential activity of the Ego; it is equally the essential activity of thought and of all motion and change. The infinite succession of all objects of sense in time involves both change and creation; this dialectic is at once infinite activity and infinite negativity—a coming-to-be and a ceasing-to-be—involving an infinite process, for processless or inactive being is impossible. It is permanent, active and negative. The simple negative is what Hegel calls negation—the negation of the negation; the absolute affirmative is the inner permanent activity of thought (the Ego).

Kant's metaphysical and transcendental conceptions of time, space and physics (Natural Philosophy) do not at first form part of his Transcendental System of Logic, but they are treated as if independent; as if they existed externally to thought or Pure Reason. At the same time, he speaks of time and space as unlimited and infinite. How could he have conceived of space and time, as unlimited or infinite if thought itself, as one with reason and self-consciousness, were not unlimited? If space and time are infinite, as he states, then nothing could exist outside of or beyond them; but already his thought, his reason as the all-comprehending unity of the totality of being is embracing space in all directions, and time—past, present and future; the eternity of space and the eternity of time are both within his thought. No one can conceive of space and time as having either beginning or end; time is eternity—duration without beginning or end. The permanent in all time and space is, then, thought or spirit, which, to use the words of Paul, is ' All in all.' Infinite time and infinite space are now present in human thought, without which any human experience would be impossible. The eternity of time and the eternity of space would have no meaning apart from the eternity of thought. It does not, of course, follow that every separate individual has these thoughts consciously in his experience, but they are implicitly present, and only so is man a person—a being of infinite worth. Man is only a person because he thinks the infinite thought of God. This infinite thought now present in man did not begin with the empirical birth of an individual, neither will it perish at his death. There is nothing better or greater than thought; God is the best, therefore God is thought, and without thought He could not be God.

Ego is the body, soul and spirit of infinite space, which is infinite extension, just as ego is the term of greatest extension and greatest intension; it is at once infinite quality and infinite quantity, for quality is the essential nature of quantity; measure consists in the substantial unity of quality and quantity. In speaking of matter, Leibnitz remarks : ' It is not at all improbable that matter and quantity are really the same thing '; and Hegel adds : ' In effect these notions differ only in this—that quantity is pure notion, while matter is the same thing in outward existence.' Ego is thus infinite space and infinite time, since it includes both ; infinite space contains all finite spaces, and infinite time includes all finite times, just as infinite thought contains all finite thoughts; thus it is that infinite thought, infinite space and infinite time as such are permanent, and are only known by reason-thought, which transcends all finite limitations. But as known to us in their particular or transitory manifestations, thought, space and time are objects of sense-perception as creations in time. Hegel's 'Daseyn' is applied to the transitory forms of being—the finite changeable forms which belong to finite time—Being as being is permanent, while 'therebeing' is transitory.

This brings us to the consideration of what Kant terms his 'dogmatic slumber.' He had evidently become deeply interested in Newton's theory of universal gravitation, with its opposing forces of attraction and repulsion, otherwise named centripetal and centrifugal forces, which were conceived by Newton to act independently. These two forces gave to Kant the idea of a possible metaphysical construction of matter, from which he developed the nebular hypothesis to explain the origin of the universe. These forces he called the metaphysical elements of the construction of matter; but an examination of Kant will show that he simply accepted the two forces of gravitation. He did not in reality construct matter from these forces, but accepted matter as being already there, and used them after his fashion to explain the various motions of the heavenly bodies. For His construction of the universe Kant assumes the existence of a nebulous matter. This explains why Hegel says that with Kant God is only an Architect, not a Creator, for with Kant both matter and forces are assumed; they are not logically or scientifically developed. Kant's acceptation of this construction of the universe constituted what he calls his state of dogmatic slumber. He conceived that he had demonstrated metaphysically the construction of the universe from these two forces, but when Hume claimed to show, in dealing with the relation of cause and effect, that we had not the slightest knowledge of the tie between the two—that in the effect we cannot discern the tie which binds it to the cause, or vice versa, then Kant woke from his dogmatic slumber. Hume declared that the supposed necessary tie was only known to us by custom. Kant saw that Hume's reasoning resulted in scepticism. As Kant could not rest philosophically on mere custom, he was driven to the *à priori* basis of his transcendental philosophy, for by *à priori* Kant meant universal necessity. This *à priori* he found in his categories and in his original transcendental unity of apperception, for he held that the categories had their source in the transcendental unity of apperception. His inquiry began with the question, ' How are synthetic judgments *à priori* possible ? ' He endeavoured to attain synthetic judgments *à priori* by the analogy which he held to exist between the succession in time and the necessary sequence involved between cause and effect. (All sequence in cause and effect takes place in time, hence the idea arises of the necessary connexion between these.) To show by analogy the identity of the two sequences, Kant constructed a huge machinery—his schemata. Mere analogy, however, does not show the universal necessity, which indeed can only be found in the Absolute Infinite Reason-thought of man, that is, in the living thought of God manifested alone in this world in the finite self-consciousness of man. The principle of absolute identity can only be found in the immanent logical dialectical process of reason, and in this form of evolution alone can be found the principle

of demonstrated science. Kant's theory excluded
a knowledge of the universality of thought, and therefore, as we could not know the thing-in-itself, the
existence of God was necessarily unknowable. If
logic as the realm of pure thought, of logical thought,
fails as a demonstrated science to prove the existence
of God as universal concrete reason, then all moral
reflection about what ought to be, or about the moral
categorical imperative, is a mere makeshift. With
Hegel the demonstrated science of logic is what he calls
the logic of the ' pure self-evolving consciousness.'
' Nay, the Logic, he tells us, is to be understood
as the realm of pure thought—as God ' (Stirling's
Categories, p. 61). ' This realm is the Truth as it is
without or veil or hull—absolute ; and so it may be
said that this is the Darstellung Gottes ; the expression of God as He is in His Eternal essence before the
creation of Nature and a finite soul.' Thus Hegel
says : ' From the logical Idea the concrete Idea is
distinguished as Spirit, and the absolutely concrete
Idea as the Absolute Spirit.' Kant used his reason
to show that while we cannot prove by reason the
existence of God, yet the atheist cannot prove his non-
existence ; thus, God remains unknowable. The
aim of Hegel's Philosophy, on the contrary, is to
demonstrate that we possess a real knowledge of God,
and this is expressed by Stirling when he says :
' It (the Ego) alone is the middle term that is the
entire secret of the universe.' He who grasps fully
the science of the notion of the ego has obtained the
fundamental principle of personality, for only because
God and man are egos are they persons. The real
and essential nature of man consists in his intellectual
capacity of consciously thinking the infinite. Man
is therefore at once finite and infinite, because in
thought he transcends all limitations and thinks and

knows God. Thought is at once intuitive, reflective and logical, and the philosophy of personality, self-consciousness, ego, spirit, and thought reveals the fact that thought in man is infinite, and so far demonstrates substantially the identity of Divine and human personality. The Ego or I not only thinks, but the I itself is Thought as Spirit thinking itself as infinite. Now man is absolutely certain that thought as infinite did not come into existence at his birth. Infinite thought is one with the eternal, therefore the essential principle of human personality is one with the personality of God. Only so can man transcend the limits of his finite existence and know consciously in his thought that there is an infinite past, present, and future. Such thought is an infinite eternal ' now ' in man. This thought is the unity of man's personality in the personality of God. So there is only one infinite—the Finite I in the infinite I—at once Absolute and Relative. It is only a confusion of thought to say that this implies ' two infinites,' and it is also quite illogical to think that the idea of infinite thought in man is equivalent to saying, ' Be man no more ; be thyself God.' It is the thought of the infinite in man that distinguishes him from the animal. Green says that to know God we must be God ; on this mode of reasoning it would be as correct to argue that to know an animal we must be an animal, or that to know a tree we must be a tree. Every man, woman and child is a person or ego ; fundamentally the nature of every human being is identical, but even to the most superficial observer great differences can be seen between one person and another. What is it that constitutes the difference ? They differ in personality to the degree in which they have attained to the experiential and theoretical knowledge of God. No man has a true knowledge of God who has not experienced the love of God in his heart; this experience can only be realized by 'having the love of God shed abroad in his heart by the Holy Ghost given unto him.' We can only truly know God when we know what love is, and this knowledge of love is as certainly a matter of thought and intellectual apprehension as is the knowledge of any other fact in the common experience of human life. It is only when men and women thus truly know the love of God, and thereby realize in themselves the 'fulness of Him that filleth all in all,' that they rise to the full stature of their personality, or, as Paul says, ' come to the unity of the faith, and of the knowledge of the Son of God unto a perfect man, unto the measure of the stature of the fulness of Christ.' One of the saddest facts of this age of our boasted Christian civilization is that so few have attained to a real knowledge of the meaning of personality ; thus we have the glaring injustice of the denial of the full civil, political and religious rights to women as persons; and other hideous injustices are rampant.

In dealing with Newton's Mathematical proof of his theory of Universal Gravitation, Hegel might appear to anyone unacquainted with his philosophy to be attacking Newton's theory, but in reality he is doing no such thing. In his paper on *Whewell and Hegel*, Dr. Hutchison Stirling shows clearly that Hegel never in the slightest degree wished to detract from Newton's greatness as a mathematician. Hegel is not so much concerned with the physics and mathematics of Newton ; it is Newton's metaphysics alone with which he is dissatisfied and which he wished to replace with his own metaphysical doctrine of the notion. When the mathematico-physicists who believed that Newton was the greatest philosopher of his time thought that Hegel wished to cast doubt on the greatness of Newton's achievement, they declared that Hegel was not sufficiently versed in mathematics to be able to criticize Newton, failing to see that Hegel's Philosophy aimed at establishing the spiritual nature of gravitation. They began to pour contempt on his system of philosophy. This was especially the case with Dr. Whewell, Professor Tait and Robertson Smith, who did their utmost to misrepresent a philosophy, the aim and nature of which they never properly understood. Their furious denunciation tended to produce a widespread prejudice against Hegel's system. Robertson Smith's second reply in his counter-attack on Hegel and Stirling can only be dismissed as vulgar abuse, and was treated by Stirling as unworthy of notice. As Dr. Stirling says : ' Hegel is merely busied on metaphysical explanation and accepts physical facts and mathematical demonstrations towards it.' ' What Hegel seeks is the necessary demonstration of reason,' and this he finds in his doctrine of the Notion or the Ego. By the notion Hegel meant the nature of God, which neither Newton nor Kant included directly in his system of nature. ' No mathematical operation is adequate to discovery of a wholly new qualitative fact' (*Whewell and Hegel*, p. 90). Calculations based on mathematical analysis can in no sense explain the nature of gravitation, and this is what a science of truth requires. After Dr. Stirling's reply to Whewell's attack on Hegel it might be considered unnecessary to defend Hegel's position with regard to Newton, yet quite recently Dr. Peake remarks that Dr. Robertson Smith fully showed that Hegel and Dr. Stirling were both unable from a mathematical standpoint to criticize or even to understand Newton. No one at all acquainted with the works of Hegel and Dr. Stirling can doubt for a moment that both of them were as great mathematicians as, if not greater than, Dr. R. Smith. The latter thought he could reply on the mathematical point, as he says, without understanding Hegel's Philosophy; this lack of comprehension, however, puts him entirely out of the field, as he was quite unable to see the bearing of Hegel's philosophy on Newton's mathematical proof. Hegel only wished to vindicate the glory of Kepler as the discoverer of the laws of free motion of the heavenly bodies, and this vindication Whewell turned into an attack on Newton's mathematics. The following quotation from Dr. Hutchison Stirling's *Whewell and Hegel* makes Hegel's position very clear: ' Now, really, Hegel has nothing at heart but his metaphysic here; he has not the slightest idea of calling the physics or the mathematics as such bad, but only the metaphysic they involve. He admits that " Newton's form has not only its convenience, but also its necessity for the method of analysis "; but he observes, " this is a mere difference of mathematical formula," meaning thereby that the *reason* which he sees in the celestial motions is untouched by the mathematical processes, let them be what they may. It is only in reference to the single rational notion present in the phenomena that he demurs to the splitting up of that unity for mere mathematical purposes into lines this way for centripetal forces, and lines that way for centrifugal forces. Such fictions lie not in the notion, he intimates, and are mere conveniences for the mathematical operations which, in their own way, are certainly correct ' (p. 98).

Both Newton and Kant in their systems tended to rest satisfied with the merely physical as an explanation of the construction of the universe. Hegel held that no system of nature was rationally complete which did not include a knowledge of God as its substantial basis. With Newton and Kant God occupied too much a position outside of Nature as an external governor or regulator; with Hegel, on the contrary, God as Spirit constitutes the substantial essence of nature. No science of nature, God and thought that fails to recognize and explain the active power and essential freedom of thought or spirit is a complete science of logic or a science of truth. Freedom implies activity and denotes power in the manifestation. It is the unity of actual and potential energy of rational thought, and so denotes process. The process is the free power of thought, and as such it is the seat and spring of all natural and spiritual life. This, then, is the immanent dialectic of the Ego, or the movement, process and development of thought in notion, judgment and syllogism. Such a process contains in itself the principle of creation. There is no known object either in heaven or earth that is not full of thought—on one side finite and on the other infinite—external and internal; every object is a category of thought, and so a middle term in an absolute syllogism; for God as Infinite Thought is All in All. Even the materialist can have no scruples in speaking of universal gravitation as All in All, though he knows not what the force of gravitation is. The only force known in self-consciousness is the power of thought; all physical force is in its essence spiritual, and is essentially one with God as the self-consciousness of the universe. Just as human thought is essentially divine, so a philosophy of nature and of truth is utterly impossible apart from the logical philosophy of Thought or Spirit.

CHAPTER II

THE MEANING AND SCOPE OF PHILOSOPHY

BUT what is philosophy ? Considering the general employment of the word, it may appear superfluous to ask its meaning. The loose use of the term, however, by the pulpit and press at the present time shows the need for a fuller and more definite explication of its scientific import and scope.

It is often said, philosophy cannot do this, and philosophy cannot do that, in a way which shows only a dim conception of the real meaning of the term. Its etymological meaning is generally known, and is, so far, good—' Philosophy is the love of wisdom '—but just as Christianity requires us not only to love but to know God, so philosophy requires us not only to love but to know wisdom. Wisdom and love are, in principle one, without which no man is a man in the true sense of manhood, just as without wisdom and love God would be no God. True wisdom contains true love, and true love contains true wisdom, but neither love nor wisdom can exist independently : they are both necessary parts of thought, while, in turn, thought is impossible apart from personality, the personality of God, the personality of man, or of a being made in the image of God. Personality is the deepest, most essential and vital element of man's likeness to God ; wisdom and love are two most important attributes of God's nature, to be without which denotes in man the lack, in an important sense, of the true moral image of God, who is at once thought, love and wisdom.

Man, then, being a person, is a moral being with a knowledge of good and evil, and he is this even when he cannot be said to be good morally. Personality is fundamentally the intellectual image of God in man, in and through which alone, by the grace of God, he can attain to moral excellence, or, in other words, can realize in himself a true knowledge of the wisdom and love of God, and so, in the highest moral sense, ' be made a partaker of the divine nature.' Only a person can love wisdom, and so only a person can be a philosopher.

Love is not mere feeling and affection—for the animal possesses the instinctive impulses of feeling and affection—but its being, its life, its soul is thought. Thought also is the life and soul of wisdom, as it is the life and soul of personality and of the universe. Love, wisdom and truth are elements in true knowledge ; but in knowledge there is an important distinction between a knowledge of moral good, and a knowledge of moral evil. Will as will, as freewill, is thinking will, and as such can will either good or evil. The animal, because it is not a rational being, cannot will either good or evil.

There is also the distinction between a knowledge of facts and a knowledge of the relations of ideas —which is the essence of facts. The animal knows only sense facts, but cannot know their rational necessary nature. Only a being whose thought is infinite and absolute can be a moral being and can know the truth in its universal and fundamental nature. A knowledge of mere fiction may be very extensive, but it is not a knowledge of the Truth, and therefore not philosophy. Philosophy, then, properly understood in relation to man, is not merely earnest human search for the knowledge of the Truth, but is possession of the Truth itself. In the history of human inquiry after truth there have been many false theories advocated, and thus theory as theory has come to be very disparagingly spoken of, as if a true theory were impossible. We cannot but take for granted that the existence of truth is a fact; that there is a true theory of truth, and further, that this theory may be known with absolute certainty by man. If truth, then, exists and can be an object of human knowledge, it must of necessity take a theoretical form which must also be logical, for the science of Logic is fundamental in all true science.

Philosophy, to be worthy of the name, must be capable of being reduced to a logical system, otherwise our knowledge will be a mere aggregate of odds and ends, connected only in a rhapsodical manner. True philosophy is not only systematic knowledge, but it is essentially logical throughout its entire range, for the illogical is necessarily the untrue. Sound philosophy, then, may be named logical philosophy. According to Dr. Stirling : ' It is to thinking or thought that philosophy as a whole is due.' By his brilliant and elaborate exposition of the Science of Logic, he has revealed in the fullest sense the sure path by which a knowledge of the real and true may be obtained. He says : ' The proper name for Philosophy in this case would be Logic.'

Logic in an important sense is the science of thought, because thought is the ' middle term ' that contains in a rational unity All that is. Further, logic is the science of reason, because reason is the essential element of thought. Again, logic is the science of truth, for truth is the essential element in both reason and thought. In a higher sense and including these three definitions, logic is the science of the Ego and the Begriff (Notion), for, as Dr. Stirling says : ' Hegel's Begriff is conditioned, so to speak, by the personality of the Ego.' This logic, however, must not be mistaken for formal logic, or the logic of the understanding : it is the Logic of Reason—Concrete Logic ; the unity of form and matter. If the science of Logic is the science of the Ego, the science of the Ego must be the science of God, for God to be God must be perfect thought and perfect reason. Indeed, as Dr. Stirling says : ' The all of things would simply be reduced to Logic. Nay, Logic would supplant and replace Theology itself. The chaos of this universe, in fact, that stands before ordinary intelligence, would shapingly collapse into the law and order and unity of a single life—a life which we should understand—a life in which each of us should participate—modally.' ' And why should not Logic constitute the principle of the whole ?—what God has created must be an emanation of His own thought, of His own nature ; and do we not know that man, so far as he is a Spirit, is created in the likeness of God ?—why, . . . then, should not Logic, which is the crystal of man's thought, be the crystal also of God's thought, and the crystal as well of God's universe ? '

Logic, then, being the science of truth, reason, and thought, is also essentially speculative philosophy. The term ' speculative ' properly means to see, that is, to see the whole as whole—not merely in fragments, for the whole is seen in the part. It is reason-vision, and therefore exactly the opposite of mere guessing, conjecture, or hypothesis. It has no place for mere opinion any more than has mathematics. Speculative philosophy, then, is the absolute unity and process of intuition, and reason in true reflection. (Speculative philosophy belongs more especially to the exposition of the Ego, and is treated more exhaustively elsewhere.)

The Bible teaches the knowledge of God both as a possibility and a necessity in the attainment of human welfare, and certainly God can only be known in and through thought, which to be true must be logical. Paul teaches : ' that which may be known of God is manifest in them ' (men), ' for God hath shown it to them,' and ' the invisible things of God are clearly seen ' (in reason-vision) ' in the things that are made,' ' for the Spirit searcheth all things, yea, the depths of the Godhead.' The Spirit is thought, reason, which alone constitutes the substantial nature of man. Man's thought, man's reason, only needs to be purified or cleansed from all erroneous and impure thoughts, and then he will see God, for ' the pure in heart shall see God.' Rightly understood, logic is the true purifier, for God reasons with man in order to make him ' whiter than snow.' ' With the pure, God shows Himself pure.'

It has been said that states are not ruled by logic : no, but they ought to be. Until this is the case we will continue to move on false lines in seeking a true knowledge of pure Reason, of the nature of pure thought, of the essential nature of God and man, and of the essential nature of the universe. Apart from a close study and an acquired knowledge of Logic, science, in its subordinate sense, can never have a solid and substantial basis, but will be based chiefly on shifting hypotheses.

It is not difficult to see that the chief aim in Dr. Stirling's writings is the vindication of the truth of the Christian religion. He says : ' Kant and Hegel are the very reverse of the so-called " German Party "

with which in England they are very generally confounded.   It is the express mission of Kant, in effect,
to replace the negative of that party by an affirmative;
or Kant and Hegel—all but wholly both, and one
of them quite wholly directly—have no object but
to restore Faith—Faith in God—Faith in the immortality of the soul and the freedom of the will—
Faith in Christianity as the revealed religion—
and that, too, in perfect harmony with the right of
private judgment, and the rights, or lights, or
mights, of Intelligence in general.'   Again : ' Christianity is the revelation.   It revealed to a world
that sat amid its own ruins, with its garments rent,
and its head in ashes, the religion of Vision, of Love,
of sweet Submission.   The Hegelian system sup-
ports and gives effect to every claim of this religion.
And this, too, without any necessity to put out the
eyes of the mind and abdicate reason.'   ' The philosophies of Kant and Hegel only give definiteness and
distinction to the religion of Christ.   In Christ
the Vision was so utter into the glory and the beauty
of all, that it passed into love ; which, in its turn,
was so rich and utter that it passed into submission,
also itself the richest and sweetest ; and thus Perception, Emotion, Will, coalesced and were the same,
and the triple thread of man had satisfaction in
every term.   Now to all this Vision, and Love, and
Submission, Kant and Hegel give only the definiteness of the intellect ; that is, they assist at the
great espousals of Reason and Faith.'   With regard
to this principle Hegel says : ' In the Christian
Religion, however, this is peculiar—this person of
Christ, his Character to be the Son of God, does
itself belong to the very nature of God.   Were
Christ for Christians only a teacher like Pythagoras,
Socrates, or Columbus, then there were no universal

message, no revelation, no instruction respecting
the nature of God, in regard to which alone we desire
instruction.' ' God has revealed Himself in the Christian Religion—given us to know what He is ; so
that He is no longer something secret, something hidden
from us. With this possibility to know God, there
is now imposed on us the *duty* to know Him.'

If, then, Logic is the Science of Thought, Reason,
and of God, it must also be the Science of Man, of
Christ, and of Nature : and in the ultimate, all
must be involved in the Science of the Ego of ' I.'
As man in his thought is Ego, he is the starting-point
of philosophy.

The ultimate goal of philosophy, then, is the
exposition of the fundamental nature of Christianity.
This involves an exposition of Logic, Nature, and
Spirit, in their absolute essential relation. Christianity is based entirely on the Person of Christ, for
essentially Christ is Christianity, and Christianity is
Christ : and Christ is God, the God-man, Son of God
and Son of Man.

The philosophy of the Person of Christ is fundamental to the philosophy of Nature, the philosophy
of Spirit, and so also to the philosophy of Religion.
The philosophy of Christianity is the philosophy of
the totality of Being—or of All in All—the Ego (I).
It is the business of philosophy to expound the
rational nature and relationship of the individual,
the Church and the State. Logical philosophy is
thus required to explain the nature of the universal
bond of the totality of Being which is essentially
Thought, in and through which all things consist or
hang together. ' In a word, philosophy demands
an explanation of existence as existence ' in its
necessity and freedom ; as truth, in opposition to
error, it is the absolute idea, developed logically

from a single principle into a universal system of cognition—and that principle is the absolute self-conscious Ego, the Universal I ; and self-consciousness is Personality, which has its true manifestation in man, the image of God.

CHAPTER III

THE NEED OF A SOUND, CONCRETE, LOGICAL PHILOSOPHY

THAT a sound logical philosophy is a great and pressing need of the present day must be evident to all careful observers of the various conflicting currents of thought with regard to the nature of philosophy, of science, and of religion. For want of uncontrovertible, apodictic principles of thought, agnosticism, a term understood to refer chiefly to the unknowableness of God, meets with too ready approval and acceptance. Most of the earlier philosophers professed not only to believe in, but to know God : the main theme of our latest philosophers and scientists is that, logically, God cannot be known.

Huxley used the word ' agnosticism ' to denote the ' New Philosophy.' The term is utterly out of keeping with the ideas of true science, philosophy, and logic. No scientist, philosopher, or logician can be a ' consistent ' agnostic. What does Huxley mean by the term ? for he certainly claims to think, to reason, and to know. He speaks of four ignorances : first, we are ignorant of that which constitutes the necessary relation between cause and effect ; second, we do not know what substance is—we know the qualities of things but not their substance ; third, we know of no fixed element of certainty in the external world—all things are in essential change, therefore, for anything we know to the contrary,

25

anything may become anything; fourth, ' What
consciousness is we know not,' ' What I can know
must be in my consciousness,' but consciousness is
constantly changing, ' matter and spirit are but
names for the imaginary substrata of groups of
natural phenomena '—' matter ' and ' spirit ' are
names ' for an unknown and hypothetical cause or
condition of states of consciousness.' ' Fact I know ;
and Law I know ; but what is this Necessity, save
an empty shadow of my own mind's throwing ? '
He says : ' One great object of my essay was to
show that what is called " materialism " has no sound
philosophical basis.' ' The fundamental doctrines
of materialism, like those of spiritualism, and most
other " isms," lie outside the limits of philosophical
inquiry,' yet he says : ' With a view to the progress
of science, the materialistic terminology is in every
way to be preferred,' and ' We may express the
phenomena of matter in terms of spirit ; or the
phenomena of spirit in terms of matter.' Thus, in
spite of his ' agnosticism,' he is a dogmatist for the
gnosticism of what he calls science, which he thinks
gives him knowledge enough to demolish all certainty
of knowledge of theology and religion. He goes so
far as to say : ' Candid persons will admit that in
a different condition of things two and two may
not be four, and that two straight lines *may* inclose
a space.' Then he says : ' With scientific Theology
Agnosticism has no quarrel ' : but adds, ' The
scientific theologian admits the agnostic principle.'
If science were truth, this might be, but the science
which Huxley names demonstrative and which rests
merely on ' an inductive hypothesis ' is not truth.
Referring to Darwin's Theory of Evolution, he says :
' Its logical basis is precisely of the same character,'
' rests upon exactly as secure a foundation as the

Copernican theory of the motion of the heavenly bodies.' *His* ' New Philosophy,' his Reason and Logic are as utterly illogical and baseless as his so-called ·demonstrative evidence. Further, he says : ' I do not very much care to speak of anything as unknowable ' ; but confesses he ' once or twice used the word in this sense, even with a capital U.' If Agnosticism only means a confession of ignorance, why all this fuss ? It is no New Philosophy or new light. It is, however, intended to mean much more than such confession involves. According to Huxley, a sound philosophy does not concern itself with ' the truth of a particular form of Theology,' but with the logical philosophical form of Theology, but no trace of any attempt to find such a theology exists in his works. We may note here he prefers Hume to Kant. He holds that Hume was ' the most acute thinker of the eighteenth century—even though that century produced Kant.' Why does he do so ? Is it because Kant seeks in his *Critique of Pure Reason* to refute the scepticism of Hume's philosophizing ? It is also pertinent to ask why does he quietly ignore the *à priori* necessity and universality of Kant's cognitions and prefer Hume's false or empirical *à priori*, and then claim to have Hume and Kant on his side ? Yet Huxley, in all his reasonings and conclusions claims to be a philosopher as well as a scientist, and in defence of his Agnosticism appeals for confirmation of the soundness of his reasoning to Hume, to Kant's *Critique of Pure Reason*, Hamilton's *Philosophy of the Conditioned*, and to Dean Mansel's Lectures *On the Limits of Religious Thought.*

Herbert Spencer, the agnostic philosopher of evolution, considers his own system sound and good, but evidently thinks, with regret, that it has not been generally accepted because of his doctrine of the unknowableness of God. From the first, he professed to follow on the lines of Mansel, so far at least as Mansel's *Exposition of the Limits of Religious Thought* was concerned, while Huxley, though only late in life, tells us how he had been influenced by his early study of Mansel. Fiske, too, as we learn in his *Cosmic Philosophy*, based his [system chiefly on the ideas of Mansel, the acknowledged pupil of Sir William Hamilton; and the main theme of all these men is that logically God cannot be known.

Most influential of all Agnostics during the last half century was Darwin, who wrote much on evolution by natural selection, wishing thereby to explain and prove what he named the origin of species; yet in the end he professed to *prove* nothing, for he says : ' In fact the belief in natural selection must at present be *grounded entirely* on general considerations—we *cannot prove* that a single species has changed; nor can we explain why some species have changed and others have not,' and—' The cases discussed . . . are valuable to me (though odious and damnable) as showing *how* profoundly ignorant we are on the causes of variation.' Can this theory truly be called science, when the cause of the variation is unknown ? Is not science knowledge that is fixed, certain, established ? If not, then what is named science has no surer foundation than the ' superstitions ' which these scientists so much deplore in the Christian Church. Locke, Hume and Kant each limited the term *experience* to an immediate knowledge of finite objects. With them God was not and could not be an immediate object of experience. Only sense objects are to them immediate matters of fact, and exist independently of any known relation of ideas. Even with Locke the idea of God is not innate, and is not and cannot be matter of experience. With Hume matters of fact are limited to the testimony of our senses; so with him the mind can never possibly find the effect in the cause, even with the most accurate scrutiny and examination.

Kant says: 'All our knowledge begins with experience, but it does not follow that therefore it all derives *from* experience. For it is just possible that experience is itself a compound.' The other element of experience to which he here refers is the *à priori* element in his 'Transcendental Logic.' He holds that all our real knowledge is confined to objects of sense; transcendental logic is understood by him to supply the certainty in all our phenomenal knowledge. Further, he says that when Reason transcends the limit of our sense knowledge it loses all its substantial reality; for, with him, notion without perception is void. Thus the teleological and ontological arguments or proofs for the existence of God (He being not a matter of experience) are void of reality, and at best are only a basis for a blind faith in God.

We see, then, that in one form or another the philosophy of these men was agnostic in reference to the existence of God. Mansel bids us turn to the study of the Bible, where we find a revelation of God, especially through Christ, and he makes its divine authority to rest on the evidential value of miracles and prophecy. But if, in consequence of the limits of human thought, I cannot have a real, logical and experimental knowledge of God, a study of the Bible will avail me nothing. If the idea of God is not in man, no amount of study can create it in him; so my chief contention is that reason-knowledge infinitely transcends all sense-objects and is as truly a matter of experience as is a knowledge of sense-objects : consequently a sound theoretical philosophy alone can furnish to man a real and true *experience* of God, ' unto all the riches of the *full assurance of understanding,*' ' unto the perfect man,' and thus only can he ' be filled with all the fulness of God,' ' the fulness of Him that filleth all in all.'

All forms of philosophy are false which deny to man a true *experience* of God as *Infinite.* Equally false is any system that denies the essential and inseparable oneness of true religion and morality in Church and State. In fact, all knowledge, be it true or be it false, is matter of experience. Our aim is to show that logical philosophy is the demonstration of the real possibility of man realizing a true experience of God.

We must remember that no particular science of physics, chemistry, or of biology, nor all such sciences collectively, nor any natural experimental psychology so-named, has explained or can explain the eternal foundation of things. Yet without such an explanation it is impossible to understand the real distinction between true and untrue knowledge, true and untrue wisdom, the spiritual and natural man ; why the things of God are foolishness unto the natural man ; why a man's wisdom and knowledge may pervert him, as forcibly declared by Isaiah ; and why ' the spiritual man searches all things, even the depth of the Godhead,' according to the words of Paul ; or ' understands the mysteries of the kingdom of God,' according to the words of Christ. A sound logical philosophy cannot slur over these great sayings of Paul and Christ. The words of Hegel, which Dr. Hutchison Stirling makes his motto in his *Secret of Hegel,* express the same belief in the possibility of understanding these mysteries of life : ' The

Hidden Secret of the Universe is powerless to resist
the might of thought; it must unclose itself before
it, revealing to *sight* and bringing to *enjoyment* its
riches and its depths.' According to the present
general teaching of science, philosophy, and religion,
the above teaching of Christ, of Paul and of Hegel,
deals with subjects beyond our knowledge, in consequence, it is affirmed, of the limited intellectual
capacity of man, or because spiritual things are
beyond the sphere of logic.

It is also generally maintained that our knowledge
ultimately rests on hypotheses, among which the two
most important are the hypothesis of creation and
the hypothesis of evolution, the latter being declared
to hold the field in preference to the former. But
mere hypothesis is no more than mere opinion, and
so is not science, as it is absurdly claimed to be. We
hold that the hypothesis of evolution cannot be presented as a logical system of philosophy : our object
is to show that ' creation is no mere hypothesis, but
may be presented as a logical system of truth. Men
have come to regard deep and vital questions as mere
matters of opinion ; indeed, it is commonly said that
on these points there must be a difference of opinion.
This is not the verdict of reason, but a decision of false
philosophy. Reason only says there is a difference
of opinion, not that there must be ; or at least it does
not affirm that mere opinion is truth. ' An opinion,'
Kant says, ' is a view of any subject held on insufficient evidence,' while Grote says : ' Every opinion of
every man is true '—' as things appear to me, so
they are to me, and as they appear to you, so they
are to you,' and he wishes to confirm the truth of
opinion by saying, ' The reason of one man differs
most materially from that of another.' This shows
he had not grasped the true conception of Pure

Reason, which, as Milton says, ' is man's being.' Much the same confounding of opinion with reason is seen in Macaulay, for he asks, ' Whose opinion is to decide that ? ' Dr. Stirling says in reply to this: ' If it were a question of an Algebra, a Geometry, an Astronomy, a Chemistry, I suppose it would never occur to ask about the wisest and best, and whose opinion is to decide that.' He (Macaulay) did not know that a logical philosophy must be an exact science. We find, however, Paul's view is not in agreement with the idea of the necessity of difference of opinion. He prays that ' all may be perfectly joined together *in the same mind* and *the same judgment* '; and that is what is meant by ' keeping the unity of the Spirit in the bond of peace,' and ' if in anything ye be otherwise minded, God shall reveal even this unto you.' Paul, as a true philosopher, recognizes the possibility of men knowing the truth, for he speaks of their hearts being comforted, ' being knit together in love, and unto all riches of *the full assurance of understanding* to the acknowledgment of the mystery of God, and of the Father, and of Christ.' Thus, opinion is banished with Paul as in true Philosophy, when *the full assurance of understanding* is gained, just as is the case in any exact science.

The method adopted by the critics in what is called the Higher Criticism of the Bible, both before and since the time of Darwin, has never been strictly scientific. It has resulted in a mere collection of various opinions founded on insufficient evidence, and cannot, therefore, be called an exact science. This equally applies to what is named Christian agnosticism and evolution, for no evolutionist nor Higher Critic of the Bible dare venture to call his theory an *exact* science. They themselves cannot, with full assurance, call their methods logical, nor can the result of their investigations be named a logical philosophy. No theory or principle of interpretation of either Nature or the Bible can claim to be truly scientific if it is not strictly logical. If Nature and the Bible contain truth, then their truth, as such, must be logically rational, and must be based on true reason. True scientific principles are eternal. Every commentator and translator of the Bible is, in a sense, a philosopher, whether all his principles are logically sound or not. Each translates and explains according to a theory of knowledge which he possesses. As is well known, many translators differ in the meaning they give to many words ; thus, while there is much agreement among translators and commentators, there is also much difference of opinion. This is natural enough, for the same word, in all languages, has many different meanings. Hence, all agree that the spirit of the word is more vital than the letter, and yet many differ greatly in the treatment of both the letter and the spirit of the written word. It is obviously necessary to know the true meaning of both spirit and letter, for undoubtedly different persons attach widely-varying meanings to the same things when expressed in words. We are not aware that anyone seriously proposes to dispense with the letter of the word altogether. What, then, is its real value, and how can it be known ? What, indeed, is the spirit of the letter, but the true meaning of thought conveyed in the words ? We find, however, that a Catholic (Anglican or Roman), a Calvinist, and a Methodist, each has a different philosophy, and, as a consequence, a different theology and creed, each attaching a different meaning to the same word, in accordance with his philosophy. Yet there is only one true logical philosophy. Each

4

Church believes its adherents and members need to be taught, but the teaching of each differs in some important aspects. This could not be to the same extent if each Church possessed the one sound philosophy. All must admit that there can, in the very nature of things, be only one genuine philosophy or one true theory of the universe, and therefore one true philosophy of religion. All religious people profess to pray that they may be taught, illumined and guided by the same divine eternal Spirit. Romanists receive their religious teaching almost entirely through the priest, and they are not taught the need of the direct witness of the Spirit in themselves. Anglicans explain the Bible chiefly by the doctrinal teaching of their prayer book, though this is admitted to be a compromise between truth and error on many essential doctrines, so as to allow of different interpretations. Lutheran and Presbyterian Calvinists have been characterized by a strong suppression of emotion or feeling in their religious life, and have relied, it may be, too exclusively for their religious convictions, on cool metaphysical reflection. Their creed teaches the doctrines of the witness of the Spirit and the assurance of faith, yet the direct witness of the Spirit has not generally had a sufficiently prominent place in the individual religious life, and emotion has been too much suppressed. Methodists, while attaching in some respects great importance to preaching, to individual study of the Bible, and to what are considered its fundamental doctrines, have greatly undervalued metaphysical philosophy and have made ' the witness of the Spirit ' to depend too much on emotional excitement in prayer, without having sought sufficiently to understand the deep logical philosophical import of this doctrine. Nevertheless, the prominence given to the doctrine has made Methodism, whatever its lack may otherwise have been, a new force in the spread of a purer Christianity in the world. Yet, unless this doctrine is grounded on a sound philosophy, the danger is that a person may think he is taught by the Spirit when he is only led by the promptings of his own fancy. The history of the Evangelical Christian Churches at times of great spiritual awakening, furnishes many examples of fanatical zeal due to this lack of a sound philosophy. Fanaticism is a real danger, though many who have been called fanatics have been in reality the most sober-minded of men and women ; even Christ and Paul were called ' mad ' and ' beside themselves,' yet their love was real and deep—not a mere impulse, but a *real* thought full of burning zeal.

The same great need for a sound philosophy is evinced by the way in which prayer has been extolled in place of preaching the word, and to the depreciation of deep thought and study. Prayer is certainly an essential exercise in the cultivation and development of man's religious life and in promoting the universal spread of the gospel, for our dependence on God's Spirit is absolute. The philosophy of prayer must always form a vital part of the philosophy of religion—but to expect God, through our prayers, to become *more* willing to save and help men, presupposes too much that we are more loving and more anxious to save men from sin and ignorance than He is. Although God is already willing and anxious to do for every one of us all that He can, it is nevertheless a fact of reason that ' prayer moves the Arm that moves the world.' Still, Christian men need to learn that God has adopted the only way in which He can save the world, and that He requires them to be the light of the world. If God could have saved men by a direct influence exerted upon them apart from the influence of Christian character and the light of the written and spoken Word, there would have been no need for the work of Christ, nor for the toil and incessant self-sacrifice of Paul and the other apostles. No ! the same arduous training, study and labour are needed now as then. A great gathering of men to God is still the burden and work of His spiritual body—the Church on earth—and it is only by the knowledge of a sound logical philosophy of nature and of the Christian religion that His Church can be perfectly equipped for the work. A Church may have ' a name to live ' and yet be dead. This is sadly too much the case at present : hence we hear of the monstrous thing called Christian Agnosticism. God, too, is named a being higher than personality, supra-personal, while what is currently called Natural-ism has taken the place of Biblical Christianity.

This same great need for a sound philosophy is apparent when we consider the conflicting views as to what constitutes a true conscience ; for different consciences cannot all be true and good. Men have perpetrated the most horrible persecuting deeds in the name of conscience, of God, and of Christ, and in the professed interests of the Christian Church, believing they were ' doing God service.' Paul in his conscience believed he was doing God service by haling the followers of Christ to prison, just as the religious Jews and their teachers thought they were doing God service in killing the Lord Jesus. A man fancies his motive is good and pure because his chief aim is good ; in this way the terms ' good intentions ' and ' good motives ' are used as excuses or reasons for many wrong actions. In fact and in truth, no higher motive can actuate a man than to do God service, or to serve man in God's name, by clothing the naked, succouring the poor and needy, and preaching the Gospel to the poor ; yet men may have these motives ruling in their minds while doing evil acts and thinking evil thoughts. In their blindness, they fondly think they are doing God service, yet at the same time they are marring both themselves and their work. The thought that they were doing wrong in crucifying Christ and in persecuting his disciples never entered the mind of Paul or of the Jews. This blindness is too common in all our Churches at the present time.

It is also very important to understand the true meaning of ' Private Judgment,' especially at the present time, when what constitutes right judgment is often regarded as a matter of opinion. This is a good and sound principle when rightly understood, but a judgment is not right and good merely because it is private. Both private and public judgment may be wrong. The Roman Catholic Church condemns the right of private, or individual judgment, but the agreed judgment of millions of individuals may be wrong while the judgment of one man may be right, as Paul's judgment with regard to the intercourse between Jewish and Gentile Christians was right, while Peter's was wrong, although the majority of the Christian Jews held similar views. Luther's, Wesley's, and Bourne's private judgment was right, while the Catholic, Anglican and Wesleyan Churches respectively were decidedly wrong in their treatment of these men. The judgment of the Roman Catholic Church on very vital Christian doctrines has very frequently been wrong : in fact, the judgment of any Church, Protestant or otherwise, or of any single individual, is only right when it coincides with the universal judgment and will of God, and this requires that all men individually should have a correct conception of *right reason*, or of *logical* philosophy. We find that although at the Reformation the right of private judgment was affirmed as a principle in contrast with the Roman Catholic doctrine of Church authority, it was not philosophically explained on the principles of true reason. The same is true with regard to the *Aufklärung* or eighteenth century enlightenment, falsely called the ' Age of Reason.' The men of this period boasted of being ' Free Thinkers,' which was their mode of interpreting the right of private judgment. It must, however, be seen that true private judgment is not merely subjective, but also objective ; and that the individual judgment is only truly objective when it is one with the universal will of God.

Many false and conflicting views are at present prevalent as to the nature of faith. Faith is commonly regarded as mere ' assent and consent ' to any tenets, even though there may be no knowledge of their meaning or truth. But ' assent ' and ' consent ' are often given to tenets and doctrines which are false as well as to those which are true : yet this is called faith. True faith is grounded *alone* on truth, whilst false faith is based on untruth or error, and, in fact, is mere superstition. Baptismal regeneration, priestly absolution, transubstantiation, papal infallibility, and many other accepted doctrines, are elements of mere superstition, even though buttressed by the sanction of a Christian Church. Such doctrines are not grounded on true reason, and no amount of mere ' assent and consent ' can make them true. The same is true with regard to the now popular faith in the doctrine of evolution. Since Darwin, this doctrine, or theory, has assumed several different forms, but none of its advocates dare declare that it is scientifically established. It is only a hypothesis, not an absolute certainty (which alone is true science), yet this is the foundation doctrine of the faith of thousands who profess to be above ' bold guessing ' and superstition, whether in physical science or religion.

Cardinal Newman despised reason and sound logic, and thought he was honouring God by relying on the authority of the Church. He says : ' Faith assents, not because it sees with the reason, but because it was told by one who comes from God.' This is the ground of the Oxford Movement in England ; and there is no remedy but in a sound philosophy. True reason is God, just as God is light, love and truth. To regard faith and reason as antagonistic is to have a false view of both, for the two contain essentially the one the other. Take either apart, as absolutely separate, and they are mere empty names, void of any genuine reality and ideality. Christian faith is not a void, or matterless thought, but contains a substantial body of doctrines ; it is not blind or reasonless, but is intellectual sight, or insight. When Paul, the Christian philosopher, said : ' We walk by faith, not by sight,' he did not mean that the true Christian walks blindly—ignorantly, but rather with intellectual insight—not by mere sense sight. True faith, then, is *confidence* in reason-sight : *seeing* the eternal and invisible, that is, seeing the permanent in the transitory. With Paul, ' Faith is the *substance* (or reality) of things hoped for.' It recognizes that Pure Reason is the universal substantial reality of the universe in a universal pure Personality, an increasing knowledge of which every pure-hearted person hopes more and more to realize. ' Faith,' too, ' is the evidence of things not seen.' Faith sees and shines in its own light ; it transcends the limit of mere sense-knowledge, and as such it 'understands that the worlds were framed by the word (or thought) of God, so that what is seen hath not been made out of things which do appear.' It realizes increasingly 'all the full assurance of understanding of the mystery of God, and of the Father, and of Christ.' This faith was most fully and clearly possessed by Christ Himself as the Son of Man. If faith did not contain reason-vision and 'the full assurance,' Christ would not have declared that men's lack of faith in Him was sin. What is named 'your most Holy Faith' cannot refer to, and mean the acceptance of and reliance on, gross error. Faith that rests on mere hypothesis is not Christian Faith, whatever else it may be. Christian Faith and religious superstition have 'no part or lot' with each other. An increase in Christian faith always involves an increase of true knowledge ; a lack of faith means a lack of understanding of God and of Christ. When Christ increased the faith of His disciples, He did so by opening their understanding through giving them a fuller exposition of the things of God and of the Scriptures concerning Himself. Progress of faith calls for a deeper insight into logical philosophy, and this is the greatest and most vital demand of the present age : a demand greatly ignored.

A true science of reason, of thought, or of logic, or whatever it be named, has been the great lack of all the ages. This, Hegel and Dr. Hutchison Stirling have discovered and completed as a Concrete Logic, so far, at any rate, as its fundamental principles are concerned. Until Hegel, Aristotle furnished the nearest approach to a concrete logic of God, of man, and of nature—not in what is regarded as his formal logic, but in his metaphysics. Kant's transcendental logic contained, in principle, the Concrete

Notion, but it lacked the concrete logical development of the categories of Being or Thought, the reflective and relative determinations of the essence of Being, and the logical functions and determinations of subjective thought, wherein and from which their objective reality demands and acquires its permanent validity and apodictic certainty. In Kant's system, experience is without a fixed basis for a subjective and an objective knowledge of the truth, and thus is as untrustworthy and unreliable as the ever-changing wind of mere opinion and the various freaks of fancy. Indeed, a true experience in the fullest sense can only be realized when based on a sound philosophy.

Above all, a sound philosophy is essential to efficient government both in Church and State, especially in its bearing on a sound national system of education. The training of the youth of a country ought not to be in any sense sectarian, but rather truly national and efficient. All schools, colleges and universities should be under the direct control of, and financially supported by, the State. The true instinct of reason is in man, in and through which he may rise, if he will honestly follow the divine impulses; still, training, instruction and discipline are not thereby rendered unnecessary. Hence the necessity of State government and educational institutions being based on the principles of sound logical reason, or, let us say, of divine logical philosophy. Neither the head of a State nor any subject enjoys true freedom if the government be not based on sound reason. In the strict sense of the words, either an autocratic or a democratic form of government is impossible, and it ought not to be necessary for the King or President to be either an autocrat or a mere dot on the 'i.' His veto should be constitutionally limited.

Government by majority has come to be a kind of fetish, in spite of the fact that the majority of a nation is necessarily the most ignorant part of it, and includes those who are the least acquainted with what is necessary for the highest development of the State. Sound philosophy would set aside that form of party government which requires a man to vote for or against a measure, or to be neutral, merely to retain his party in power. By the minority is not meant the rich, for these are seldom the most enlightened : riches for the most part promote conceit and highmindedness through their deceitful working in the mind of their possessor. The real enlighteners of a nation have always been few in number, seldom rich, but generally persecuted or ignored, until by sheer force of thought, and not without great anxiety and pain of mind, they have compelled attention. The few have always been, and always must be, the instructors of the many : though, as true knowledge becomes general, the few will become many. Christ in His teaching clearly revealed what ought to be, but He could not persuade the rulers, teachers, or the people generally, to understand and accept His teaching, and this has been the case in every age and country. It is the same to-day. In matters of government and education no people can rise above its real intellectual apprehension of Truth. The Greeks killed or banished their philosophers, and as a result their national power and skill gradually declined. Reason demands that the State must recognize the constitution and sphere of Church government, while the Church must recognize the State as a divine institution. Both are fundamentally divine, and necessary the one to the other, while the sacredness of the family and the individual is necessary to both Church and State. The corrup-

tion of Church doctrine leads to a corruption of
State legislation and of the State administration of
law, while injustice from the State to the Church
injures the State itself. In carrying out its divine
mission, the Church must possess property in land,
just as the family and individual do : a Church building cannot be erected in the air. Both Church and
State, however, often act unwisely towards each other,
the one trying to coerce or overrule the other ;
hence have arisen many cruel persecutions. This
is the conflict between truth and error, knowledge
and ignorance, honesty and dishonesty, which conflict is practically and theoretically the cross of
Christ.

Before it can exercise a due influence in the government of either Church or State, a sound philosophy
must be known, and only so will false ideas of
liberty give place to the true. While there is so
much talk about honest doubt, and ' philosophic
doubt,' human society cannot reach its true goal.
What is required is a genuine, which means a rational,
intelligent faith : not a blind faith, which is mere
superstition ; not a faith based on hypothesis, but
a philosophic faith based on reason at once divine
and human—and that is the Divine Ego in its logical
exposition.

CHAPTER IV

THE NEW THEOLOGY—UNSCIENTIFIC

THE public religious mind has recently been much perturbed by what is called the New Theology. The Rev. R. J. Campbell is recognized as its chief exponent, who himself says of it, ' The new theology is the religion of science,' meaning thereby that it is based on the two theories of agnosticism and evolution, which theories have captured the higher criticism. Dr. Orr has best shown from what source these new views took their rise, but it is to be feared that agnosticism, evolution and the higher criticism of the Bible have got too deeply seated for his views to be seriously regarded. Unscientific theology has now the pull, just as a distinguished author was once warned by his publisher that it was ' the No-God men who had the pull at present,' so at the present time *opponents* of these new views are not likely to be listened to. Professor Orr says : ' The kind of theology of which Mr. Campbell has made himself the mouthpiece—one might say, the trumpet—is at present in the air. It represents a tendency, a type of thought, a mode of speech begotten of the age, constantly being met with in books, newspapers, magazine articles, public utterances of would-be public men, that needs to be taken account of. As everyone that has eyes to see must be aware, the thing has been smouldering below the surface in all the Churches for a considerable while, and was bound to come out. I am only thankful it has broken out where it has, and not elsewhere. There was needed a clearing of the atmosphere, which this book of Mr. Campbell's, written with such a surge of passion and earnestness, that speak to the author's intense belief in himself and his message, will help to bring about. This is where good people mistake, who fulminate at Mr. Campbell as if his so-called " New Theology " was only a perverse outburst of his own, instead of being, as it really is, a very significant indication of the spirit of the time.' There you have the whole case in brief. I prophesied forty years ago that sooner or later the present confusion in philosophical and theological thought must arise. It is principally to be attributed to the spread of a falsely-named scientific philosophy.

Now we affirm that the New Theology is unscientific, and why ? Because the New Theology is based on what is now named the New Philosophy, which denies that man's thought is infinite, and this involves the denial of the true conception of Human Personality, and therewith the true knowledge of the Personality of God. The new philosophy is based on a false conception of Induction and Deduction. True Induction begins from the Ego (I), as the term denoting the absolute universal Thought or Notion, which is at once the term of greatest extension and greatest intension. The Ego as thought includes All and means All ; as such it is ' All in All ' ; it includes all thought and all being. Induction is the thought of absolute being that brings into, and realizes in itself, the Absolute and Infinite particularity of the universe as the one Totality of Being and Thought in absolute unity. Deduction begins from absolute Being of Thought, and is, when fully carried out in all its logical detail, the absolute specification of every category of being and thought of the Ego in all its infinite detail. In principle induction and deduction are the same as the Thought or Notion of the greatest extension and the greatest intension. They resemble, *so far*, the integral and differential calculus—the one denoting absolute unity, the other absolute difference—all in the unity of the Ego ; or, speaking logically and theologically, all in the unity of the Godhead, the absolute Creator of all things visible and invisible in heaven and in earth. The ' I,' then, of absolute universal *thought* is that which Stirling says ' shall be the ultimate of the universe ! It, and it alone, as it is the *last* of *induction*, shall be the *first* of *deduction*.'

The New Theology is unscientific because it rests on mere induction based on a collection of more or less superficial analogies. It is in its form and content devoid of an absolute universal middle term, without which demonstration is impossible. Aristotle saw clearly that all scientific investigation and demonstration has reference to the discovery of the Middle Term. Induction based on particulars alone proves nothing, even though the particulars are such general terms as animal and plant. The only true universals are such as explicitly express the universal and real *nature* of thought, reason, spirit, self-consciousness, Ego, personality, man, God. In the perception of the necessity of an absolute universal middle term in true science, Hegel was forestalled by Aristotle. In our modern inductive science the infinite personality of thought in God and man is only rated at the value of a mere *abstract infinite* or non-finite, a general mist—the unknown God of agnosticism.

The self-conscious thought of the universe is concrete, and self-conscious concrete thought is spirit, is personality. Apart from the thought of self-conscious spirit, no true demonstrative science is possible, for that is not true science which cannot be demonstrated. Spirit as Spirit, in its very nature, is essentially concrete, never purely abstract. The human spirit in its thought is absolutely Universal and Individual and contains in itself the Absolute and Infinite Particularity of the Universe in its Absolute Totality, and is therefore absolutely one with the Thought and Being of God. To rate the self-conscious spirit of man as an *abstract* infinite is ' the lie and the bad,' because it involves the denial of infinite concrete thought in the personality of man, and therewith the denial of a *knowledge* of the infinite concrete personality of God. It is the same ' lie and bad ' that Christ refers to when He says, ' If I should say I know Him (God) not, I should be a liar like unto you.' He said to the Jews, ' I know that ye have not the love of God in you.' The personalities of man and God are abstractions or abstract infinites, so though all think God, they only realize their true personality when they truly love God and their fellow-men. Love is the bond of perfection ; the means by which man attains to a real knowledge of God. Thus their ' lie ' consisted in not loving God, even though they professed to believe that He was their Father. So Christ said, ' If God were your Father, ye would love Me, for I proceeded forth and came from God. Ye are of your father, the devil. For he is a liar and the father of it.' Paul refers to the same fact when he says, ' All have sinned and come short of the glory of God,' and that man in his vain glory had changed ' the truth of God into a lie.'

Again, the New Theology is unscientific because it limits the conception of morality to the love of man, whereas morality consists essentially in loving God with all the heart as the supreme moral governor of the universe. Thus God is the essence of morality and of religion, which have their identity in the perfect law of love, manifested in and through the perfect personality of Christ, whom Paul names ' the perfect man.' Thus ' the lie and the bad ' in philosophy and the Bible consists in not loving God supremely. A philosophy or science that denies to man the concrete thought of the Absolute and Infinite is unsound to the core, for it denies to him a knowledge of God as Infinite Personality, named by Hegel ' the Universal-est Personality ' ; such knowledge is not the direct sense-knowledge of some corporeal object, but of God, the absolutely universal object as Spirit of all Spirits.'

(Hegel's philosophic exposition of ' the lie and the bad ' is an extraordinary feat, though not presented in very intelligible language.)

The New Theology denies to man a knowledge of the personality of God, but professes to know that an infinite and eternal energy exists. When a man intelligently says, Energy, it must be evident he thinks it, and knows the meaning of the term. We speak of potential and active energy, but what is potential is only known by its essential unity with active energy. Potential by itself is an empty abstraction ; apart from actuality it is Nothing ; but in man's thought it is in himself a well-known active power in his real Being. So when a man with intelligence says, ' Infinite and Eternal Energy,' it is evident that he not only thinks what energy is but also what infinite and eternal energy is. The infinite is a real actuality in thought and being, and includes eternity, while eternity includes absolute infinity. Infinite and eternal energy, then, are three thoughts in man ; three thoughts in one ; and it is man who thinks this infinite and eternal energy, which again is the infinite and eternal thought of man, otherwise he could not say it, any more than can the animal. This infinite and eternal energy is infinite and eternal reason, infinite and eternal spirit, infinite and eternal self-consciousness, infinite and eternal personality or Ego (I) the infinite and eternal God, whose thought and being in man make him a person in the image of God. Man's thought of the infinite is not an infinite abstract, but an infinite concrete. As we have said, man is only a person because his thought is infinite ; deny that man's thought is infinite, and you deny the personality of man. All beings who think the infinite, think God, and this involves at once the substantial personality of both God and man.

The modern critical exposition of the first three chapters of Genesis is based on the principles of the new philosophy and the new theology, and is therefore unscientific.

We are told by an evolutionist that ' The Copernican astronomy upset the geocentric theory on which the Church built so many of its earlier assumptions,' and that ' Geology played havoc with the infallibility of Genesis.' But the geocentric theory of Astronomy is not taught in the Bible. The Roman Church accepted the Ptolemaic theory, the false science of a previous age, and then endeavoured to palm it off as the Bible theory. It accepted many other false doctrines, just as now the leaders in our Protestant Churches would have us believe that the Darwinian theory is in perfect accordance with the teaching of the Bible. The geocentric theory had not been scientifically established, nor has the theory of evolution been proven. To say the least, it is very rash and unscientific to declare that ' Geology has played havoc with the infallibility of Genesis.' If this refers to a supposed creation of the Universe in

5

identical, and by the light of knowledge the darkness of ignorance is made visible. So because the light of God is eternal and God is the Eternal Creator of all things visible and invisible, day and night, light and darkness, belong eternally to mere natural things, and can by their externality be revealed to the Spirit of man by the Spirit of God.

It may be doubted by some whether the words, ' the earth was without form and void,' are a correct translation, as this seems to convey the idea that the earth could once have existed without content and form. Some translators think that the phrase would be better rendered, ' the earth was not a desolation,' but be this as it may, the words, ' the spirit of God moved upon the face of the waters,' make this more than probable, as being more in accordance with the nature of things as the work of God. Certainly astronomy teaches that law and order everywhere prevail in the movements of the heavenly bodies. Matter, form and reason cannot in the nature of things be separable, just as the created worlds of light and darkness are inseparable. Then, since God must be eternal light, and light and darkness are essentially objects of sense-sight, the natural inference is that the first five verses of the first chapter of Genesis were to the writer a mere statement of matters of fact in necessary relation of ideas of sense-perception and reason in the unity of reality and ideality. In this way the writer presents God as the rational and logical beginning of the universe, whether visible or invisible. Man as a rational being is absolutely sure that very little of Nature is open to sense-vision, but the whole, as whole, is open to reason-vision. The detail of the whole, though not expressed philosophically, is always present and open to logical knowledge, in the same way as are the details of geology, astronomy, and other sciences. The writer of Genesis here only states the philosophy of Nature in brief universal terms.

The science of astronomy in its wide range of sense-vision, in unity with infinite reason-thought, points conclusively to the infinity and eternity of the universe as the creative work of God, for God as *Eternal Creator* is the necessary demand of Reason. Geology has not destroyed the truth of Genesis, namely, that God is the *eternal beginning* of this earth of ours and of the entire universe. It is mere assumption to say the Bible teaches that heaven and earth and all therein were created in six natural days : it plainly says, ' they were created in the day that the Lord God made the earth and the heaven,' and that is an eternal day.

With the writer of this account, the invisible bond and subsistence of all creation in all its parts was God. The invisible God as Spirit was to him the real-ideal, or the ideal-real of all things visible to sense-sight. Thus man made in the image of God as a self-conscious being was the crown of creation, for only such a being is capable of dominion. Of course, the geological history of the world was then necessarily unknown ; besides, it formed no part of the purpose of the record to give an account of the eternal history of the earth, sun, moon and stars, excepting to make it clear that God is the eternal beginning of all things.

The new philosophy, on which the New Theology is based, ridicules the idea of the supernatural in Nature. Huxley says : ' I am unable to perceive any justification for cutting the universe into two halves, one natural and one supernatural.' The terms ' natural ' and ' supernatural ' have always meant the one physical and the other spiritual. Yet Huxley himself says : ' In itself it is of little moment whether we express the phenomena of matter in terms of spirit; or the phenomena of spirit in terms of matter; matter may be regarded as a form of thought, thought may be regarded as a form of matter—each statement has a certain relative truth. But with a view to the progress of science, the materialistic terminology is in every way to be preferred.' To speak of ' cutting the universe into two halves ' may appear smart, but who has ever attempted to do so, even speculatively ? It is simply an utter misrepresentation of the attitude even of the old metaphysical philosophy of theology. Now, the whole of Huxley's science and philosophy in his demonstration of the theory of evolution rests on what he calls an inductive hypothesis. Darwin, in a letter to Hooker, speaks of having been ' much struck with Huxley's philosophy of induction." His (Huxley's) strong point in proof of his inductive theory of evolution is the evolution of the hoof of the horse. The horse he holds to have been derived from some quadruped which possessed five complete digits on each foot, which he considers to be analogous to the five digits of the human hand and foot. Four digits somehow die off, and the middle one, being more exercised during untold millions of years—how many is of no moment—becomes the hoof. This kind of reasoning is also applied to the cases of the ass, zebra, and quagga. It is unnecessary to follow him through his entire process. The whole of his argument rests on ' inductive hypothesis,' and we may add, on widely disconnected superficial analogies, such as that between the toes of a man and the toes of a quadruped. In reference to this case he says: ' This is what I mean by demonstrative evidence of evolution.' Now, Induction based on particular facts furnishes no demonstration, and is no more than a mere hypothesis.

Huxley's analogy between the theory of evolution and the Copernican system is false, because what he calls, and mean by, 'demonstrative evidence of evolution' is *not* demonstrative evidence, and never can be, and its logical basis is *not* of precisely the same character as the Copernican theory of astronomy. His evidence of 'the evolution of the horse from the Orohippus' is not logical, because he can furnish no proof, whereas the Copernican theory was logical from first to last and was not based on a mere Inductive hypothesis, as is the theory of evolution. The Ptolemaic theory was based on false reasoning from sense facts, but, according to Kant, 'The Copernican theory started from logical principles, by which reason according to unvarying laws compelled nature to reply to its questions,' for, as he says, 'Reason must not approach Nature as a pupil, but in the character of a judge, and must compel Nature to reply to those questions which he himself thinks fit to propose. To this single idea must the revolution be ascribed.' With Kant the idea of reason was supreme in philosophy, for, as he says, 'Objects must conform to thought, and not thought to objects.'

Strictly speaking, Hume is the founder of this so-called New Philosophy, and not Kant, to whom Huxley wished to ascribe it. Hume stated the problem of philosophy as follows : 'All our reasonings concerning matters of fact seem to be founded in the relation of cause and effect,' 'the mind can never possibly find the effect in the supposed cause by the most accurate scrutiny and examination. For the effect is totally different from the cause, and consequently can never be discovered in it.' 'It may, therefore, be a subject worthy of curiosity to inquire what is the nature of that evidence which assures us of any real existence and matter of fact beyond the present testimony of our senses or the record of our memory.' Hume ignores the à priori of Kant.

Now this position of Hume drove Kant to the à priori, that is to say, to his dialectic logic, *the system of the categories*, and to their source in ' the original synthetic unity of apperception,' which he called ' the transcendental unity of self-consciousness (the Ego).' If Kant had logically developed his system of philosophy from the Ego, as did Hegel, he would have solved the problem of Hume, for the whole genuine system of logical philosophy has its foundation and source in the Ego, the original unity of self-consciousness. Unfortunately, he failed to see the real depth, breadth and fullness of this simple ground principle of philosophy, and resorted to a supposed analogy between what he regarded as succession in pure time and the sequence of cause and effect, although he says, ' *Time cannot be perceived*,' and further, ' the " I am " and " I think " is neither a perception nor a notion, but a mere consciousness,' so that the personalities of man and God became in his hands mere unknown things in themselves. This result of Kant's critical philosophy is substantially the new philosophy of Hume and Huxley. Hegel, however, saw that Kant's Original Identity of the Ego in Thinking (the Transcendental Unity of Self-consciousness) as the special ground proper of the Categories was substantially one with the old theology, wherein the real personality of man and God are known in their truth. The old theology always recognized the strict omnipresence of God as substantially one with what Hegel means by *Der allgemeine Begriff der Logik*, or the universality of the Ego, or of God, even though the nature of God as absolute Spirit had not been, so far, logically expounded. Hegel would have nothing to do with an *unknown* God ; God with him was a *known* God, ' in spirit and in truth,' just as is taught in the Bible.

To attempt to philosophize with an unknown God shows the unscientific nature of the new so-called scientific philosophic theology.   The God of the Agnostics is beyond the real self-conscious thought of man, and is, in fact, no God at all.   The term *subconsciousness* has become very popular with the adherents of the New Theology and the new philosophy, though in reality it is absurd, for there is nothing below, beyond, or above consciousness.   It is used to signify what is improperly named conscious or consciousness, for it is unscientific to speak of a consciousness below consciousness in man, or to call any chemical process in man's physiological organism a subconscious activity.   *Subconsciousness* and *pragmatism* have in them no real scientific principle.   The subconscious mind is absurdly supposed to throw valuable light upon the mystery of human personality, and to be the seat of inspiration and intuition, while Pragmatism absurdly teaches that man can only know the difference between truth and error after they have shown their good or evil effects in practice, and that the only test of truth is, ' Does it work well ? '

Pragmatism is said to have been a disturbing force in Oxford through its opposition to Hegelianism there, though the Hegelianism of Oxford was never anything but a caricature of Hegel's Philosophy.   The philosophy of T. H. Green was named Neo-Hegelian, as if it were an improvement on the *principle* of the philosophy of Hegel, though in reality it was a distortion of Hegel's teaching under the guise of a correction. Professor James himself, as we have already noted, has told us that he does not know what Hegel means by Dialectic : while Dr. Horton, another new theologian, in a recent book, says that the philosophy of Hegel will turn out to be nothing but a narcotic—not a stimulus. This shows how little Hegel's philosophy is understood by leading Nonconformists.

The New Theology claims to give a vaster and grander conception of God than the old theology, and speaks of God as being that mysterious Power which is finding expression in the universe; this mysterious power is 'infinite', but what 'infinity may be we have no means of knowing,' and so 'the most devout Christian is just as much an agnostic as Professor Huxley.' This, we are boldly told, 'is the religion of science.' Thus we have no means of understanding the immanence of God excepting in 'finite forms,' and in the person and teaching of Christ. But if God is merely the immanent unknown Power, and is not known as an infinite Person, then He as the immanent Power in Christ is still unknown. Now this mode of presenting the Immanence of God is utterly unscientific, even though the claim of the New Theology is that it 'is the religion of science.' It is absurd to say, 'To define is necessarily to limit, and we are thinking of the illimitable,' or, to say, 'The act of creation is eternal,' if we do not know the meaning of the Eternal Personality of God. A science based on agnosticism is an absolute contradiction of terms.

We are told 'The Infinite Consciousness sees itself as a whole,' though this is just what the Agnostic denies. If this is so, why say God is nothing but the mysterious power of the universe and then speak of an Infinite Consciousness? Surely no one is warranted in speaking of an infinite consciousness unless he knows what it means. If the writer knows that God is an Infinite Consciousness, the same Being who is an Infinite Self-consciousness must be an

Infinite Personality. Surely man who thinks this Infinite Being must be in thought infinite, and for this reason a Person. This being so, personality cannot logically imply limitation. It is said, 'There cannot be two infinities, nor can there be an infinite and also a finite beyond it.' Just so, the infinite must include the finite, and the finite must contain the infinite. When it is said, ' All being is conscious being,' then a stone or a tree must be a conscious being ! Absurd ! An *animal* possesses sense-consciousness and is in thought limited, because it is not a self-conscious being. Man is the only self-conscious being in the world who is in thought infinite, and therefore he is a person consciously free, moral and religious.

We are told that a finite creation is a fall. If this be so, God by an act of creation loses His greatness and majesty, falls from His high estate, and thereby becomes a fallen being, which is absurd ; similarly, then, man will fall by creating any finite object, as a watch. But the real fall is the moral fall of man, not the fall of God.

When the Rev. R. J. Campbell says, ' Our true being is eternally one with the being of God,' and ' to be separated from a full knowledge of that truth is to have undergone the fall,' he is stating the true Biblical position, but not the evolutionary idea, which holds that man has risen from lower types, not ' fallen ' from a higher : besides, he elsewhere implies that man cannot separate himself from God. In one sense this is true, but the restoration of the true idea of the Atonement and of the Cross of Christ belongs to the philosophy of Hegel and not to the so-called New Philosophy of Theology, for Hegel teaches that the evil done by man can be undone through the love of God in Christ.

Under the influence of this unscientific science of

evolution, which is said to teach ' a vaster and grander' conception of God,' we are asked to believe that God was so weak that he required eternal ages to create man by evolution, for it is now the fashion to speak of creation by evolution, as the new theologians do not wish to break away altogether from the idea of creation. Darwin, however, more consistent with his theory, would not have creation in any form. Lyell could not give up the idea of creation even to please Darwin, who in writing to Lyell frankly said : ' I grieve to see you hint at creation of distinct successive types as well as of a certain number of distinct aboriginal types. Remember, if you admit this— you cut my throat; and your own throat; and I believe you will live to be sorry for it.' Creation and evolution are mutually exclusive ; Huxley said it must be Evolution *or* Creation—not creation by evolution, yet strictly he would have no *or*; only evolution.

The True Immanence of God is the logical Idea of the system of the categories of the Being and Thought of the Ego ; and the true Transcendence of God is the Idea of the Absolute Self-conscious Spirit of the universe in essential identity with the absolute logical Idea ; and this identity is the Absolute Personality of God. The false conception of the Immanence of God is what the New Philosophy and the New Theology name the mere abstract, infinite and eternal Power or Energy of the Universe ; and which maintains that the only conception or thought man can have of Personality is Limitation. The former is scientific theology, the latter unscientific ; that is, the former is substantially the old theology, while the latter is the sophistical new theology.

Let any man realize to himself what self-consciousness means, and he has a true conception of the infinite transcendence of God, for a merely immanent God without the transcendence of self-consciousness is no God at all.

To summarize: The whole difference between the old theology and the new, and between the fundamental principle of the old philosophy and the new, may be stated thus: the former begins with the idea of the omnipresence of human thought in essential unity with the thought of God as an omnipresent personal spirit, while the latter starts from an inveterate conviction that human thought is necessarily finite and limited on all sides. The former is the theology and philosophy of the Bible and logical Reason. The latter is 'the lie and the bad,' which has its origin in the blinding and bewildering influence of guilt, arising from the consciousness of having knowingly yielded to the doing of an evil action, as decisively stated in the words of Christ, 'This is the condemnation, that light is come into the world, and men loved darkness rather than light, because their deeds were evil, for every one that doeth evil hateth the light.' [1] The former is speculative philosophy, thinking the infinite as that which is positively rational, the opposite of what is falsely called rational. It is the substantial element in real mysticism which is at once subjective and objective, the light of God. Speculative is another name for the true rational. The latter is the scepticism wherein man has lost the knowledge of his true oneness with God. Thus the loss of man's knowledge of his unity with God is the real Fall of Man. The New Theology may be named the doctrine of the Fall of Man, and is even a

[1] It is remarkable that the teaching of Aristotle is essentially one on this point with the teaching of Christ: ' For wickedness perverts the judgment, and makes men err with respect to practical principles ; so that no one can be wise and judicious who is not good ' (Aristotle, as quoted by Bloomfield).

more subtle and delusive danger to the Christian and Protestant spiritual life of the nation than Roman Catholicism, for the poisonous nature of the latter is more generally known in England than the former, though they both deal with the Bible according to the unscientific spirit of each, and both ignore the science of Concrete Logic, or logical philosophy.

Guilt implies a fall into sin, for sin and evil are inconsistent with the real nature of man's being—the image of God. The disposition to do evil actions implies a fallen state. Sacrifice also implies a fallen state, with a desire to obtain forgiveness of sin, but in the case of Christ, His sacrifice of Himself in a sinful world is the manifestation of the wisdom, power and love of God as the means of man's restoration to a knowledge of loving fellowship with God. Reconciliation to God is by the Cross of Christ, the bearing of which is the condition of discipleship. The Cross, then, is the fundamental principle of the Atonement of Christ.

Logical Science, Logical Philosophy and Scriptural Christianity are essentially identical.

Logical Philosophy is the wisdom of God, and is fundamentally the principle of evangelical theology.

The so-called New Philosophy and New Theology are the wisdom of this world, which knows not God. They are the wisdom of this world, which is foolishness with God.

The so-called science of the new philosophy of theology is the same false principle of wisdom which Paul calls ' the wisdom of this world, that knew not God, and that comes to nought." It is a clear and distinct fall on man's part from the wisdom of God, which is one with the Concrete Notion of Kant, logically expounded in the philosophies of Hegel and Stirling,

CHAPTER V

LOGICAL PHILOSOPHY—THE WISDOM OF GOD

THE science of logic, being the science of thought, plainly does not rest on, or begin from, any mere assumption or hypothesis, but starts from plain, clear, self-evident matters of fact.

There are no two matters of fact more certain than that 'I think' and 'I am.' I do not infer that *I am* from the fact that *I think*, nor that *I think* from the fact that *I am*. Each of these two facts stands firmly and indubitably on a third, namely, I am sure beyond all doubt that *I know I think* and that *I know* that *I am*. I or Ego, think or thought, am or being, know or knowledge, are the four terms which it is the business of logic to explain and whose essential relation it must show. All four, however, are thoughts, and as such, are matters of fact in human experience, or in other words in human cognition; all thoughts are matters of experience, whether true or false. Of course, the business of logic deals only indirectly with error or the untrue—its real province is to determine, What is Truth? or, in other words, What is Science? for whatever is called science, but is not in its real nature True, is only 'fuel for the fire.'

There is a wide difference between elementary and advanced science. The former is not untrue because it is not advanced, but advanced always implies elementary science. Furthermore, however advanced a man's knowledge of any science may be, he is always obliged to be using his most elementary knowledge. For instance, in arithmetic he is always adding, subtracting, multiplying and dividing; or in geometry he is always dealing with points, lines, planes, circles, triangles, squares, oblongs and curves, however advanced the problem to be solved. So in the science of logic, seeking for an understanding of the mystery of God, and of the Father, and of Christ, he is always dealing with notions, judgments, and syllogisms in the manifold forms of thought, understanding, and reason or ideas.

As science begins in seeking to know the relation in matters of fact, these latter are, so far, elementary science. It is of the utmost importance to recognize distinctly that all matters of fact are such only because they are essentially relations of ideas. There are no facts devoid of ideas, and facts only become scientific knowledge when the ideas and the relations they involve are clearly brought to light. Burke said, 'One fact is worth a thousand arguments,' but we say, one fact explained is worth a thousand unexplained. It is a gross error to proclaim that only mathematics involves relations of ideas. Every sense-fact rests ultimately on logical ideas; if this were not so, no branch of physical science would be possible. Thus the science of logic as the science of thought, ideas, judgments and syllogisms is the metaphysic of physics; the science of thought is also the metaphysic of every branch of mathematics. Indeed, apart from thought, science is an idle name. We have seen that matters of fact and relations of ideas stand or fall together. The one is nowhere without the other; for as Dr. Stirling says : 'Even in mathematics there is eyesight sensuous quite as

well as eyesight intellectual, and the difference between them is, that the one is but sight, the other
insight.' Without *both* sight and insight 'the whole
estate of geometry' would be, as it were, a blank.
All ordinary concrete existences—bricks, stones, mortar, mud—imply relations of ideas quite as apodictic
as any relations in mathematics. Yet the most
fundamental and vital of all questions is, What is the
full import or meaning of 'I think' and 'I am.'
In the same reference Kant asks, 'How is experience
as science possible ? ' 'How are *à priori* synthetic
judgments possible ? ' He endeavours to answer
these questions in his Transcendental Logic. He
tells us, ' Our cognition has, on the part of the mind,
two sources,' and that 'neither sense-perceptions
without notions, nor notions without sense-elements,
are capable of furnishing a finished perception,'
' pure perceptions (space and time) or pure notions
are alone possible *à priori* ; empirical ones only *à
posteriori*,' for ' in all the Rational Theoretic Sciences
Synthetic *à priori* Judgments are present as Principles.' ' I call all cognition *transcendental* which is
occupied not so much with objects, as with the process by which we come to know them, in so far as that
process has an *à priori* element.' Consequently,
' the sure criteria of *à priori* cognition are necessity
and strict universality.' The result, so far, is based
on what he names sensation, the *matter* of sense-
cognition, while pure notions (categories) constitute
the *à priori* form under which an object in general
must be thought, so with Kant, ' Thoughts without a
content of perception,' are void ; 'perceptions, without
a focus of notions, are blind.' As yet, with him,
perceptions and notions are outside and independent
of each other. His aim is to show how their conjunction is possible, and for this purpose synthetic

6

judgments *à priori* are necessary. His only means of conjoining notions and perceptions is imagination. His vast machinery of Schemata is a *fiasco* if the unity is not already essentially one with his ' original synthetic unity of apperception,' the ' *I think*,' which he calls ' the transcendental unity of self-consciousness.' To save his synthetic unity of imagination from being too palpable a *fiasco*, he brings in the concept of Time (though pure time does not itself, empirically or *à priori*, in any way act on objects). ' Ideas, in matters of fact, are relations of substance, causality, and reciprocity and these cannot be separated from motion, impenetrability, and inertia,' and yet Kant rejects these latter because they are ' not quite pure and independent of empirical sources.' But most surprising of all—he reduces the Ego—I *think, I am* (and therewith the reality of personality), to ' the simple reflection,' as Kant himself names it, which ' is neither perception nor notion, but a mere consciousness falsely converted into a thing.' Why cannot the real substantial personality of man be proved *à priori* ? Simply because he holds that man in his thought is not infinite, and therefore does not and cannot ' step beyond the world of sense,' whereas man is an Ego, a Person, just because he in thought is infinite and transcends in immediate self-consciousness all sense limits. But that, says Kant, would be ' to have penetrated into the sphere of the noumena '—to which we may add, this involves, further, a knowledge of the essential unity of phenomena and noumena, that is, of *things*-in-themselves, which, again, involves a knowledge of God in spirit and in truth : as Christ said, ' Ye shall know that I am *in* My Father and ye *in* Me and I *in* you,' and ' the words (thoughts, notions, ideas) I speak unto you, they are spirit and they are life,' all of which to know 'is life eternal.' Therefore to know truly matters of fact (phenomena, existences) is to know truly 'relations of ideas.' So, if God created the world and the finite spirit of man, then all created things (matters of fact) are the manifestations of matters of sense-sight and of intellectual insight, for when their true meaning is understood, they are seen to be relations of God's Ideas. Man, being *a rational being*, sense-sight and reason-sight are with him in essential unity, though through lack of caution he often reasons and acts illogically. (To reason illogically is not reason.) The logical error of Kant, as already noted, was that he treated sense-thought and the *à priori* notions of intellect as if they some-how existed independently of each other until brought into unity by what he calls 'the transcendental synthesis of imagination.' Logical thought with him is a mere abstract empty form; it 'abstracts from all matters of knowledge.' Yet in spite of his depre-ciation of the Ego, he regards it as the seat and source of all his judgments, categories, and *à priori* cogni-tions. Indeed, his transcendental logic is deduced from the Ego. Understanding is a function of the Ego, and judgments are functions of the understand-ing; and Reason is the function of the Ego that conjoins all judgments, notions, categories into syllo-gisms of necessity under an intuitive or perceptive understanding that knows the objects of sense in the same act of consciousness in which it knows itself as universal (infinite) thought, for man's thought and knowledge are never purely subjective and finite. Thus it is manifest that if man knows what an original or intuitive perception is, it belongs as truly to him as to God. Kant says the problem proper of pure reason is, ' How are *à priori* synthetic judg-ments possible ? ' Now human thought is essentially a synthetic unity of differents; for self, world and God constitute the original absolute identity of man's thought, judgment and reason. Therefore the supreme problem of philosophy is not so much, ' How are synthetic judgments *à priori* possible ? ' (for such judgments are matters of fact, involving necessarily the relations of ideas), as how to explain logically the essential relation of these three ideas of reason while preserving their absolute distinguishing character, for beyond all doubt, neither man nor the world is God. The thought of the world is objectively and subjectively present in man's thought, though the world is not man and man is not the world; the substantial personality of all men is identical and yet different, just as although the thought of God is present objectively and subjectively in the thought of all men, yet the personality of God is distinctively different from that of man. Infinite difference in identity is thus the supreme *à priori* synthetic judgment of infinite Being, or of the totality of Being. The above is no less an indisputable matter of fact than that judgments, notions, ideas, categories, understanding, and reason are matters of fact in the self-conscious Ego, or the I think. The relations of ideas in thought constitute the essential connective tissue of the universal Ego, and are not less fixed and certain than the propositions of Euclid. Such relations of ideas are matters of fact. It is said that what is intellectually, is much higher than what is sensuously, seen; that the former is necessary and apodictic, the latter only contingent and probable, and that the contrary is possible. This is so, nevertheless all contingent matters of fact are only what they are because they contain absolutely necessary relations of ideas. It is said, it is a contingent truth that I am in existence; just so, but

I am nevertheless a whole world of necessary relations of ideas. Indeed, a world at all necessarily implies ideas of contingency and absolute necessity. Man's birth and growth is a chain of necessary relations, notwithstanding his subjection through life to manifold contingency. Yea, though a cabbage is a very transitory and contingent object, its existence and growth involves manifold necessary relations of ideas. That I think the world is not a whit more a self-evident fact of existence and thought, than that I think God ; or the fact that I am or exist as a self-conscious Person involves equally the necessary relations of ideas in myself as a self-conscious Ego. Man can no more rid himself of the idea of the existence and thought of the world than he can rid himself of the idea of the existence and thought of God, or of the existence and thought of his own Being. They are an essential Trinity in unity in man's thought. This unity in the self-conscious thought of man constitutes at once the infinity of human thought and of human personality. This conscious threefold unity the animal does not possess, and so it is not a person. The personality of man is the image of God, and therein, the personality of God is the image of man. This is the fundamental reason why man cannot but think God. Consequently, it is just as impossible to prove the existence of God as it is to prove the existence of the world, or the existence of man. They are each self-evident matters of fact in man's thought involving the original absolute necessary relations of ideas in all existence ; consequently, I do not assume my own existence, the existence of the world, and the existence of God any more than I assume what are generally recognized as well-known ' Matters of Fact,' or as well-known ' Relations of Ideas.' Kant maintains that ' mathematical judg-

ments as such are always *à priori*,' ' natural philosophy possesses synthetic judgments *à priori*,'' and in
metaphysic synthetic cognitions *à priori* simply must
be,' 'and at least in its aim metaphysic consists of pure
à priori synthetic propositions ' and ' has, as the special
aim of its inquiry, only three Ideas ; God, Freedom and
Immortality, and so that the second united with the
first shall lead to the third as a necessary conclusion.'
' Here, in the fulfilment of our great design, we proceed from what experience offers us immediately
to hand-psychology, to cosmology, and thence to
the cognition of God.' He, Kant, says, ' A complete
insight into them (God, Freedom, Immortality) would
render Theology, Morals, and, through union of both,
Religion, solely dependent on speculative Reason.'
In the science of metaphysics Kant has three
important threefold Ideas in Speculative Reason.
First, God, Freedom, Immortality ; Second, Psychology, Cosmology, Cognition of God (Erkenntniss
Gottes) ; Third, Theology, Morals, Religion. But
says Kant, ' These Ideas are not required in aid of
natural science, but to transcend nature.' We ask,
In what sense do they transcend nature, and are not
required in aid of natural science ? Is he not contradicting himself ? for he says, ' There are certain
laws, and that *à priori*, which first make nature
possible,' and ' The categories prescribe laws *à priori*
to nature ; nature, for law and order, depends on
Categories.' Besides, why must the cognitions or
Ideas of God, Freedom, Immortality, Psychology
and Cosmology be regarded as unavoidable problems
unless they are essential elements of human thought ?
Nature is itself a matter of fact in the unity of ideas,
and therefore cannot be transcended. Nature is
the external expression of these Ideas. Indeed, as
Dr. Stirling so well explains, ' That has been the

one error of all time to fix oneself in the existences and so blind oneself to the *relations*.' This exposition of the identity of matters of fact and relation of ideas by Dr. Stirling in *What is Thought?* is, I believe, one of the most important ever made in the history of philosophy. The ' relations of ideas ' is ' the transcendental *Schein* ' when reason transcends sense ; but matters of fact are the *real Schein* of the categories in absolute identity with the relations of ideas in the totality of Being in Thought and Reason. Hegel says, ' Appearance, show, is essential to essential Being.' But Kant, in forgetfulness of himself, has said, ' All our knowledge (cognition, Erkenntniss) begins with experience and is a compound of sense-knowledge and knowledge *à priori*.' Now this compound, experience, is strictly the relations of ideas in matters of fact, that is, synthetic judgments *à priori* ; that is, again, there are no matters of fact in heaven or earth, or matters of experience, or of cognitions independent of *à priori* principles of knowledge. Kant, however, says that ' Certain of our cognitions rise, or completely transcend the bounds of all possible experience.' But how can this be so if all cognition is experience ? All conscious thought is matter of experience, and as such is matter of cognition. To speak of thought as empty form, devoid of content, is nullity or non-sense. Then, it is none the less untrue to speak of mere formal logic, as if logic could be or ever was devoid of content-matter. So when Kant says, we cannot know things in themselves but only appearances, we cannot believe and accept this ' ghost-stuff ' he offers us as if it were real logical scientific thought. No, the soul, ego, I think, personality of man, the world of nature, and God the Absolute Spirit are of a value intrinsically, infinitely more substantial than the fairy, richly bespangled phantasmagoria such as his whole system amounts to ; or, as Dr. Stirling says of Kant's system, ' The entire world of Knowledge is but as a soap-bubble between two wholly unknown and merely supposititious X's —the X of an unknown and supposed thing-in-itself on one side for *Sensation,* and the X of an unknown and supposed *Supreme* Being (Thing-in-itself) on the other side for Belief.' Kant says, ' I must abolish *knowledge* to make room for belief.' Now, to talk about belief without knowledge, even in the name of reason, is the climax of superstition, and destroys at once the foundation of morality, religion and theology. But true faith is intellectual insight, or what Paul calls ' the eyes of your understanding being enlightened,' which is the real seeing and knowing God in spirit and in truth. Hegel's philosophy from first to last is the witness of God's Spirit in man's spirit. Kant calls the work and matter of two of his immediate successors mere ' ghost-stuff,' nothing to ' clutch,' yet it is with compunction, in the light of his *reine Apperception* and categories, that one can name his own system such, for in spite of his false reasoning otherwise, these make his *material* genuinely real.

Consequently, in the main, Hegel turned the form and content of Kant's transcendental logic, ego, pure notions *à priori,* categories, pure understanding, dialectic, ideas of pure reason, so to say, upside down and inside out. With Kant, acts of the understanding, that is, to think and cognize through notions, are reduced to judgments, and all judgments are functions of unity to the variety in a cognition ; the functions of thought are reduced to four heads, with three moments under each. *À priori* cognitions rest on *à priori* notions of understanding, and this pure synthesis rests on a ground of synthetic unity *à priori.* Then he says, ' By synthesis, in its most general sense, I understand the uniting of various units in a consciousness the one to the other in single cognition.' This last synthesis is evidently what he calls, ' the unity in it, the transcendental unity of self-consciousness,' ' the I think.' Thus the two systems (of Kant and Hegel), though different, are in substance one. The secret of one is the secret of the other, for the problem of the one is the problem of the other, and that is not only the tie between cause and effect, but the absolute unity of the totality of Being. With Kant the problem is how to explain the universal and necessary validity of human experience. The nature of the universal attraction propounded by Newton had a great fascination for him, so, too, had the lofty idealism of Malebranche, that ' God comprehends within Himself all eternal verities, the Ideas, and Perfections of things,' and that ' we see all things in God.' He sought to combine the theories of Newton and Malebranche in a philosophy of Nature, and to deduce Matter from what he regarded as two forces of Attraction and Repulsion. He derived repulsion from what we conceive as the impenetrability of matter, and affirmed that no matter without attraction and repulsion could possibly exist. These he regarded as metaphysical elements of matter. In the end, however, he seems to have abandoned this form of exposition because he failed to grasp the real essence or nature of attraction. With him design (thought, spirit) was not a constituent element in substance, therefore God was only an Architect, not a Creator ; design only applies to contingency, is only regulative of phenomena, and so, he maintains, we cannot know things in themselves, in their real nature, so that even the Ego, soul, I think, personality and logic are neither perceptions nor notions, but mere consciousnesses ' falsely converted into things.' Kant evidently holds that the soul is, in some sense, more than a thing, although to him it is neither a perception nor a notion, but ' a mere consciousness.' ' To be able to treat the ego as an object and apply categories in its regard, it would have required to have been empirically given in a perception.' So ' we cognize our own subject only as sense-appearance, and not according to what it is in itself.' Now Hegel saw in the ' I think ' what Kant called ' the mere consciousness ' of the soul, ' the universal Absolute Notion,' and he also saw that man possessed ' the perceptive understanding ' (which Kant thought belonged only to God), ' spirit thinking its own inner being,' and that therein ' the categories constituted the system of the logical ideas or absolute Idea ' (though Kant only regards them as mere empty thought-forms). Kant held that the soul as a mere consciousness may, like any other transitory phenomenon, vanish by degrees, and that things as they are in themselves cannot be known by the understanding. But a man does not cease to be a person when in the unconscious state of sleep, in a swoon, or even in a state of insanity. Kant argues that the category of extensive quantum by remission of degrees of intensity may vanish, so the soul, if regarded as a thing, may also vanish, but Hegel says, ' the soul is not a thing, but Geist (Spirit),' and ' to the Spirit there belongs certainly Being, but of a quite other intensity than that of intensive quantum,' and we must ' perceive how in the eternal nature of Spirit there arises consciousness, finitude, without this Spirit thereby becoming a thing.' The soul, therefore, is not a mere thing, a mere dead thing, it is more than substance, it is self-conscious, it is a subject and active, and evolves distinctions from its own nature. Kant was right in emancipating the soul from the old abstractions; these were not good enough for the soul, which is much more than a mere simple, unchangeable thing. It is not too much to say that his estimate of the soul, and therefore of ego, spirit, personality, in his exposition of the Psychological Idea, forms the central defect in his *Kritik of Pure Reason*. It is the root cause of his unsatisfactory exposition of the Cosmological and Theological Idea (God) which follows. This is the more astonishing because the Ego, Reine Apperception, is the Alpha and Omega of his whole system of philosophy. For, as Hegel says, ' Kant's allegation is that the categories have their source in the Ego, and that it is the Ego gives the forms of universality and necessity.' Yet he (Kant) reduces ' the categories ' to what he calls ' mere (void) thought-forms.'

It is worthy of note that both Kant and Hegel, in the highest sense, begin their philosophy with the Ego, though both have two other very different beginnings. Kant professes to begin from experience, which he holds is a compound knowledge of sense and of what are called *à priori* principles of reason. Hegel professes to begin from pure Being as the most abstract form of Thought. Dr. Stirling focuses Hegel's Ego in these words, ' Hegel's Begriff (Notion) is the Immanent Dialectic of the Ego's own Self.' The science of logic includes the nature of Thought as Spirit, and is the principle of self-movement in thought and reason, and at the same time includes in itself notion, judgment, and syllogism, while dialectic means the absolute self-activity of logical thought in the universe as the principle of all natural and spiritual life. Thus thought is at once both negative and positive, as in magnetism, or it is a permanent in all change—the outward perishes while the inward outwardly renews itself as the temporal and eternal, or the unceasing ever-ceasing, the positive-negative and the negative-positive. Thus God, as Spirit, in His free eternal necessary Being manifests Himself in the creation of nature and a finite spirit in His own image.   There is a free necessary motion in the heavenly bodies, for all motion implies freedom.   The essence of Spirit is freedom— it sees in its own light—and ' freedom is the truth of necessity,' for substance is that in itself which the Notion is in its manifestation, so the Notion is the Immanent Dialectic of the Ego's own Self, thus the Notion of the Ego as Spirit is the truth of substance. Dr. Stirling says, ' All lies in the I—Me,' or ' Thought is the Absolute Ratio between the I and the Me.' Without the Ego the universe would not only be dark and silent, but non-existent.   But it is all in all.

Of course, this is the Absolute Idealism of the Absolute Realism, for an ideal that is not real is out-and-out nonsense.   The common ordinary ideal is an ungraspable Will-o'-the-wisp.   The true ideal is the glorious universe, substantial in whole and part, in which we mortal-immortals live, move and have our substantial real being.

Hegel grasped clearly the real logical significance of Kant's Ego, the Reine Apperception, the synthetic judgments à priori, and the substantial nature of the categories.   He declares : ' This (Kantian) philosophy specifies the Original Identity of the Ego in Thinking (the Transcendental Unity of Self-consciousness) as the special ground proper of the categories.'   ' I, Ego, Thought, Thinking is accordingly infinite, because in thinking it refers itself to an object that is itself.'   ' The principle of connection is Ego— this is a great consciousness, a most important recognition.' 'The unity of notion and being it is which constitutes the notion of God.' God, then, is in His personality the absolutely universal Personality.' 'The absolute Notion, that thinks itself, that goes into itself—it is that we see, through the Kantian philosophy, appear in Germany; and so that all essentiality and truth falls into self-consciousness. Synthetic judgments *à priori* are nothing else than the union of opposites through themselves, or the Absolute Notion,' the Ego.

To set forth the exact philosophical position of Kant and Hegel, especially that of the former, in relation to God, man, and the world, is no easy task. The difficulty in reference to the position of Kant is, what while it contains so much that is really very excellent, it contains also much that is very very unsatisfactory. The difficulty in doing full justice to Hegel arises from the wide extent and elaborate detail of the subject-matter of his numerous writings. It may be, however, that the greatest difficulty is to make clear the real meaning of his Dialectic. Mr. McTaggart has not grasped its true meaning. This is evident in his Cosmology on the personality of God. Professor James confesses he has been unable to understand what Hegel means by his dialectic, but thinks it would be of very little value if he did. Of the many interpreters, Dr. Stirling is the only one who can be credited with a full insight. The dialectic is the deepest secret of Hegel's philosophy, and until it is seen, his philosophical system will continue to be more or less misunderstood and misrepresented.

The Immanent Dialectic of the Ego's own self involves the conception of Creation, and therewith the secret power involved in the reality of the miracles of the Bible. The dialectic is the self-active, self-creative power of the universe, and therefore identical with causation. Creator involves creation, wherein what is created can never be independent of the Creator; therefore Nature and man in different forms are necessarily manifestations of the eternal power of the eternal and infinite Godhead of the one living, personal God. Herein is the new conception of Logic which Hegel has discovered and given to the world. Ego is a rational thinking being, therefore Being is Thought—Being without thought is nothing. There is nothing in heaven or earth without or separate from thought. Nature apart from thought is nothing, but since Nature really is there, as a matter of fact, this Nothing is Being. This is the true conception of Hegel's identity of Being and Nothing and Becoming—for in all change there is in thought the immanent movement of Being passing into Nothing, and the passing of Nothing into Being, wherein they are absolutely identical. Thus Nothing is as certainly a noun, as thought and being are nouns, that is, they are names of realities. Hegel's Nothing is a thought, and since Nothing is the name of a thought, it is Being. Being is the present participle denoting process, the verbal noun. It is one form of the verb ' to be,' and as such it is called the *substantive* verb. This is the reason why the verbal noun ' Being ' plays such an important part in Hegel's philosophy. It denotes process, the self-activity of Thought, of the Ego and the activity of the universe. Process is at once both positive and negative; so it is that Nothing is the negative of Being, and as such, Hegel's logical dialectic is the unity of Being, Nothing, and Becoming, the first concrete-abstract, or abstract-concrete Notion. Yet in another sense Being is the most concrete Notion, for it is infinite All, all that is. We must here notice that Hegel, unlike Kant, regards God as Creator, not merely as

Architect, for he says, ' God be praised ! we can abstract from Nothing and then Being remains, for the creation of the world is but an abstraction from nothing.' ' Christian metaphysic, in rejecting the position ' From Nothing comes Nothing,' necessarily maintains a transition from Nothing to Being,' which is the very essence of Becoming (Creation). Thought is Being and Being is Thought, infinite creative energy ; so the theory of evolution by natural selection is an absurd guess, ' the mere accident of an accident.'

We remarked above that Kant says, ' All our knowledge begins from *experience* ' (observe, he does not say *experience* begins with knowledge) ; but he does not make it quite clear what he means by *experience*. He has much to say before his meaning is brought to light. He early tells us it (*experience*) is a compound of the objects of sense-perception and a knowledge of principles *à priori*, and that ' necessity and strict universality are sure criteria of *à priori* cognition.' At first, however, these two sides of experience are quite independent. To bring them into unity a synthetic judgment *à priori* is required, and this is only attained by what he names ' the transcendental synthesis of imagination.' His pure perception (*à priori*) of space and time are not notions ; his pure notions of the understanding are the categories. Transcendental, according to Kant, is the *à priori* element in experience and knowledge, and the *à priori* notions alone make cognition absolutely valid, or give the universal and certain criteria of the truth of all and every cognition. Here, then, the ' relations of Ideas ' is the real nature of all matters of fact, that is, of all objects of sense-perceptions : that is, experience is a ' compound.' Kant and Hegel, however, both agree that experience only tells what is, not how objects must or should be, yet, strange to say, the real and avowed aim of both philosophers is to demonstrate the universal and necessary element of experience in all sense-objects. Although Kant says the two elements of experience are sense-perceptions and ' *à priori* cognitions,' he makes no attempt to explain how sense-matter, sense-objects, come to be matters of fact. Creation, as we have noted, forms no part of his philosophy, for, as he says, ' the notion of design exhibits God only as an Architect, not as a Creator '—not as One that created, but only as One that gives form to matter. He leaves too much the impression that experience begins from sense-perception, and that the *à priori* faculty of cognition is a quite subjective element added to our experience, for he says, ' We shall understand by cognitions *à priori*, not such as are independent of this or that experience, but such as are totally independent of any experience whatever,' and ' empirical cognitions are only possible *à posteriori*, or from experience,' while ' those *à priori* are quite free from any empirical admixture.' We see here he has forgotten that what he called ' experience' is necessarily ' a compound.' Further, we may ask why did not Kant say that ' beyond all doubt all our knowledge begins with and from *à priori* cognition ? ' Obviously because he conceived the two elements of experience existed somehow entirely apart. Then he proceeds to give his criteria of the essential difference between sense and *à priori* knowledge : ' Necessity and strict universality are sure criteria of *à priori* knowledge and are inseparably found together,' and ' it is to show that there actually are in our knowledge such necessary and in the strictest sense (consequently pure) *à priori* judgments.' ' If we withdraw from an object all properties known to us from *experience*, we shall still be unable to withdraw from it those by which we think it as substance.' 'We must admit the notion of substance has its seat *à priori* in our faculties of cognition.' From these quotations we see clearly that Kant can only mean by 'from experience,' from some form of sense-perception. His aim is to show that all certainty of knowledge is based on *à priori* notions, for, he says, 'How should there be any certainty in experience were all the rules in it only empirical and (consequently) contingent ? It were hardly possible, evidently, to allow any such rules the name of first principles.' Here I remind the reader, contingent events and objects are matters of fact in universal relations of ideas, and these constitute the 'synthetic judgment *à priori*,' which Kant attempted to explain in his Transcendental Logic.

In Kant's system, though not intentionally, time comes almost to supply the place of God. 'Time determination' seems almost almighty, to contain all fullness, and manipulate all the categories. 'The Schemata are nothing but transcendental Time-determinations *à priori* on rules ; and these relate, in the order of the categories, to Time-series, Time-content, Time-order, Time-implex, in regard of all possible objects.' If the Ego, divine and human, in the absolute unity of Thought, Stirling's I—Me, had been given the place of Kant's 'Infinitude of Time,' how much more consistent with pure reason would he have made his system of philosophy ! Though time is infinite, the Ego alone is the infinite power in all.

The meaning of Transcendental is so peculiar, that to express it clearly is not easy. Though beyond special sense it is not beyond, but in, experience. It is precisely that element which renders our experience *à priori* possible. Transcendental, with Kant, always means either *à priori* perceptions—space and time—or the pure *à priori* notions of the understanding—the categories. He says, ' Pure understanding is as such, neither empirical nor sensuous ' : and ' all acts of the understanding may be reduced to judgments.' Then ' all judgments are functions of unity to a variety in a cognition.' ' General logic abstracts from all matter of knowledge.' Now as a matter of fact, neither pure perceptions of time and space *à priori*, nor pure notions (the categories) *à priori*, are possible. They are each and all matters of experience, and are therefore never devoid of empirical and *à priori* matter of content. Therefore all knowledge is a matter of experience, and as such is a compound of sense-perception and *à priori* ideas. Each apart would be empty, blind, truthless abstractions. But they are not empty abstractions, but full concretes. They are only what they are through the absolute necessity of the Relations of Ideas, apart from which no mathematical, physical, metaphysical, and so no logical science, is possible ; for all science consists in the absolute unity of matters of fact, in an essential necessary relation of ideas ; on the one side sensuously, and on the other side intellectually, perceived ; on the one side constitutive of categories which are empirical and contingent, and on the other side constitutive of categories of thought and being which are eternal, infinite, apodictic necessity and certainty. Possibility and impossibility, necessity and contingency, are among Kant's categories, the strict criteria of which he holds are universality and necessity. So, contrary to Kant, space and time are at once empirical perceptions of sense and *à priori* notions of the understanding and reason, for, on the empirical side they are sensuously seen (perceived) as finite, while on the side of reason-thought they are intellectually seen (perceived) as infinite. Space, measured by yards and miles, is limited, finite, but intellectually apprehended in reason-thought, it is unlimited and infinite. So time, sensuously perceived and measured by days and years, is limited and finite, but intellectually apprehended by reason-thought, it is unlimited and infinite —it is eternity—duration without beginning and without end. Even so, both God and man can be sensuously seen, God through Nature, and man through his works. The visible heavens declare the glory of God, and the visible works of man, the glory of man who, in spirit, is ‘ the image and glory of God.’ It is, however, on the side of conscious reason-thought that God and man can be truly, intellectually perceived. On the intellectual side God and man in thought are Ego, the universal subject ; throughout all space and time there is but one I—one universal thought. The absolute-infinite is the thought that includes and overlaps in itself all space and time— in a word, it contains *all that is*—it is the universal compound experience of sense and reason in the cognition of God. It is an error to suppose, with Kant, that we can think of the non-existence of matter but not of the non-existence of time and space, for we can no more think of the non-existence of the one than of the non-existence of the other, for the reality and ideality of the one necessarily involves the reality and ideality of the other. Real idealism is not the transformation of God, man, and the universe, as some irrationally suppose, into a sort of fanciful ‘ ghost-stuff ’ or chimera of the brain. An ideal that is not real is not ideal, Kant’s fanciful ‘ thing in itself ’ has blinded him to real idealism, as also to his own metaphysical theory, that objects must conform to cognition *à priori*, or, conform to thought. True idealism is ' an original perception such that through it the very being of its object is given.' It is the perceptive understanding. Kant says, ' All that is perceived by sense is always, so far, sense-appearance.' This applies only to the sense-perception of an animal, not to man, for man is an ego, but the animal is not. ' The consciousness of one's self (apperception) ' says Kant, ' is the simple cognition Ego.' This is his fundamental error, for the manifold of sense is real only in essential coherence in the unity of the Ego, and is only cognized in the intuitive light of the Ego's own self.

We now come to a more vital point, touching the very complex foundation of the Kantian philosophy. First, Kant professes to begin from experience : this we have in part explained. He next starts from the understanding and says, ' Pure understanding is as such neither empirical nor sensuous,' and therefore ' is no faculty of perception proper.' Then he says, the ' understanding itself may be defined, a faculty to judge,' and thus ' The functions of the understanding will be the functions of unity in judgments.' Now, for all that, he holds that the understanding furnishes only the forms of judgments, not the matter, and these form the notions *à priori* in the pure understanding. Here, then, according to Kant, we have a matterless form ; this, however, nowhere exists. Yet, in spite of this, he declares, ' perceptions without notions are blind, and notions without perceptions are empty.' He professes to derive from these empty notions twelve judgments : three judgments of quantity—universal, particular, singular ; three judgments of quality—affirmative, negative, infinite ; three judgments of relation—categorical, hypothetical, disjunctive ; three judgments of modality—problematic, assertoric, apodictic. Out of these empty notional judgments he derives twelve *à priori* notions which he calls ' categories,' the pure notions of the understanding. These pure notions, however, are as empty as are his judgments of the ' pure understanding.' Both are, he says, ' as such neither empirical nor sensuous,' yet ' furnish conditions of the very possibility of all our perception.' Therefore, as yet there is no conjunction of notions and perceptions, though ' they presuppose conjunction.' He comes next to the ' I think,' which ' must be capable of accompanying all my perceptions; for otherwise there would be something placed in my consciousness which could not be thought; and that is as much as to say that the perception itself would either be impossible or else nothing for me.' He calls this ' pure apperception,' and further, ' the transcendental unity of self-consciousness.' All this notwithstanding, with Kant perceptions are not yet conjoined in thought. For this unity he still requires ' a transcendental synthesis of imagination,' ' a faculty which *à priori* acts on sense-objects,' ' in accordance with the synthetic unity of apperception.' ' In this wise the categories, though mere thought-forms, get objective reality.' True, for the complete realization of synthetic judgments *à priori*, outer and inner sense and *à priori* forms of space and time are yet required, but of these further remark here is unnecessary. The nature of the unity in the above specified judgments is now the chief point demanding explanation.

In spite of all Kant's empty-abstracts, a great many unities are implied on all sides in the circle of his exposition of Pure Reason. Hegel says Kant's exposition is barbarous. I suppose the reason why he condemns it so strongly is because it reduces the

Ego of God and man to mere unsubstantial phantoms of imagination. Kant's system is certainly almost the most ingenious and complicated piece of theorizing ever devised. In it there is no real knowledge of the world, or God, yet one is made to feel it is not the work of a charlatan, but of an honest, deep-thinking man striving earnestly to get at the reality of all existence. Nay, further, that his writings contain much that is of the highest value. Indeed, after reflection, we find that much of the material used in the construction of Hegel's system has been derived from Kant, although the whole structure appears to be entirely new. To comprehend Hegel's system we must keep in mind the nature of the Ego, *i.e.* of the three judgments of quantity, for with Hegel the notion of quantity and the notion of the Ego are substantially one. The result is that the universal, particular and singular of quantity constitute the universal, particular and singular of Hegel's Notion and are essentially the three functions of the Notion of the Ego. This, in fact, is Hegel's Infinite Absolute Notion, properly named Ego. These three moments of the Notion and Ego form the *three categories* of quantity, viz. unity, plurality and totality, or, as Schwegler arranges them, totality, plurality, unity. The order of arrangement, however, is not of vital importance, for unity is at once both singular and universal, just as totality is at once universal and singular, either all and one or one and all, just as the Ego is logically one and all, and the Notion is logically one and all. The three judgments of quality, affirmative, negative and infinite, are logically one with the three qualities of the Ego and Notion ; and at the same time are respectively one with the three *categories* of quality, viz. reality, negation, limitation (including illimitation), which

are at once the finite and infinite. So far as the
categories are of sense, they are finite and transitory;
so far as thought is their real essence, they are infinite
—man being one with external Nature, his outward
man is mortal and perishes. Kant's is not the true
infinite, for finite is not without the infinite nor the
infinite without the finite. Kant does not logically
deduce his twelve categories from his judgments,
but somewhat dogmatically inserts them. The judgments are treated as notions, and the categories as
notions and judgments of the understanding. These,
however, are empty until somehow filled with content supplied by objects of perception.

We cannot attach too much importance to the
fact that the real and true sense of the universal is
infinite (for example, I can form no conception of
universal gravitation but as an infinite thought).
It is a simple matter of fact that the Ego thinks the
infinite, for the thought of the concrete totality
of Being, or of *all that is*, is a true definition of the
infinite, and also of the Absolute Relativity of the
absolute unity of thought and being. The term
' universal ' is often used in the sense of general, as
all trees, all birds, all fishes, all animals, but the true
absolute universal stands for All-That-Is, and is
the true Infinite-Thought. The term infinite is
often used to signify a relative-infinite in the sense of
infinite space, infinite time, an infinite series, or the
mathematical infinite, that includes all mere relative-
infinites. In this sense, the quality of thought is
the universal affirmative reality of reason and spirit.
Kant's definition of the infinite is not the logical one,
for if anything is removed from ' the infinite number
of things ' the amount is *not* ' still the true infinite.'
Hegel has the true conception of the infinite, but it
cannot be adequately expressed in a judgment, for

therein the subject and the predicate must be different, though in substance identical (as, God is ' absolute Spirit,' or, the Infinite is absolute Thought and Being). The true notion of the Infinite is best expressed in the absolute syllogism—the logical Idea, Nature and Spirit.

The order of these elements of thought is, with some important additions, entirely re-arranged by Hegel. He deals in his Logic with the categories in three different forms; in his doctrine of Being he takes them in their simplest form; in his doctrine of Essence they take the form of reflexion-determinations; and in his doctrine of the Notion he gives them the more specific form of notions. This change is of very great logical value. It must be noted, however, that with Hegel the real substantial nature of the categories assumes several other forms, especially in his philosophy of Nature and Spirit. To him the categories are never merely subjective. In his logic he takes no account of time and space, they being regarded by him in this branch of his philosophy as quite irrelevant and as pertaining only to the science of Nature. Kant begins his system by a metaphysical and transcendental exposition of time and space. In Hegel's logical exposition of the science of Nature the categories first assume the mathematical, mechanical and chemical forms of external bodies in their various modes of motion, especially of matter in its sensible forms of light, heat and sound. They take another form in their bearing in relation to the growth and life of plants and animals, and yet another and higher form in relation to the qualities of Spirit in Art, Religion, and the constitution of national State Government. For a proper acquaintance with the various shades of difference in Hegel's logical exposition of the categories his writings require to be studied and not to be taken second-hand from any man.

In Kant's system there is an impassable gulf between his form and content, so in his final result he has failed to show ' How synthetic judgments *à priori* are possible.' In Hegel's philosophy *form and content* are identical from first to last. We do not say it is complete in every detail, but this incompleteness does not arise from the nature of his logical dialectic, but from what we may call his mis-calculations. We do not blame the science of arithmetic for the miscalculations of the fallible arithmeticians, for ' to err is human.' The error in this case belongs to the philosopher—not to the nature of his scientific theory. Of Hegel, however, it ought to be said that in his later mature writing he will seldom be found tripping.

The division of Kant's categories into two classes reveals a deep chasm. The first six of quantity and quality he names mathematical, the second six, of relation and modality, he names dynamical. His first group are ' intuitive,' ' constitutive,' ' apodictic ' ; his second group are only ' discursive,' ' regulative,' ' contingent.' In the first he professes to demonstrate necessity ; in the second, only an uncertain matter of contingency. As a matter of fact, all the twelve are equally intuitive, constitutive, apodictic, and equally dynamical. They are all equally constitutive and necessary elements of thought in the free self-activity of the universal, omnipresent Spirit as manifested in the self-conscious logical dialectic movement of the Notion, the Ego's own Self. The Ego is the principal and immortal germ of all individual and personal life throughout the totality of Being. For what does the notion of Relation in the form of judgment imply but the unity of infinite quantity and quality of universal thought and being ? Indeed, Kant professes to derive his categories of Relation from his three judgments of Relation, all of which have their substantial reality in the Ego, the Infinite Absolute. The relations of thought in the judgments and notions of the categories 'are : first, The essential relation of the predicate to the subject ; this is the categorical judgment, as for example, substance and accident—rose is a plant, man is a rational being, God is absolute Spirit ; thus the categorical judgment is essentially infinite. Second, The relation of antecedent to consequent, the hypothetical judgment—cause and dependence, cause and effect. Here the relation is infinite and absolute throughout all space and time. The third relation of thought is the disjunctive judgment denoting communion, co-existence, reciprocity of action and reaction. Here, again, the relation is infinite and absolute, embracing universal Being. ' The categories are root notions of the understanding and all the categories are judgments as functions of the Ego. The categorical judgment expresses the immediate unity of subject and predicate. The hypothetical judgment only says that if the subject is, the predicate is; if the cause is, the effect is; or if creation is, the Creator is. The disjunctive judgment is the third form of the judgment of necessity where, in the universal as the absolute genus in its complete specification, two sides are identical—the genus is the totality of the species, and the totality of the species is the genus, and the unity of the universal and of the particular is the Notion and the Absolute content of the Ego ; or, to express the moments of the Ego otherwise, the categorical judgment is assertorical, the hypothetical judgment is problematical, while the disjunctive judgment is completely apodictic, because in this judgment everything is constituted according to its notion in the unity of particular, universal, singular ; one, many, all—the absolute Allness.

The truth, however, of the unity of these three judgments is best seen in the absolute syllogism in the absolute unity of the logical idea, nature and spirit—the Absolute Ego. In reference to this three-fold unity of the Absolute Ego, viz. the Logical Idea, Nature, Spirit, we quote the following from the *Secret of Hegel.* ' If, then, we have correlated and co-articulated into a whole, the subordinate members or moments of Reason, it is evident that the completed system, now as a whole, as a one, will just similarly comport itself to its other, which is Nature. In like manner, too, as we found Reason *per se* to constitute a system, an organized whole of co-articulated notions, so we shall find Nature also to be a correspondent whole—correspondent, that is, to Reason as a whole, and correspondent in its con-stitutive parts or moments to the constitutive parts or moments of Reason. The system of Nature, too, being completed, it is only in obedience to the general scheme that Reason will resume Nature into its own self, and will manifest itself as the unity, which is Spirit, and which is thus at length the final form and the final appellation of the Absolute ; the Absolute Spirit. And Spirit, too, similarly looked at and watched, will be found similarly to construct and constitute itself, till at last we reach the notion of the notion, and will be able to realize, in whole and in part, the Idea, that which is, the Absolute.' With Kant the Ego and the categories are not constitutive but only regulative of Nature. But he endeavours to show by ' the transcendent imagination ' ' the possibility of a transition may be made.' Still, God, man, and nature are with him quite independent and separate—that is, God is only Architect, not Creator.

Kant, however, professed to deduce three unconditioned transcendental Ideas from experience, viz. psychology, cosmology, theology—the soul as thinking subject—the world as sum of all appearance—God as the highest condition of all things, ' das Wesen aller Wesen.' Then out of the formal logic of experience Kant derives three forms of reason-syllogisms (*Vernunftschlusses*), the categorical—the psychological Idea; the hypothetical—the cosmological Idea; the disjunctive—the Idea of God or the Theological Idea. It must be clearly recognized that the idea is the unconditioned and infinite. It belongs to psychology, cosmology and Theology—in other words, either to the soul (Ego, self-consciousness, Personality), to the world, or to God. The unconditioned is not the soul nor the world, but God. The unconditioned or infinite is not only the subject of the two premises but also the subject of the conclusion, therefore the subject and object in the disjunctive syllogism, notwithstanding their difference otherwise, are identical. With Kant the unconditioned was not infinite, and so was only an abstract universal indefinite; but the conditioned is concrete and absolutely infinite; and this alone is the true conception of Reason, of the absolute Idea; the Idea of the Infinite to Kant was no more than an Instinct of Reason.

As the ultimate outcome of all Kant's very clever, subtle, ingenious, complicated reasoning, his ideas, notions, perceptions, have no real being, for ' being is no real predicate ' (Seyn ist kein reales Prädicat). Yet it is surely correct to say I think, and also that Thought is Being, and therefore I am Being, and that Being is a predicate of the Ego and also a predicate of thought. Indeed, Being can be predicated of all that is—everything is Being. It is identical with Being. In this sense, to say I am is the least I can say of myself, and therefore the poorest predicate of man. 'I am' is at once subject and predicate of a true judgment, I and Am are identity and difference in Ego and Being. Yet both are absolutely universal, infinite, absolute. Ego is essential Being, Thought and Reason, and therefore in thought man is essentially one with God, for God cannot be outside of the infinite thought of man. Infinite conscious Thought is the ground principle of the personality of God and man, the ground principle of logical philosophy, the ground principle of theology as the science of God and Divine things, and the ground principle of every particular science of Nature.

The one supreme aim of Kant in his *Kritik of Pure Reason* was to explain logically the nature of that which is the necessary and universal bond between cause and effect. In spite of all the excellent things (and they are many) found in his writings, he failed in his aim because he failed to grasp the fact that man in his thought is infinite ; and for the same reason he failed to realize the essential nature of the Ego and personality of man and God. For if man in his thought is only finite, then the infinite God is necessarily unknowable by man. Hegel begins and ends with the idea that man in his thought is infinite and knows God. So, to know God is to know Wisdom, Reason, Truth.

CHAPTER VI

PERSONALITY—INFINITE

DR. Stirling says, in *What is Thought?*—'Man, in that he is of sense, is finite; but man, in that he is of thought, is a spirit and infinite.' These words express in brief the fundamental principle of human personality which is one with the supreme principle of divine personality. The pith of both is contained in the two words, ' infinite ' and ' thought,' that is, infinite-thought. Both personalities being in thought infinite, and so far identical, are yet in an important sense widely different. Infinite thought in God means omniscience, while infinite thought in man, though containing the concrete totality of Being, is, in different men, of a more or less abstract character; that is, thought is in its substantial nature concrete, never a pure empty abstraction; in other words, though in man a concrete infinite, thought is always in part abstract, because, however great his knowledge, he can never be omniscient in the sense of knowing *All in its infinite detail.* This distinction in the nature of personality is all-important; without it the logical difference and identity of the two personalities cannot be explained in their true character.

Again, the words in the first chapter of Genesis which state that ' God made man in His own image and likeness,' express in brief the fundamental intellectual principle of personality, Divine and human. God necessarily means a self-conscious being, infinite in thought, and so a Person; and man made in the image of God equally means a self-conscious being, in thought infinite, and so a Person. Man knows himself to be a self-conscious being, he knows that there is no limit to his thought, and that, therefore, he is, so far, in the image of God, and, like God, a Person. Paul expresses the same principle of divine and human personality when he says, ' Man is the image and glory of God,' and ' God is manifest in men.' The divine personality of man is also expressed in the words, ' Thou hast made him but a little lower than God, and crownest him with glory and honour: Thou madest him to have dominion over the works of Thy hands.' This thought of personality is confirmed by Christ in His words, ' Is it not written in your law, I said, Ye are Gods? ' It is only because man in his personality is infinite in thought that he is a person, and thinks God. This is the attitude of Calvin in relation to man's knowledge of himself and of God. In his *Institutes* he tells us that man can only know himself through his knowledge of God, and can only know God through the knowledge of himself. A true logical insight into the genuine nature of man's personality is of vital importance.

The general teaching of the Old Testament recognizes the fact that man in his thought is in an important sense, infinite, otherwise the words contained therein would be devoid of any true meaning. To illustrate this point, we quote here a few passages— of which there are many more to the same effect: God is ' the high and lofty One that inhabiteth eternity '; ' Great is our Lord and of great power, His understanding is infinite '; ' from everlasting to everlasting Thou art God ' ; ' the eternal God is thy refuge ' ; ' I am that I am ' : to Abraham God was the Lord, the everlasting God. View these words as we may, they express an infinite and objective thought as constituting the nature and personality of God, which must have been present in the minds of the writers as an essential subjective intellectual principle, otherwise they could not have given expression to it. Their real meaning is so plainly expressive of the one infinite thought in God and man, that nothing but an illogical philosophy could render thought only finite when applied to human personality.

Properly interpreted, the Bible teaches that man in his thought is infinite ; this same thought forms the foundation of logical philosophy. It is necessary here to show that Personality constitutes the most universal concrete basis of philosophy and forms the real foundation of all existence. That man is a person is admitted without question, but what it is that constitutes personality has been clearly and properly grasped even by few philosophers. Popular and current science and religion know it not. The definitions generally fall very far short of its deep and full meaning. This is very evident from the way in which the term personality is applied to God, or, rather, from the way in which it is denied to God. Because man is a person, it is thought to give a more exalted view of God, to say He is more than a person, or that He is above personality, as if to call God a person reduced Him to the level of man. The term ' supra-personal ' has been applied to God ; but this only tends to reduce man's conception of Him to a kind of ethereal mist or something indefinite. There has been, especially among theologians, an unwillingness and even a repugnance to speak of

God as the ' Unknowable,' in view of the fact that the Bible speaks so much, not only of the possibility, but also of the absolute necessity, of man knowing God ; and true knowledge is not abstract but concrete. Still, the phrase ' Christian agnosticism ' has had considerable vogue. The chief cause of the spread of such pernicious ideas has been the general prevalence of an unsound philosophy, and an imperfect conception of what constitutes human personality. Indeed, if men have a false conception of human personality, it must be impossible for them to have any other than erroneous ideas of the personality of God and of Christ. Many men, who have cherished and maintained very exalted views of the dignity and value of human personality, have yet utterly failed to see it in its true light. Indeed, Personality in its true light has only recently entered the consciousness of the Christian world.

In discussing the nature of Personality, it may be advisable first to refer to some of the so-called philosophic views which have hitherto prevailed with regard to this subject. Locke says, ' A person is a thinking intelligent being that has reason and reflection,' ' a rational being.' ' The personality of an intelligent being extends beyond itself, beyond present existence to what is past, only by consciousness.' He holds, that man as a person has no positive idea of the ' infinite,' because man cannot add to that idea. Now the idea of *all that is*, is an infinite concrete idea in man, and certainly cannot be added to. And man, we affirm, is ' a rational being,' and so ' a person,' just because he has the concrete idea of the infinite (with all that idea involves and contains) as the absolute relativity of *all that is*. The animal is not a person, because it cannot think the infinite, or because it has not in it the infinite as a conscious

8

thought. Rational thought is concrete, is in and for itself infinite, and therefore contains God, religion, law, moral government, thus constituting man a rational moral being, or in a word, a person. The concrete thought of the infinite is the only thought that distinguishes man from the reasonless brutes.

To speak of an infinite in thought, and yet of the infinite as beyond thought, is without any real definite meaning, and is only a speaking into the air. To deny that man has a definite thought of the infinite, is the same, in principle, as to deny that he has or can have a real knowledge of God : or it is the same, as to deny that man is a person. Hegel says, ' It is the highest form of untruth, the lie and the bad.' To deny that man in his thought is infinite, is the source and spring of every theory of agnosticism and scepticism. To say that man knows not the infinite, is proof that he thinks and knows it, just as when he says, ' There is no God,' he proves that he thinks God. The animal neither thinks that there is or is not a finite or an infinite, or that there is or is not a God.

M'Cosh holds strongly to the conviction that a true conception of the personality of man is vital to philosophy and theology, and that man has an intuitive conviction of the ' infinite,' but he regards both these terms as abstract, as merely, in some way, side by side, and not in absolute relation. We maintain that thought, ' personality,' ' infinite ' are nowhere independent of each other. He holds that personality cannot be defined, because it is an intuition. An intuition, with him, is simply an original, self-evident, indefinite principle of the mind, of which no more can be said than that there it is, as a fact in human thought. He says, ' Fichte, Schelling, and Hegel, taking with them *no belief* in the personality of self, never could reach the personality of God.' Philosophically M'Cosh himself did not reach the true conception of the personality of either God or man. He was wrong in charging Fichte and Schelling with not having a *belief* in the personality of man and God; and in regard to Hegel he was also wrong, for Hegel attained to a clear knowledge of the personality of both man and God : with Fichte, Schelling, Kant, it was mere *belief*, not cognition.

If by definition is meant the absolute separation of one object of thought from another, then all definition is impossible. So far as definition even of man is considered, eliminate the idea and knowledge of the infinite from human thought, and no intelligible definition can ever be given. In such a case it would be like defining a square without an angle. Certainly to define a person as a rational being is not enough, unless it is added that rational thought is one with the consciousness of infinite thought.

Mansel, writing on Personality says, ' It is an original intuition,' ' is indefinable,' ' is superior to definition,' ' it can be made no clearer by description or comparison,' ' the only human conception of personality is that of limitation,' yet it is this limited finite indefinable personality that he asks us to conceive of as being a fitting representation of the infinite personality of God, for he holds that we must conceive of God as a person, and believe that He is infinite. So with Mansel also, it is *belief*, not cognition. He places personality as the fourth and last of his limits of religious thought. The other three can, however, only be makeshifts, for if ' personality is essentially limitation,' and if ' we cannot transcend our own (so-called limited) personality,' then the other three limits prove nothing if man's thought is necessarily finite. Necessary *distinction* and *relation* in human knowledge, so far from implying limitation, are the absolute condition of the existence of infinite thought, and of personality both in man and in God. The distinction and relation between objects, between subject and object, and the limits between objects, in the infinity of space and the infinite duration of time, have no real bearing on the limitation of thought and personality, for it is only because thought is infinite that personality is infinite, since unlimited time and space cannot limit the nature of thought and personality. Human thought includes, overlaps and pervades all relations and all limits : it is always infinitely beyond every point that a person might wish to fix in thought, either in time or space. Infinite thought is always here and now consciously present in a Person as that which constitutes personality.

Mansel's view of intuition is as erroneous as his estimate of personality, for increase of clearness of knowledge in relation to what is intuitively known is both possible and necessary for the full development of man. Man's intuitive knowledge of the infinite admits the possibility of an increasing clearness, by means of logical or speculative philosophy. To affirm the contrary is proof of a deficient insight into the science of thought. Mansel does not evince in the least a rational knowledge of personality, nor does he give a logical exposition of the nature of personality. The reason he gives to prove that human personality is only finite in thought is full of logical contradiction, and proves the very opposite of what he labours to prove. The logic of the relativity of human knowledge proves that man is a person, and therefore in his thought infinite. Relativity is at once Infinite and Absolute.

In modern times Kant was the first to discover

the Concrete Notion. This he expressed by saying, 'Sense and understanding are two stems of human knowledge having *a single common root.*' It is his 'percipient understanding'; it is his 'metaphysical Copernican conception of Nature,' in which objects conform to thought, and not thought to objects; it is his 'transcendental unity of apperception,' in and through which the categories of thought give necessary and universal validity and stability to all phenomena of Nature; it is the 'ground and substance of his 'transcendental logic and philosophy.' Dr. Stirling says, 'Kant identifies consciousness with understanding, understanding with judgment, and judgment with thought or thinking itself.' He also identifies the thinking-self with self-consciousness and Ego. Kant says, 'That man can have Ego in his apprehension exalts him *infinitely* above all other living beings on earth. Thereby is he a Person . . . even when he cannot speak the Ego.'

In Kant's theory or conception of Personality, as contained in his philosophy, there are three essential elements:—concrete thought, freewill, and a vague notion of the infinite, named by him the indefinite. Abstract thought is neither infinite nor free, and therefore it is not the Ego. Because man in his thought is infinite, concrete, and free, he is a spirit, and therefore Ego. As stated in the last chapter, though Kant was the first to see and say that a being that is Ego is a Person, he never attained to a true conception of Personality; so, although he made this great step in advance in philosophy, his logical development of this new principle was very defective, for with him, *personality was an unknown thing in itself.* His transcendental logic was a great improvement on formal or abstract logic, as far as it went, for it introduced the *concrete notion* or the abstract judgment of *allness* (all in all) into the science of deductive logic, yet in his hands it, logic, became neither absolutely concrete, free nor infinite ; *not concrete*, because he treated the categories as merely subjective notions and as if they were in themselves devoid of all objective reality ; *not free*, because it excluded from reason a real objective knowledge of the world and did not attain to a logical idea of an *infinite* personal God. On these grounds his principles of *necessity* and *universality* in human thought were completely overthrown, for thought that is not infinite is not universal.

In the hands of Fichte, some of Kant's defects were considerably remedied, though not altogether scientifically removed : for his (Fichte's) logical exposition of the Idea of the Infinite was burdened with the obstacle of an endless succession of finites wherein the absolute notion of the infinite was never reached ; whereas the true concrete notion of the infinite is really always present, and is thought's own self. In spite of Fichte's comparative failure, Hegel credits him with the first reason-attempt in the world to deduce the categories from the ' I think.' It cannot be easily maintained that Fichte's view of Personality was very much better than Kant's, though they both had a much more rational estimate thereof than Schelling. Indeed, with Schelling there was not, in reference to God, ' a shred of intelligible personality left.' His system is full of glaring contradictions ; Ego, with Schelling, was devoid of consciousness, was not personality ; and he concludes, ' there is not a personal God, because consciousness is impossible without an object, and for God, that is, for the Absolute Ego, object there is none, for this Ego would cease thereby to be absolute.' He talks absurdly about going ' further than a personal God,' whereas personality is self-consciousness, and is at once both subject and object to itself. No person can by any possibility avoid making his own personality, his own self, his own thought, the object and subject of his own thought. A being that does not know itself as object in and to itself in its own thought, is not a person. Besides, there is nothing ' *further* ' than personality, or better than a personal God. Schelling held that ' the Ego is the Absolute,' ' the Ego is the unconditioned,' but Ego that is not personal is not Ego. He seeks in his later philosophy to derive the ontological Idea of God, in opposition to Hegel's exposition of this Idea, ' from the Seyn (Being) that is beyond all thought." But where is that Being that is beyond all thought ? It is the Being of an ' actual ' God to which he is referring. The Being of God, however, is all in all ; the actuality of thought. If this were not so, God were not. He says, ' We demand from philosophy the actual God—not the mere idea of God ' ; but the Idea of God is the one eternal, real true and actual Idea—the Idea that can never not be. Only so can God be the Absolute Ego, the Absolute Self-consciousness of the Universe —the Absolute I.

Now, sense-perception *alone* can no more reveal an ' actual ' God than sense-perception alone can reveal a man. Yet God can no more be excluded from the external world of sense, than the idea of design in the world and reason in man can be excluded therefrom. In man there is the threefold essential unity of sense-perception, understanding, and reason. Man is the microcosm of thought in which are seen at once in absolute unity, design in the world, personality in man, and the absolute self-consciousness of God. Just as the world and man are only truly seen in all their glory in reason-vision, so in like manner can God only be seen in all His glory in human thought. To attempt to speak or think of anything as being beyond or outside of thought is the climax of folly or madness. How can there be anything outside of, or beyond human thought, when the thought of *all that is*, is in man's thought as a definite infinite thought ? There cannot be more than *all that is*. As a thought it is more distinct and definite than the *thought of any finite object*, for every finite object in its qualities crosses every other infinitely in every direction. So man, in a manner, more clearly apprehends the infinite than the finite. The chief point here, however, is that the concrete, infinite idea in man constitutes the substantial nature of man's personality and the personality of God.

The categories all denote relation, consequently they are all concrete notions, while personality is the one absolute concrete Notion, the Notion of Notions, the universal Notion, the Ego. A merely subjective category, or a merely objective category is an empty abstraction—the one as empty and void of reality as the other. Although man is an empirical personality, or empirical Ego, he is in thought infinite ; of this he is conscious. Into this empirical Ego the universal personality of God is reflected ; in and through this, man is a person. Dr. Stirling has pointed out that a water-drop as a finite object can have reflected into it the whole visible expanse of the heavens. Sense-perception, however, cannot tell how far this reflection extends, but we are sure that reason-thought extends infinitely beyond the objects of sense-thought and takes into itself the totality of Being. The least that can be said, though not forming a proof, is that material reflection lends some evidence to show that the finite Spirit has reflected into it the thought of the Infinite Spirit, and thereby proves the possibility of the finite comprehending the infinite; the real proof, however, is to be found in the light of the Spirit's own self, which is 'the light of every man that cometh into the world.'

The world is the outwardness of the Absolute Personality wherein 'the heavens declare the glory of God.' 'Without a world,' as Hegel says, 'God is not God,' man is not man ; and without the Absolute Self-consciousness of Spirit (i.e. Personality) a logical philosophy of nature is impossible. Personality forms the basis of the logical system of the categories. A category, as a judgment, is essentially both subjective and objective, and includes both form and matter ; to view it otherwise renders the use of the term category wholly untrue and unnecessary. The world is in reality the external manifestation of the complete system of the categories of rational thought, and thus constitutes the unity of sense-perception, understanding and reason ; for everything is essentially quality, quantity, measure, substance, in one totality of being, in one Universal Thought. As Hegel says, 'The fullest is the concretest and most subjective, and what withdraws itself into the simplest depth is mightiest and most prevailing. The extremest, most pointed of points, is the Pure Personality.' 'As man has personality, so there is in God the attribute of Personality—Absolute.' 'The Spirit of God is the eternal life of the Christian, in which he is conscious of himself as this Spirit. In religion, the Absolute Spirit, the form of God is not taken from the human, for God Himself, in the true Idea, is the Absolute Self-consciousness.' 'As man has personality, so there is in God the attribute of Subjectivity, Personality, Spirit, Absolute Spirit.'

Kant and Fichte started from the Ego, but they neither attained to its true logical idea. As Dr. Stirling puts it, ' Hegel's Begriff is conditioned, so to speak, by the personality of the Ego, and neither Kant nor Fichte had ever risen to that.' This statement has an important bearing on the later development of the Kantian principle of philosophy. It is through the exposition of the Ego that a true knowledge of personality, whether of man, Christ or God, is attained. We see how and why both Hegel and Stirling regarded the personality of God as the culminating point in philosophy, and this through the logical exposition of the empirical Ego ; for therein the Infinite I is demonstrated to constitute the substantial nature of the Finite I—the Infinite is demonstrated to be in the finite, just as the universal is in every particular ; in other words, the universal is the soul of all particularity. Every particular in the universal, however, is not a self-conscious being. Man in this world is the only self-consciousness. He alone can philosophize, because he alone is thinking-reason. A reason that rejects a knowledge of the infinite and absolute is falsely named. A reason that confines itself for positive knowledge merely to what is empirical and finite is fatal to philosophy. To such reason, the eternal and supersensible, is a sphere of emptiness and dream. Because man is essentially thinking-reason, or, in other words, is in thought infinite, his professed rejection of a knowledge of the Absolute impels him to an infinite striving after a ' wisdom ' that becomes ' foolishness,' or to a striving to maintain forms of Christian teaching which are open to every gust of subtle sceptical thought.

How the personality of man is full proof of the personality of God is well given by Dr. Stirling :

' Now, the Begriff, the Notion, is actually empirically *existent* in man, and man is the finite Spirit. Man is the only actual *existent* (i.e. sensibly existent) that says I to itself, or can say I to itself. But if every *singular* self-consciousness is only a *particular* self-consciousness to the *universal* self-consciousness, then, God is. God is—not sensibly, mortally, finitely is, but absolutely, immortally, infinitely *is*. Let there not be one single *existent* " I " within the compass of this whole huge universe, and still there will be—absolutely—the one I—I am that I am—alpha and omega, the first and the last, Dynamis, Energeia, Entelecheia.'

The following translations from Hegel by Dr. Stirling show clearly that Hegel's system recognizes the personality of God :

' God, then, though only felt and believed, is still the universal quite abstractly taken—even in His personality the absolutely universal Personality. . . .'

' I, Ego, is the pure personality in which every particular is negated and absorbed, this ultimate singleness, and the pure oneness of consciousness.'

' God is not blank vacuity, but Spirit ; and this attribute is no mere word or superficial phrase ; Spirit clothes itself ; in that God is recognized as essential Tri-unity. . . . . Without this attribute of Tri-unity God were not Spirit, and Spirit were an empty word.' Here knowledge is not the direct sense-knowledge of some corporeal object, but of God, and God is the absolutely universal object, the universalest Personality, not, certainly, any one single particular—knowledge of God is the thinking of God, for thought is that act for which the universal is.'

Hegel was the first to attain to a logical scientific knowledge of the personality of man, of Christ and of God. How it is that he has been charged with denying the personality of God and the Divine Christ can only be accounted for by the fact that his own express statements have been carelessly slurred over. The idea that his system finds no place for a personal God, or that it is logically opposed to the conception of a personal God, can only have arisen from a failure to grasp the real logical character of his system of philosophy. Though Kant and Schelling started in a manner from the Ego, their view did not involve the idea of a logical dialectic of the Infinite, as with Hegel. They did not attain to a logical knowledge of what even the personality of man really meant; the result was that neither of them developed a true logical conception of a personal God. In justice we ought to note, Fichte's conception of a personal God was so far logically developed that his ' idea of the Godhead ' was ' *an I* that through its determination of self is the determination as well of all that is not self.' Hegel, however, attained to what they missed, because he completed the concrete notion of Kant into an absolute system of concrete logic. If Kant had worked out his transcendental philosophy instead of remaining content with his transcendental logic or his *Critique of Pure Reason*, he might have found out his mistake.

It is remarkable how even philosophers in this and every age have stumbled at the terms ' finite notion,' ' finite I,' and ' empirical Ego.' Finite notions are nothing but parts of the one absolute concrete notion : they are particular elements of universal Being, *for a universal without particulars is pure nullity. A full exposition of a finite notion is necessarily a logical exposition of the absolute Notion,*

*and is therefore essentially concrete, at once objective
and subjective.* It is at once finite and infinite in
the unity of pure reason, for the logical exposition of
a finite category (Notion) necessarily rises to infinitude. As a rational whole it implies personality.
It is the same with the Finite I. Every man is
an I, and as such, he is in his essential nature a
rational being. He is an ' I,' especially because of his
conscious relation to the Infinite I, and that because
there is no other possible Infinite than a being that is
infinite in thought. It is the same with the notion
of an empirical Ego. The empirical is what, on
one side, depends on many contingent circumstances,
though there is on the other side a non-contingent,
and so far, a non-empirical element in all contingent
events and forms of being. While there is in man
a divine non-contingent principle, many contingent
circumstances surround his birth, life and death.
However, in spite of all contingency, man is an I, an
Ego. Indeed, without contingency man as I, as
Ego, as personality, could never have existed. Contingency is an essential principle in all finite existences, for it implies change. Let anyone try to
realize to himself a world without change in man,
animal, vegetable, water or air. It would be a mind-
less world. Such a world is impossible. As it is,
however, personality is morally above the external
control of contingency. Man can die rather than
yield to the immoral, and die like Christ. Man, then,
as an I, an Ego, a Person, is the living embodiment
of the unity of finite concrete notions and the infinite
concrete notion. A thorough investigation of the
finite categories leads necessarily to ' the metaphysical notions of God, with proof, even in the
necessity of it, necessarily also of the existence of

God. And these, surely, are pregnant findings, crucially critical, too : not without a light from them in which what to Hegel was Notion, Category, God —all are express.' All of which bring into consciousness the true conception of Personality.

CHAPTER VII

THE EGO

A SOUND philosophy begins and ends with the logical exposition of the Ego.

In his book *What* is *Thought?* Dr. Hutchison Stirling makes it quite clear that Hegel had two beginnings in his mind—one, Ego, the other Being in its purest abstraction. The former Hegel kept too much in the background, while the latter is well to the fore. Though not explicitly stated, we find that Hegel regards the I or Ego as the term of greatest intension, the most concrete Notion, and Being as the term of greatest extension, the most abstract notion, meaning thereby, neither more nor less than what nothing means. In one sense they absolutely include each other. It is, however, of the highest importance distinctly to see that the I is the term of both greatest intension and greatest extension, for in it the extremes, or the most abstract and the most concrete, meet, and fully include each other, though few have recognized this essential unity. Being, to him, is not something outside the I, but is simply the poorest thought in the I itself. In one sense Hegel was quite right in beginning his logic with the most abstract Notion, and in following up the dialectic logical development of thought to the most concrete Notion, the I. Hegel names this movement of logical thought, ' the progress of the Notion to its exposition.' At first we are at a loss to know what he means, for both his Notion and Dialectic are as yet unexplained. He ought, however, to have made his beginning from the I, as the concrete Being of the Infinite I, more clearly explicit, and this he could have done, because the process through which he attained to this knowledge must have been clear to himself before he commenced to write his logic. If his readers were to understand, to lay bare this process was all-important. Dr. Stirling's chief aim in *What* is *Thought ?* is to bring the idea of Ego, the I, boldly and fully to the forefront. His (Dr. Stirling's) philosophy is not a mere abstract form, but the absolute concrete form (as a critic of Stirling said). 'His criticism of Kant from the standpoint of Personal Idealism, is true and well put, but in *What* is *Thought ?* Stirling does not advance beyond individualism.' On this Stirling says, 'My individualism is the individualism of the absolutely personal God whom Christ has vindicated into concretion from abstraction by the assumption of humanity.' 'And he who rejects such a philosophy has some reason to fear for the security of his Theism.' This point his reviewers generally have missed, and so have failed to see the force of his criticism of Kant's analogies in reference to the principle of causation. For much the same reason they have failed to see his doctrine of contingency in his criticism of Schelling, and the irresistible light it sheds on the 'unreason' which Schelling refers to as being in the world. He shows the vast importance of Hegel's seemingly contradictory statement that 'the unessential is essential.' It can scarcely be doubted when fairly looked at, whether from the Divine or the Human side (for the one contains the other), that the Ego, being of the greatest intension and extension, is in itself infinite.

This contains, at bottom, the ontological Idea of the proof of the existence of God. Stirling's exposition of the ontological argument in his Gifford Lectures is of great and vital importance.

1. GENERAL STATEMENT

Hegel regards the I (Ego) as the term of greatest intension, the most concrete Notion; and Being as the term of greatest extension, the most abstract Notion : by the latter he means, neither more nor less than what nothing means. Then, since Nothing is a Thought, Nothing is Being, because Thought is Being, the Being of Thought is Reality. In Logic, the science of the nature of Thought, Ego, Being, absolutely include each other; but it is of highest importance to see distinctly that I (Ego) is the term both of greatest intension and greatest extension, that in it the extremes meet, or the most abstract and the most concrete are one and fully include each other. Even Being in its purest abstraction is not something outside the I, but when considered in the abstract it is the poorest thought in the I itself. So far, however, as Being includes the Concrete, it is itself the Absolute Concrete, and therefore includes the I; thus Being and I (Ego) are identical with Thought, and so Being as Concrete is also the term of greatest extension and greatest intension : Ego without Being and Thought would be nothing but a truthless abstraction. Hegel nowhere defines the Ego as the Being of greatest extension and intension, but it is clear from his remarks in his *Phänomenologie des Geistes* (p. 199) that he held that the extension of a term was no greater than its intension, and conversely : this idea is evident all through his philosophy. It may not inappropriately be named the secret of the *dialectic* development of his philosophy.

9

Whether he named his beginning Notion or Being, he had the Ego always in his thought, and with him this was the Absolute and Infinite, or Ideality as sole Reality. If he had only stated clearly at the beginning of his logic that his aim was to give a logical exposition of the Absolute Notion of the Being, of the Ego, and that Being was the most Abstract, or undefined, Notion of the Ego, then he would have made it easier for his readers to grasp the beginning and exposition of his logic, in the dialectic logical development of thought from the most abstract notion to the most Concrete notion, the I. Hegel afterwards incidentally names this movement, ' the progress of the Notion to its exposition,' and says that ' of this (Notion or Ego) Logic is the exposition.' At first, as already stated, we are at a loss to know what he means, for both his Notion and Dialectic are yet unexplained. He ought, however, to have made his beginning from the ' I ' more clearly explicit. This he could have done, for he afterwards stated that ' The Absolute Being is the Self-thinking Self-consciousness, Ego.' He also tells us, ' The unity of notion and existence constitutes the Notion of God.' This is the Notion of the Being of the Ego, ' I am that I am ' of Moses. His system is logical, not natural or physical, evolution. It may be named metaphysical or spiritual evolution, but it is in no sense the origin of Spirit from matter.

Since the Notion of the Ego is of the greatest extension and intension, such Notion or Thought must necessarily be infinite. The term ' All,' when fully examined, may be used to express the same idea. In one sense it may mean a limited All, as when we say, All men, All trees, etc.: but if I say, *All that is*, then the meaning is absolutely universal or infinite ; the whole embracing or including in its unity, God, man, nature. There is not, cannot be anything outside of, or beyond, this All. This all is an infinite thought, and the being that thinks it is infinite, and therefore a person. Such a being is man.

Since concrete logic is the exposition of the concrete Notion of the Ego, it must equally be the exposition of the Absolute and Infinite. Its purpose is not to expound the Infinite in all its finite details—this is the work of the various finite sciences—but rather to expound Thought in relation to the Totality of Being as a rational or intelligible whole. Thus as the Ego is the Absolute Concrete Notion, so it is the Absolute Apodictic Judgment and the Absolute Syllogism—each of which includes the Infinite, the Absolute Totality of Being.

2. PARTICULAR STATEMENT

We have already said that Kant discovered the Concrete Notion. Now, how did he come to see that Notion was Concrete ? He did so by deducing the categories from the ' I think,' or rather from the judgments given in the text-books of logic. Dr. Stirling says that he deduced them ' in a manner.' This means that the deduction was not strictly logical. (The direct logical deduction of the categories from the Ego or I was first begun by Fichte.) Yet if we cannot affirm that the manner of Kant's deduction was logical, it was not, for that reason, wholly false. At any rate Kant felt justified in maintaining that as he found twelve judgments in what he named general logic, so there must be twelve categories, which were also notions in the Ego, or in the I think. This latter he named, ' the original unity of self-consciousness.' The categories, then, with him, were conceived to have their root in the Ego. So far his conclusion was correct, whether he

arrived at it in a strictly logical manner or not.
If this mode of reasoning can be admitted to be
valid in its conclusion, then the categories themselves must be *concrete* notions and the Ego itself
must be the one supreme Universal Concrete Notion.
If we admit, for the nonce, that there is a difference
between a judgment and a category, then the categories must be a step further towards reality than
the estimate which Kant forms of the judgments.
With Kant, however, both the judgments and the
categories must have their seat and root in the Ego.
If the categories can legitimately be named notions,
can they not with equal legitimacy be named judgments ? If so, then all categories are judgments
of the Ego, and constitute at once the substantial
form and matter of the Ego's own self, whether viewed
on the subjective or objective side.

A category, as we have already noted, is only a
category, and so only a notion, because it is in itself
both subject and object. Subjectively looked at,
it is notion : objectively, it is being, for a notion
that has no being is not a notion at all. Thus it is,
that all categories are concrete notions, and thus also
because the Ego, the transcendental unity of self-
consciousness, contains all concrete notions, it is the
absolute Concrete Notion, the Absolute Ego : the
Universal I. So a notion that is not concrete, that
does not contain both matter and form, is not a real
notion, and an I that does not contain concrete
notions is not a real I. This is equally the case
whether the I be infinite or finite—but the finite is
only I in and through the infinite I, the absolute
self-consciousness of the universe.

For the present, it must be seen and admitted
that man is only man because he is Ego, or I, for
whatever is not an I is not a man. Man is only a

man because he thinks and says ' I,' or can say,
' I am, or ' I think.' ' I ' is a self-conscious being, and
the fact that man says ' I am ' is proof that God is
the absolute self-consciousness of the universe, and
must say to Himself, ' I am that I am,' for man is
consciously sure that he himself is not that great
' I am.' Man, however, is an ' I am,' and therein he
is substantially one with the Infinite I am.

Kant apparently never realized the full import
of the concrete notion involved in his categories,
and as a consequence he never saw the full meaning
of the Ego. To him the categories were only empty
matterless notions, and the Ego was only the ' unknown thing in itself,' whereas in truth and in fact
there is nothing of which man is more certain than
the fact of self-consciousness as infinite, the true thing
in itself.

A correct conception of the real import of the
concrete notion forms the ground and starting-point
of concrete logic, and therefore of the logical philosophy both of Nature and Spirit. Now as man in his
thought apprehends notion as notion in its concrete
universality, so he equally apprehends in thought
that the universal notion contains and involves in its
real nature a universal matter. What, then, is the
universal matter, being, or content of the Concrete
Notion ? (for notion is only notion in and through
its content or matter). The matter of the Notion is
simply the complete logical system of the categories
of the totality of Being.

Unfortunately for the complete success of Kant's
critical philosophy, it lacked, among other things,
three initial, essential, logical relations. He viewed
logical judgments only from the subjective side ; his
categories in themselves were only matterless notions,
entirely subjective, and thereby his notions, as cate-

gories, ceased in any true sense of the term to be categories at all; further, they were altogether too limited in number to fulfil what was required of them; in reality the categories are as infinitely numerous as the relations of thought and being. Thus his notions not only ceased to be categories or concrete notion, but his Ego ceased to be Ego, man, to be man, and God, to be God. Thus Kant says the Ego ' is but a logical copula—it is wholly without matter of contents—it is but a point, but a logical idea, that is itself void, that has nothing to show for itself . . . nothing but a mere reflection falsely converted into a thing.' Still, in a sense the concrete notion is a central point in Kant's philosophy, and one cannot but be surprised that his system theoretically is so defective. However, he ' inaugurated the reign of Reason ' when he came to see the categories had their source in the unity of self-consciousness. I know of no words so brief and light-giving as the following, from Dr. Stirling's *Secret of Hegel*: ' Socrates reached the Abstract Notion, and Aristotle completed it into the Abstract Logic; but Kant discovered the Concrete Notion, and Hegel completed it into the Concrete Logic.' This single sentence tells the whole tale. The Concrete Notion, as it manifests itself in Hegel is, perhaps, at shortest, this : ' The Absolute is relative ' . . . ' An absolute is an absolute just because . . . of the relativity it contains.' ' To define God is to *think*, or express God in thought, and Logic ought to comprehend all thoughts as such.' ' The predicate then is alone substantial.' That then is Ego—the Concrete Notion—' the thing in itself ' of which ' Logic is the exposition.' ' Logic is, so far, Metaphysical Theology which considers the evolution of the idea of God in the ether of pure thought.' And that is the science of the pure Idea, the science of God and of divine things.

With Hegel the Begriff (Notion) is in part subjective, and in part objective. Even when he is speaking of either separately, he always regards it as implicitly containing its opposite. In his Logic he first deals with his theory of essence and being; the categories, though treated as objective logic, are regarded as a gradual development of subjective logic, or as a gradual evolution from the most abstract notion— pure being—to the most concrete notion, the Ego. The objective or external character of the categories is of the greatest value, since without this externality a genuine philosophy would be impossible. But the same result would follow if they were not essential notions as qualities of the Ego. Nay, they are only external because they are first of all internal and produced by the living energy of the Ego. They constitute the absolute-concreteness of the Spirit, without which Spirit would be a void name. In general, objective notions have, with Hegel, four distinct stages in Thought. First—their progressive development through the Categories. Second—their more concrete form as Mechanism, ' Chemism ' and Teleology. Third—their yet more concrete form in Nature proper : the absolute mechanical motions of the heavenly bodies, the general physical and chemical properties of matter, the organic relations between the animal, vegetable and mineral worlds. Fourth—their highest concrete form in the objective Spirit, as shown in the Laws of the State relating to property, to the constitution and to State-government in relation to religion, citizenship and family rights, and in the bearing of Freewill on the question of Civil rights. While in these four stages each has a real objective aspect and shows an advancement in concrete character, each has equally a substantial subjective side. The highest form of objective thought is the Ego or Spirit thinking and knowing its own self. It is, however, only the Ego, self-consciousness, Personality or Spirit that can properly be named Subject, and that because it is essentially conscious thought. A stone, a tree, an animal, gas, space and time are only objects for thought; because they cannot think, thought can never become an object for them, nor can they become objects for themselves : only thought is object to itself. Everything is object to conscious thought, because all that is is contained in and essentially related to thought in all its infinite particularity. Thought, however, because it alone is pure subjectivity, can according to its pleasure make and treat every object as a subject, e.g. A rose is a plant ; or, Space is boundless. Thus ' rose ' and ' space,' though objects of thought, are subjects of a judgment.

In a sense the object may be called the real, and the subject the ideal, though in their truth the idea is their substantial unity, for an ideal that is not real is not an ideal. The science of the pure idea, being the logical system of the categories, constitutes the middle term of the syllogism, for every category is at once real and ideal, just as every subject in its truth is idea.

The totality of being embraces in its unity the three branches of philosophy—the logical idea, Nature and Spirit. These have absolute unity in the Concrete Notion, the Ego, or Thought, for each of the three by itself is null and void. The subjective Notion of the subjective logic is, however, that part of philosophy which demands the most thorough investigation and exposition. Therein alone can the full import of the Ego and its Spirit be properly realized.

The subjective *Notion* of the science of logic naturally falls into three parts, viz. Notion, Judgment and Syllogism. It is the Notion proper that has received in the study of logic the least deep and thorough investigation. So far as a complete exposition of the Notion is concerned, we owe the most, by far, to Hegel and Stirling. The Notion proper is the Ego itself. As Notion, it contains three moments —universal, particular, and singular. It is only in the light of this threefold division of the Notion, that a rational explanation of judgment and syllogism can be given. The three functions or moments of the Notion furnish naturally a threefold rational division of the judgment, and also, on the same principle, a threefold division of the syllogism. These constitute in their rational dialectic development the logical evolution of the Notion, because everything rational is syllogism and judgment in the unity of the Notion; and of this the syllogism is the complete logical expression. The Ego, then, when logically fully expressed, is Notion, judgment, and syllogism (or it is subject and object in the absolute logical idea).

The Ego as thought is first, intuitive apprehension of itself as Notion in its pure universality; secondly, intuitive apprehension of itself as judgment in its particularity; and thirdly, intuitive apprehension of itself as reason in its infinite singularity. The absolute unity of these three moments makes the Notion in itself concrete. Further, its content or matter is concrete in and through its universal particularity, for its content is the particular in the universal and the universal in the particular. It is through this threefold form of apprehension that the Notion of the Ego is in itself both subject and object.

The following explanation of the extension and

intension of terms will help to make the true nature of the Ego more fully understood. It is generally stated, that as the extension of a term increases, its intension decreases. This is an error which has led to much confusion of thought in the science of logic. The intension of a term is simply its meaning. The term tree includes all trees; that is the extension; and that is also its intension. Oak-tree includes all oak trees; this term is of less extension than tree, and it is therefore less in intension, because it means less, for it only stands for the qualities which are peculiar to the oak. If it is said that oak-tree stands not only for the oak, but also for all that tree means, then it can with equal correctness be said that tree means all that is both common and peculiar to all trees; in this way the difference between the two terms in extension and intension is lost sight of, and the one term is made to mean the same as the other. Similarly with the terms metal and gold; animal and dog. The term gold is of less extension than metal; it is not used to signify all that the term metal means, for silver and lead are also metals, that is, gold is not gold merely because it is a metal, but the term gold only stands for what is peculiar to the metal gold; in the same way, though a dog is an animal, yet the term dog does not stand for fish and bird, thus the extension of a term decreases and increases just in the same proportion as the intension decreases and increases. Tree stands for all properties common to all trees; animal for all properties common to all animals; and metal for all properties common to all metals. Gold is only gold because of the special quality that marks it out from all other metals; the dog is a dog because of the special quality which marks it out from all other animals. Take away these special qualities of the gold or dog, and it is impossible to say what they are. Indeed, they are only what they are by their special qualities, and in each case, their distinguishing quality implies, in one sense, both more and less than metal and animal. These illustrations of extension and intension belong to the finite spheres of being. But the Absolute Ego embraces the Absolute sphere of absolute being, and this includes all finite spheres. Absolute Being, then, includes the Absolute Ego, and the Absolute Ego includes the Absolute Being. In this sense they are both concrete.

It follows that the Ego is the term of both greatest extension and greatest intension. There is no term or notion that includes more, and no term that means more. The finite, then, is not without the infinite, nor the infinite without the finite. Each without the other would be null and void. Being and Ego are both abstract and concrete, but Being without Ego and Ego without Being are empty names. Therefore the infinite and finite are difference in identity and identity in difference. The universe, in all its infinite diversity or difference, is God's universe. Not a single dust atom exists independent of God or of the total whole. The most minute atom is in essential relation to every other atom ; and thought constitutes the essential nature of all, for everything partakes the nature of reason and thought. The absolute unity of everything, whether viewed as the whole or in its parts, is found in the principle of design. The universe is the product of the Ego—Ego is not the product of the universe. The foundation of ' all that is ' is intelligibly Ego, Thought, Self-consciousness. Any other foundation is utterly unintelligible. 'Man is the only sentient existent Ego in the world. How is it that man alone is Ego ? Intelligibly man is an I, only because man is the only

exampler, analogue, type of the infinite I.' Only in
and by thought can anything be explained. Thought
alone can explain the world, explain God, or explain
itself. This is a fact so evident that it cannot be
doubted. Thought, then, is the only Being that is
at once in itself the term of greatest extension and
greatest intension. The greatest question, then, of
all questions is, What is Thought ? This question
can only be answered by thought's own self. ' Philosophy is the product of thought. Thought is the
seat and spore of philosophy, as it is of all existence.'
If this is so, then, the explanation of thought will be
the solution of Kant's problem, ' How are synthetic
judgments *à priori* possible ? ' and at the same time
it will reveal what is the principle of necessity in the
relation of cause and effect.

The non-solution of the secret of the relation between cause and effect has been the chief ground of
scepticism since the time of Hume. He said, ' All
reasonings concerning matters of fact seem to be
founded in the relation of cause and effect.' ' The
mind can never possibly find the effect in the supposed
cause by the most accurate scrutiny and examination ; for the effect is totally different from the cause,
and consequently can never be found in it.' He found
in mere sense-objects no connecting principle, only
a swaying to and fro of the testimony of our senses.
Custom was the only explanation he could give for
his belief in a necessary relation of cause and effect.
Kant's theory of analogy failed to give a logical
explanation. Agnosticism does not pretend to give
an explanation ; it rather takes for granted that
none can be given. No theory of evolution can give
an explanation, it can only say ' variation,' but can
give no reason for the cause of ' variation ' ; Darwin
bluntly declares that he is ' profoundly ignorant of

the cause of all variation,' while Huxley dogmatically asserts that variation is ' spontaneous.' Here is no explanation. Even for the Theist to say that God is the cause of all variation, is simply to say so, but the statement is not an explanation. Besides, we know that man is certainly the cause of much variation in the various spheres of existence. We know of no solution of these problems of Kant and Hume but in the philosophy of Hegel and Stirling. Hegel broke entirely new ground in philosophy in his Science of Concrete Logic by a new exposition of the Ego, or rather, the Begriff or Notion, as he names it.

8. Ego as Thought

It may be said that Dr. Stirling in *What is Thought ?* has discovered and explained the fundamental nature of thought, and in so doing has laid the pure and sure foundation of the great building of genuine philosophy. In the progress of human knowledge some few of the great discoveries with regard to the facts of nature were accidental, but the most important have been the result of persistent research in the various departments of Nature. The nature of thought as thought has, however, received the least direct persistent attention, and thus religion, morals and politics have moved in the most erratic ways. The physico advancement of thought can never properly supply the lack of progressive insight into the eternal and substantial nature of religion and morality. Our business at present is with thought as thought. It must be seen that it is only in logical thought that we begin to apprehend it in its substantial, essential and eternal nature. Merely to reflect on sense-perception, memory and imagination is to treat thought in a very superficial manner. The absolute assurance of the correctness and truth of any process of thought can only be found in thought's own self, and the form thereof must be the syllogism. It is only in the syllogism that rational thought first comes to the true light of consciousness; it is in the syllogism that thought first becomes truly logical, or takes the forms of the science of reason. Logic is the science of reason, because reason is the logical element in thought. Understanding, as the faculty of judgment, fulfils an important function, but it is reason that forms the solid eternal groundwork of truth in thought. Reason is the essence of thought, of truth, and of spirit: it is that in which spirit knows itself in its truth. Just as certainly as there is an eternal logical living element in thought, so it is pervaded throughout with the glorious light of intuition. The logical process of thought without this light of intuition would only be a groping in the dark. Thought is a matter of fact, and contains its own light, its own certainty, its own reason. These characteristics will never be properly seen in their true relation to each other by means of mere chance reflection. Intense earnestness in the study of logical thought is required. Yet it is in the intuitive conception of the infinite that thought rises to its own light. Intuitive and logical thought constitute in their essential unity the true nature of speculative philosophy: both are necessary to the science of logic, and in their united activity alone can apodictic certainty be realized in thought.

Thought is essentially infinite, whether in God or man, and knows itself as such. At first in man it is only the conception of a more or less abstract infinite, that is, it only knows the whole as whole, not in all its details. This is especially so when the child first attains to the knowledge of the I as concrete, even though this knowledge of the whole is very indefinite. The child soon knows that it has many thoughts in one thought or I. It knows what a clock is long before it can tell the time by it. The indefinite conception of the infinite in the I is the abstract infinite whole of thought, and, as such, it is the infinite abstract I as thought, for the thought of the I and the Being of the I are in this sense the same identical abstract infinite. The infinite itself is essential concrete : the true notion of the Concrete Infinite is only attained when it is seen that the ' I ' contains, and is *in sum and substance* the complete logical system of the categories of thought in the Absolute Concrete Logic. Logical thought constitutes its real concrete nature. Hegel calls the abstract infinite thought, the Notion : the concrete infinite thought, the Absolute Idea. The logical Idea constitutes the real filling and substantial nature of the Concrete Notion, and this is the Ego or I in its genuine rationality. Without the logical system of the categories existence is reduced to a mere mass of confused picture thought. Of course the categories are all judgments, and in themselves possess very different degrees of concreteness, but they only become truly rational when reduced to syllogism. Every real thing is a syllogism, and therein it is rational, for the rational is alone real as the Truth. The Idea as Ego is the complete system of categories.

Considered apart from Nature and Spirit, thought is abstract. Logic in the same way, when so viewed, may be regarded as abstract, just as pure mathematics is regarded as abstract, though in truth and in fact all existence is one universal concrete whole having all its parts in essential unity. The right conception of the abstract is of great importance, otherwise a logical exposition of the Concrete Absolute is impossible ; but it is equally important to have a right conception of the Absolute as the concrete whole. To suppose that any single part, or any single abstract notion or principle can have an independent and separate existence apart from the whole, is simply to render philosophy, and with it all explanation of everything, impossible. Apart from the essential unity of the totality of Being there can be no principle of identity therein, and if no principle of identity, the necessary connexion between cause and effect, or any other necessary relation, can never be explained. It is easy to see that all explanation requires thought : mere space, time, gravitation, etc., without thought, can explain nothing. So thought as thought must be well reflected on, both in its absolute abstraction and its absolute concretion. Pure Nothing has as real a meaning as pure Being, for both are pure abstract thoughts in the one concrete Thought, or concrete Notion, the I. Both mean pure indefiniteness when held fast in their abstract purity ; so far, then, pure Nothing and pure Being are the same, yet each contains a difference. They are two thoughts of which all we can think is that they are both indefinite, the one as indefinite as the other : their unity or identity is in thought— the Ego. Thought is the middle term that embraces Being and Nothing in the oneness of the Absolute Ego. Being in its pure abstractness is simply the present participle of the verb ' to be,' and denotes process ; as such it is the pure abstract becoming, that is, the most abstract form of the dialectic thought of the Ego : or it is the immanent movement of thought in its purest abstraction. As thought is essentially active in the concrete Ego, so it is essentially active as pure becoming—the abstract Ego. Pure becoming is always coming to be, always ceasing to be, and yet never ceasing, just as time is an eternal now, always passing and always coming. Pure space and pure time are each abstract Being and Nothing, though more correctly they each belong to the abstract beginning of the philosophy of Nature ; Being, Space and Time are three pure thoughts in the Ego. In a sense all these belong to the philosophy of Spirit : the highest form of Spirit is the unity of thought and feeling—feeling has no existence apart from thought : the philosophical self-consciousness of man as Spirit is love, which is with God, the absolute Spirit. As already noted, the logical form of thought is properly the syllogism, and the dialectic is the power and self-activity of thought, on one side negating itself, and on the other, through this negation and absorption of the lower abstract syllogisms, rising higher and higher into more concrete syllogisms until it attains to the Absolute syllogism. The logical Idea, Nature, and Spirit are three branches of the Absolute syllogism. It must be observed, however, that the logical Idea, Nature and Spirit form a triple syllogism, since each of these three terms in turn becomes a middle term in forming the Absolute syllogism. This has received its most complete and final form from Dr. Stirling in his exposition of the Ego, his I-Me-I, in which thought is shown to be the ratio or middle term between and within the I and the Me : I as subject, Me as object, and Thought, overlapping and embracing both, as the entire Secret of the Universe. This, as we have stated, is the most perfect and Absolute syllogism yet enunciated ; it is the most clear, simple, and immediate syllogism from which logical philosophy can make a perfectly intelligible and absolutely valid beginning. The I-Me knows itself at once to be subject, object, and middle term in the identity of thought. Object and Middle term can only be found in the subject itself. Then I itself is this three-fold unity : it contains what Hegel sets forth as the three essential elements or functions of the Notion (Begriff). The I is not I until it thinks itself I, and does not require for its cognition the introduction of any foreign element or matter ; it only needs to know itself to realize to itself the totality of Being. To know all that is in the I is the same as to know all that is. Concrete logic, then, begins and ends with the infinite and absolute quality of thought ; the I-Me with thought as the middle term ; for logic comprehends all thoughts in thought : thought alone is the whole, and as predicate it is the alone sub-stantial. So far as man's knowledge is superficial, it may be named abstract ; so far as it is deep and thorough, it is concrete : only, however, in the appre-hension of concrete logic does knowledge become truly philosophical.

According to the prevailing method of presenting or expounding the I (Thought, Reason, Self-conscious-ness or Spirit), the above statements may appear absurd, not only to the materialist and agnostic, but even to the theologian : yet if the difference between the abstract and concrete, absolute and infinite, were duly pondered and understood, we should hear less about the unknowableness of God. The whole difference is again evident between abstract and concrete thought, reason, Notion, Idea and Logic, and further involves the difference be-tween the abstract I and the concrete I, which latter is in fact and in truth the only I there ever was, is, or ever will be. To see the logical idea in the logical Notion is all-important in reference to the logical philosophy of the infinite and the finite, the ' I-Me ' or ' the I-Me-I.' The conception of the concrete infinite belongs essentially to the intuitive capacity and logical nature of human thought. But though thought contains the infinite concrete logical elements which constitute its own concreteness, it is not immediately aware of all the categories and syllogisms that constitute the complete logical I in all its fullness. This knowledge can only be gained by much study, just as proficiency in mathematics or any other science is obtained.

The three figures of the syllogism as enunciated by Aristotle were the natural demands of reason : the fuller insight into the real ground of these three forms, and why only three are possible, is due to Hegel. This he found in the Notion, or, more correctly, in the Ego. With Hegel, universal particular and singular are the three functions or elements of the Notion, and so they become the three fundamental principles of all the categories of the judgments, and of every syllogism. This is the threefold form of the Notion, or the I itself, and is named by Dr. Stirling ' the Secret of Hegel.' This threefold unity, known in a manner to the ancients, was by them named All-Many-One. With Hegel, All is the universal, Many is the particular, One is the singular. All, many, one, by themselves are not strictly in a rational or logical form. The term All is indeed universal and contains the notion of infinite particularity, but does not expressly denote the essential relation of the parts to each other and to the *all*, nor does it explain how the all and many are one. It is only in thought that their true rational and logical difference in identity is realized. Thought alone intelligibly contains the all, the many, the one, in their essential unity. With Hegel, the universal, particular and singular were each in turn made to take the form of abstract as well as concrete. It is often very difficult to follow Hegel through all these changing forms, especially when he treats the particular as universal. Kant, Fichte and Schelling each failed to see the immanent movement of the Ego in its own essential, substantial nature. Stirling's I-Me, with Thought as the Ratio, seems to me an immense simplification of the whole subject, and consequently a great advance upon Hegel. It may be thus briefly stated : ' I,' because it is in itself Thought, is universal ; ' Me,' because it is Thought, is the same universal ; and Ratio, because it is Thought, is likewise the same universal : yet in these three universals there is absolute difference in identity. From this pure clear original syllogism of Stirling's all the categories in their absolute unity and identity of internality and externality can be dialectically deduced. (This triplicity of thought must be kept well in mind in studying any works of Hegel and Stirling.)

Nature is the outward manifestation of the Ego, yet the Ego is not the same as the finite appearance of Nature. The outward manifestations are transitory and perish, but the Ego would not be Ego if it ceased to manifest itself in finite transitory appearances. Sense-objects are the creations of the eternal immortal Ego in and through the necessary free creative activity of thought ; sense-objects all perish, but the Ego, the self-conscious substantial essence of ' All that is,' is imperishable and immortal. It contains all Being in itself, perishable and imperishable, and is the seat and source of all reason, goodness, wisdom and power. ' There can be no completer unity,' says Stirling, ' than the unity of the Ego, yet in the midst of that unity there is an invisible dividing line. " I " is double, " I " means " I-I," or " I-Me." As double there is a dividedness in itself, and, in seeking to remove or level out the contradiction of it, really to create—not God—not the

Absolute Ego, which never was not, and always will be—but you and me, the world within and the world without. It is that hair-split, too, that is the source of all evil in the universe, evil physical, evil moral, pain, sin.' There is, then, a dividedness in the unity. The particular is one with the singular and with the universal, and yet it is different, and so, divided and restless, is ever seeking its full fruition in its other. In doing so it only creates itself, and thus particular succeeds particular endlessly in its dividing unity—the inseparable unity of the I—Me in its three elements—universal, particular, singular. The universe is a rational whole because Thought is the living, moving, self-creating Ratio that is in all and through all and by which all consists. Thought is the only intelligible first. The idea that thought is 'the outcome of mere material evolution' is not only irrational, but the greatest of all absurdities.

4. THE UNITY OF THOUGHT AND MATTER

It has long been the boast of mathematicians that mathematics alone is an exact science, and that the validity of all physical science rests on mathematics. We, however, maintain that all sciences, including mathematics, have their foundation in metaphysics. Mathematics is especially regarded as an exact science because it is viewed as being purely abstract and having no essential relation with either matter or thought. It is supposed that thought has no direct and immediate control over matter : the reason why Nature possesses these mathematical laws is held to be unknown and unknowable. Yet without thought there would never have been a mathematical science. The science of Arithmetic depends on thought and number, thus the unity of thought and matter is essential to Arithmetic. Algebra is the science of quantity, but apart from matter there is no quantity, and apart from thought there is no science of quantity or matter. The same is true of Geometry, the science of magnitude; and of the calculus, or the arithmetic of infinitely small differences of variable quantities, which implies fluxions or variable motion. Apart from matter there is no magnitude or motion, and no science apart from thought. No calculation in any form can be carried on without symbols, which are merely arbitrary inventions of thought : all symbols require some form of matter, and yet what would be the use of symbols without thought ? Thus not a step in any mode of calculation can be made without the absolute unity of thought and matter. Is it asked, What is matter ? and What is quantity ? In answer we quote from Stirling : ' As for matter, Leibnitz remarks, " It is not at all improbable that matter and quantity are really the same thing "; and Hegel adds, " In effect these notions differ only in this—that quantity is the pure notion, while matter is the same thing in outward existence." ' Now to this we may add a few words quoted elsewhere : There are particular matters in *existence*, each for itself and as such : but matter as matter does not exist : it is, but it is only a universal of thought, an entity in the intellect.' Quantity is only quantity because it is concrete, and it is discrete only because of its continuity, therefore quantity is the absolute unity of the discrete and concrete. There is no one that is not at the same time many. Space, time, matter, Notion, light, Ego are each examples of pure quantity, and are all in the unity of the concrete Notion, thought, or Ego. Only through this general notion of quantity is any branch of mathematics possible ; thus the ground of mathematics is metaphysical, and metaphysical science is the logic of concrete thought.

What is it that constitutes an exact science? It cannot be its completeness or perfection in every point, as this would imply that no further progress in human knowledge could be made. If this were the case, then no mathematical science is exact, for great advancement is still being made, and the possibility of further advance opens on all sides. If total completion in every detail were the test of an exact science, no science or true knowledge of anything whatever is possible, and all knowledge, named science, is a myth. All that exact science demands is that the principles on which it is based are absolutely certain, fixed and unalterable. Now concrete logic, or logical philosophy, asks and claims no more for itself than what is absolutely necessary in any other science. Hegel and Stirling are the last men in the world to claim for logical philosophy absolute completion at the hands of any man. Hegel was always haunted with the thought that many of the details of his work needed to be re-written and partially re-modelled, but he had no doubt that his system was grounded on a true and everlasting basis. Stirling says: 'As already intimated, we do not mean it to be supposed that Hegel in his work is either infallible or faultless. That of any human operation is not a thing to be said or even dreamed.' New books are constantly appearing with the aim of making improvements or some advancement in the various sciences, but they always proceed on some principle universally or generally recognized as fundamental and unchangeable. So in the progress and development of a sound philosophy, the fundamental principles of Concrete Logic must be clearly seen and recognized in their universal validity and apodictic certainty. The categories of thought, in the unity of Being, in their essential relations to each other in the Ego are the fundamental principles of logical philosophy; in them is the unity of thought and matter, subject and object. Thought has not to go out of itself to find its matter or its object, nor have matter and object to come into thought from a supposed elsewhere; thought without a content, a matter, an object, is not thought; so all the categories of being are the categories of thought's own being. This is the original unity of self-consciousness, the Ego. It has been stated that without matter there could be neither number, quantity nor magnitude, and that without thought there could be no mathematical science, nor, indeed, could there be any science without the unity of thought and matter. If this unity were not original, how did it come to be a fact in human experience? Natural evolution is no explanation. That matter is in thought is obvious, otherwise it could in no sense be an object of thought. As a matter of fact, the two are in unity from the beginning of infant consciousness: even there, the one is only known in and through the other in an original unity of self-consciousness. Sense-consciousness and self-consciousness are always in the unity of thought in human experience, and are always beyond any particular sense-object. This becomes very manifest when the child can say I; the implicit Ego in the child has now become explicit. Thought in man transcends every sense-object, but it never transcends the original unity involved in the unity of matter and thought, which is a necessary universal unity, because God is an infinite, universal and eternal Creator. God is the Absolute Ego, and man is Ego because he is in the image and likeness of God; this unity in the Ego is the starting-point of philosophy.

All the infinite diversified forms of matter are

simply external forms of thought in the unity of the Absolute Ego, so it is that we can have a science or a logical philosophy of Nature. Let Nature be independent of thought, or thought independent of Nature, or let the two be merely somehow alongside each other, then nothing worthy of the name of science, or logic, is possible. Astronomy is only a science because its nature and laws are one with the logical forms of thought. Chemistry, too, is only a science because it is the embodiment of reason and accords with the logical forms of reason in human thought. Chemistry deals with the forms of matter, with what are named its elements, and especially with the laws of proportion in their combinations and dissolvings, but no sense analysis can get down to the supposed separate, ultimate particles, whatever they may be named, to the universal all-common nature that binds the universe together and makes all one. All separation only gives another union, or another form. A formless matter is impossible, because the formless is nothing at all. Science is based on form, and this again on difference in identity. Laws imply unity, and unity difference. In every department of nature we see the essential unity of thought and matter. Since matter is, we know that it exists in an endless variety of forms and transformations, hence we see no reason to doubt the existence of a universal ether, invisible to sense, which may also be named matter, however different in outward form to other manifestations of matter. Such forms and transformations of matter are perfectly in agreement with what Paul calls the ' spiritual body,' and with the body of Christ after His resurrection appearing in a spiritualized or etherealized form, and also with His transfiguration in His bodily appearance on the mount before His disciples. It is an

obvious fact that thought is in essential relation to
what are named the various forms of matter, and also
that matter is variously modified and controlled
on every side by the thought of man; it is, then,
quite logical to regard matter in all its forms as
externalized thought and spirit. This is what the
categories of thought and being involve. A category is at once both internal and external, thought
and matter, or on the external side as matter the
categories are the externalizations of thought. The
great mistake of Kant was that he regarded the
categories as only subjective notions. True, he named
quantity and quality, intuitive and constitutive,
but even so they were with him only subjective
notions ; the rest of his categories he named regulative and contingent, consequently God was logically
an unknown Being, if He existed at all. With him
it was fundamental that notion without perception is
empty, and perception without notion is blind. He
did not attempt to prove this, and simply assumed it
as a fact needing no proof. His transcendental
synthesis of imagination really expressed the unity of
thought and matter, as did his two stems of human
knowledge having a single common root, because
imagination implies an essential connection between
the intellect and objects of sense. He evidently
did not realize that all the categories contained the
' à priori synthetic judgments ' he was in search of,
but Hegel saw clearly the nature of the unity, for he
said, ' They are possible through the original absolute
identity of differents.'   Stirling adds, ' that is simply
the Ego ' ; which is the fundamental principle of
concrete logic.

Our aim is not to give a complete system of the
categories of Concrete Logic, which would *here* be
an impossible task, but only to show some of its

fundamental principles. Many different catalogues of the categories have been given by various writers, according to their estimate of logic and philosophy, but, to our mind, the most complete system is that given by Hegel. To us a category is a notion denoting *a relation*, which is its essential nature. The categories fall in general into the particularity of the Notion. The universal and singular are no doubt categories, for they denote relations ; but particularity is their special · sphere, and so far, expresses finite relations, but since relation is as infinite as being itself, the categories of thought are innumerable. They are all, however, within the Absolute Notion, and therefore constitute the essence of the being of thought. With Hegel, logic is the pure Idea, and the logical Idea proper is the sphere of the categories, and must be regarded as the system of pure reason, the realm of pure Thought, and so the science of things in their unity in thought.

Now, thought and things are immediately in the unity of self-consciousness and are at one in the Ego.

Thought is conscious in itself that it is always essentially active, that this activity is always within itself, and yet that it is in all objects of thought; therefore it contains a double activity, internal and external, in living unity. Every known movement without is at the same time a known movement within, for that which is immediately known as *out* is immediately known as *in*. Further, activity implies change, and change denotes process. Thought, however, is always permanent, and is in permanent unity with matter in all its manifold forms of action. Activity is the process of creation in and by thought's own self. The knowledge of movement is not merely derived from the motion of external objects, but is known immediately in its own self-activity. Ego, which in its very nature is thought, is consequently the seat, source and origin of all movement, and the fountain of natural and spiritual life.

This activity of the Ego, the Notion or Thought, is what Hegel names the inner and pure negativity. External negation is the first negation, or mere ceasing to be ; the pure inner negativity is the negation of the negation, that is, creation. Without negation there could be neither motion nor natural and spiritual life ; no motion of the planets, no running rivers, no descending rain, no fertilization or growth in the vegetable and animal worlds. The negation of the negation is the restoring, creating, and perpetuating of being, motion and all natural and spiritual life. These terms express creation, birth, death and resurrection. Christ said, ' Except a corn of wheat fall into the ground and die, it abideth alone, but if it die, it bringeth forth much fruit.' In a deeper, spiritual sense He expressed the same truth when He said, ' Whosoever will save his life shall lose it, and whosoever will lose his life for My sake, shall find it.' Here death is ' the negation,' and life ' the negation of the negation.' Paul names it, ' the law of the spirit of life in Christ Jesus.' It is the love of God in Christ as the spirit of truth, and the essence of Christianity ; it implies being ' dead to sin and alive unto God.'

Such a phrase as ' the negation of the negation ' is not only new, but at first appears somewhat repellent, but it is not more strange and forbidding than the phraseology or technical terms found in every scientific text-book, and besides, Concrete Logic brings with it an entire revolution in the science of logic, and therewith introduces a new principle into science in general.

The foregoing is fundamentally Hegel's dialectic, which with Stirling is ' a dialectic that was the living internality of an Ego.' According to this principle, the universe is no longer to be viewed as dead or as the working of a huge system of mere mechanical laws, but as the living universe of the living God. The dialectic is the active power and goodness of God manifest in all creation. In human thought it is the impelling power striving to break through its finite abstract limitations, and gain a fuller knowledge of the different forms of the finite in its own infinite nature.

When Kant wrote of ' a transcendental synthesis of imagination,' ' a divine intuitive understanding,' and ' the reflective judgment,' he was near to the deeper and true conception of the absolute concrete Notion ; the unity of man, Nature and God. Creation as the work of God can never be independent of God, or without essential relation to Him. An intuitive, reflective and logical understanding and judgment belongs to human thought in and through its oneness with the divine ; for thought in its ' triplicity ' is the light of the understanding itself. If Kant had not himself possessed an intuitive understanding, he could not have seen the necessity for such in a divine understanding. It is not, however, given to man merely to be able to search and understand the deep things of God, but even to mould and control the forces and laws of nature to an almost unlimited extent. God has given power and dominion to man, He has ' put all things under his feet.' The full realization of this depends on man's knowledge of the mysteries of the kingdom of God and of Christ, and so of the unity of God and man.

The doctrine of the unity of matter and thought

touches closely the question as to the reality and possibility of miracles, which, as already noted, is no doubt at present supposed to be one of the most difficult problems to solve. According to the reported words of Jesus, these may be performed by false teachers as well as by true. Why do men question the possibility of miracles ? Fundamentally only through the unity of matter and thought are miracles possible, and, as such, they are external manifestations of the power of prayer over what is called matter. To sense-perception, a miracle has the appearance of thought acting on matter at a distance through a void space, and therefore without direct contact ; but an absolutely void space destroys at once the conception of universal matter and universal thought in their essential unity and relation. It thus renders impossible both a rational conception of the universe and the idea of miracles being performed either by God or man. The working of miracles by false prophets, without divine aid, indicates great power of thought in controlling Nature. Evidently there are invisible material forces in Nature upon which human thought acts and manifests itself in a great variety of ways. The material magnet and animal magnetism are obviously of the same origin, and form a ground for the action of what Paul calls ' lying wonders,' and ' deceitful workers.' There may be a strong faith in the power of Spirit which is not of God : the power of thought and spirit may be guided by the desire for 'the wages of unrighteousness,' by the pride of intellect and knowledge, or by the love of power. The true faith, ' the faith of God,' is ' the faith that worketh by love.' The true nature of thought will never be known until it is recognized that in reality, and in its fullest sense, it is identical with love, for ' God is Love.' Hitherto the great defect in science, philosophy, and Theology has been the failure to recognize that thought constitutes the essential nature of love and of the entire universe ; and yet thought in its unity with matter is the one invisible power known by every man to be the real moving power in all the ordinary events of human life. Without thought this land would soon become a desolation, and the universe be as dark and silent as the grave. The Ego in the ultimate contains the secret and solution of miracles and of all other mysteries ; the same power and wisdom is as necessary for the growth of grass as for the working of any miracle, and the latter is as much in harmony with reason and the laws of nature as the former. If Laplace, when reasoning out his great work to prove that ' the planetary system could not have been made on any other scheme,' had meditated more on the nature of his own intellect, he would not have concluded that the existence of God was a mere hypothesis. Man's thought is not a mere abstraction in his head. Let him reflect, and he will soon discover that he knows of nothing more concrete than his own thought, simply because nothing contains more. Spiritual unbelief is the great barrier to progress. We are told that Christ could not do many mighty works at Nazareth ' because of their unbelief,' and of some it is said that ' the word did not profit them, not being mixed with faith in them that heard it.' Hegel declares, ' The courage of Faith, Faith in the power of the Spirit, is the first condition of philosophical study,' and this involves a knowledge of the unity of thought and matter, the unity of the divine and human nature.

CHAPTER VIII

EGO—MAN, 'THE MEASURE OF ALL THINGS'

WHEN Protagoras said, 'Man is the measure of all things,' however imperfect may have been his conception of the meaning of the phrase, he therein expressed fundamentally the same thought as the scriptural expression, 'God created man in His own image.' All philosophy begins from the finite and must begin with man himself. Man must first ask and explain, 'What am I?' and then see how therefrom he can know God and Nature. Such knowledge would be impossible if man were not in himself a threefold unity of Self, God and Nature.

It must, nevertheless, be clearly recognized that Man, as 'I,' is essentially a spirit, and, as a spirit, in thought infinite. The infinity of man's thought constitutes his self-consciousness. As infinite, self-conscious, he is a rational being and essentially a person. The idea of personality belongs to and constitutes the true nature of Man, of Christ, and therefore of the Christian Religion. The essential elements of Personality are spirit, infinite and absolute thought, rationality or thinking-reason, and self-consciousness. Self-consciousness is infinite and underived. Man in thought is in absolute identity with God, for his self-consciousness is the self-create Self-consciousness of God, and therefore eternal. Man, to be man, must possess these elements of thought, as God, to

144

be God, must possess them : and thus it is that ' man is in the image of God.'

The Christian world accepts the statement that ' God made man in His own image,' but the theologian has laboured fruitlessly to show that this ' image ' was only moral, not intellectual, forgetting that there can be no moral being whose thought is not infinite. Attempts have been made to point out the limits of Human Thought, but all such attempts have failed, because man's thought is infinite and overlaps all limits. The thought of God as infinite, which is in man, is an infinite thought, therefore man is infinite in his thought. A being possessed only of finite thought—of sense-thought—is not a rational being, and so is neither a moral nor a religious being ; only an infinite being can have ' dominion over the works of God's hands.' When Paul speaks of man ' being renewed in knowledge after the image of Him that created him,' he does not mean giving him the idea of God, but the restoring of the Witness of the Spirit of God lost by sin, thereby taking the dark veil of sin from his understanding and giving him a knowledge of God in harmony with His true nature, such as He is in and for Himself. That man can have foolish and degraded thoughts about God will not be denied. A man's religion is true according as his knowledge of God and man is true. ' This is life eternal, that they might know Thee, the only true God, and Jesus Christ whom Thou hast sent.' Instead of speaking of man's thought of God being limited and finite, it would be more correct to say, man's thought of God may be abstract, obscure, indistinct, confused, or even mixed and perverted ; but to call his knowledge of God finite *only*, is very incorrect, for man can increase in the knowledge of that which he knows to be infinite. Paul grasped the true notion of the way in which man's knowledge of God may vary, when he said, ' When they knew God, they glorified him not as God, neither were thankful ; but became vain in their imaginations and their foolish heart was darkened ; professing themselves to be wise, they became fools, and changed the glory of the incorruptible God into images made like to corruptible man, and to birds, and four-footed beasts and creeping things."

The Bible everywhere recognizes and teaches that God's thought or understanding is infinite : it speaks of Him as eternal, in understanding infinite, and knowing all. It also recognizes the fact that man can know God as such intellectually, and therefore imposes on him the duty of increasing in the knowledge of His greatness, love and majesty. If he were not intellectually ' in the image of God,' he could in no sense know the meaning of these statements in relation to Him. Of course, the image of any object is never exactly the same as the object itself, still it must bear some real and striking resemblance to the original. Immense harm has been done to, and in, the studies of theology, philosophy and physical science by the endeavour to whittle away the intellectual image and likeness of man to God. If there were a positive limit to man's intellect beyond which in thought he could not pass, he would be as devoid of the notion ' infinite ' as the animal is ; but man not only knows with certainty that he has this notion, he knows with equal certainty that the animal has not. Paul's expression, ' Man is the image and glory of God ' cannot refer merely to what is named ' the moral image of God.' Indeed, man, even though morally deeply degraded, is still a moral agent, and knows intellectually the difference between love and hate, and good and evil. Man, even in his sinfulness, being intellectually in the image of God, knows God, while the animal, which is not in intellect made in the image of God, can in no sense know Him. The basis of man's moral nature is his intellectual capacity, and therefore he is still capable of being 'renewed in knowledge after the image of Him that created him.'

When we turn to the Biblical account of the nature of man, we find that the first statement is that ' God made man in His own image.' As already stated, that which is essential is the intellectual image, in and through which alone man is a moral being. He does not cease to be a moral agent because of his sinfulness, nor does he cease to be 'in the image of God ' even though he becomes immoral and sinful. It is not necessary to do evil in order to have a knowledge of God and of good and evil, for this knowledge is inherent in his nature as a rational being, but by transgressing the moral law he became acquainted with the awful, ruinous consequences of sin. By disobedience he lost the witness of God's Spirit in his heart. For the first time, he gained the painful knowledge of a guilty conscience and sought to conceal himself from God.

Some Biblical critics absurdly tell us that ' the fall of man is the birth of conscience.' This statement will not bear examination. It is evidently based on the evolutionary hypothesis that the animal, before it had any sense of right and wrong, had to become a sinner before it could develop into a man. On this line of reasoning, further transgression would increase the power of conscience ; this is not the general experience of men ; sin has rather the opposite effect of dulling the conscience. Where there is no knowledge of the moral law, as in the animal, there is no moral law, therefore such a being is incapable of committing sin. Besides, surely no man will deny that man is higher than the animal; then, if so, how is it possible for the animal to fall up into manhood ? The phrase, " The fall of man is the birth of conscience,' resembles the expression ' A round square.' It is altogether a misnomer : it is absurd. Even if these critics say that they only make use of the expression, ' fall of man,' to explain the ' so-called fall,' yet the above remark still holds good, How can the animal grow up into a knowledge of good and evil, when such is not inherent in its nature ? for the animal has no more a moral capacity than a tree or a stone : the very idea of an animal sinning is, to say the least of it, irrational. Conscience is a name for man's knowledge of good and evil, and this he had before, as well as after, his moral transgression ; transgression made him feel a sense of guilt and shame. It could not evolve a conscience, for he had that already. Man as man, being in the image of God, cannot but know good and evil, just as it is the nature of God to know good and evil. God is the moral Governor : man, a moral subject.

When Dr. Stirling says, ' Man in that he is of sense is finite, but in that he is of thought is of spirit and infinite,' by ' of sense ' we take him to mean sense-perception, which, although giving finite knowledge, cannot give the notion of the infinite. Thought as thought, reason-thought, cannot limit itself to sense-knowledge : it transcends sense-knowledge and rises to the infinite, or, rather, is in itself infinite, and sees the relation of ideas in matters of fact. The materialist admits that the sum of matter is always the same ; but it is only reason-thought, not sense-thought, that can see and realize this as a fact. The Ego, the I, the I-Me, is, however, the common root of both reason-thought and sense-thought. The difference is not merely between objects of sense-perception, for difference in identity belongs *à priori* essentially to reason-thought. Thus we see that man is both finite and infinite in so far as he is of thought; that even the transitory is permanent, for in an important sense the transitory can never cease. This is a deep thought on the part of Hegel. Such terms as becoming, process, mediation, dialectic, imply both a coming to be and a ceasing to be; at the same time implying Being without beginning and without ending. Such Being is conscious-reason-thought, and this in its truth is God, Freedom, Immortality, which again is fundamentally Man, Freedom, and the Immortality of the Soul, for man is only man because he is a conscious thinking reason-being.

Touching the nature of man, we find that Paul occupies exactly the same ground. Sense is absorbed in reason, in reason-vision. He says, ' When that which is perfect (reason) is come, then that which is in part (in sense) shall be done away '—sense is merged into reason, that is, Reason puts away childish things, i.e. speaking, understanding and thinking as a child. ' The man, when a child,' says Kant, ' even when he cannot speak the Ego, has it implicitly, and so comes to know himself as I, as though it were *the going up of a light to it.*' The ' going up of a light ' accords with ' putting away childish things,' and with the implicit Ego becoming explicit. Man only knows his true manhood when he sees himself in the light of pure Reason, of pure thought, of the pure Ego, and this alone is ' face to face.' To see nature, man, and God otherwise than in the light of intuitive reason is only ' to see through a glass darkly,' or through a veiled understanding. The ' open face ' alone can see the glory of God, of man and of nature in the face of Jesus Christ, ' in Whom dwelleth all the fullness of the Godhead bodily.' 'Now (in sense) I know in part (finite); then (in reason) shall I know even as also I am known '—that is, through the same pure intuitive reason-vision in which I am known to God. 'To know even as I am known,' 'face to face,' is a great thought, and well expresses the philosophy of Hegel and Stirling.

It is often said that man as finite cannot have a logical comprehension of the infinite God, yet it is also often said that we shall know God and see Him face to face after death. Those who say so, forget that if our finitude prevents us from knowing God now, it will equally prevent us from knowing Him *then*. With Paul, God was an object of present knowledge, and though he regretfully said, ' Some have not the knowledge of God, I speak this to your shame,' it is clear he did not believe that God was unknowable, in consequence of man's finite nature, otherwise it were no shame not to know Him.

It is remarkable how even well-educated men, in their writings and speeches, will contradict themselves in the use of the terms ' finite ' and ' infinite.' Why do they use the term ' infinite ' at all if they know the infinite is unknowable ? The very use of the term proves that their thought is infinite, and cannot be repressed to mere finite limits. Thought, self-consciousness, is always and in every direction infinitely beyond every limitated part. Let anyone in a numerical ' regressus ' or ' progressus ' in time, or in a ' progressus ' in every direction into the infinity of space, multiply time by ages, and space by miles, and then try to fix a limit to his thought in time and space, and he will find that his thought is already infinitely beyond every limit. A person might multiply for ever without making the slightest approach to the conception of the infinite by such a process.

The fact is, that the idea of the infinite belongs essentially to human thought, and is in its nature infinite reflection. Thought is just as sure that there is an infinite past and an infinite future as that there is a present: and as sure that there is an infinite space as that there is a here. To say that our conception of the infinite is merely an indefinite conception, overlooks the fact that the indefinite contains the infinite, and the infinite the indefinite. ' At the name infinite there arises to spirit its own light,' and this is the light of God. To know God, man must know himself, and to know himself he must know God. This is, as we have stated, the position of Calvin in his *Institutes*. If man had only reflected more on the nature of thought, there would not have been so much aimless wandering in search of the truth—the permanent, eternal and real. Stirling tells us that Noack sought to minimize the glory and greatness of the Ego by saying, ' The Ego is but the becoming aware or conscious that we think.' To which he replies, ' And what pray, we may ask, would you have more ? Good heavens ! just suppose it off !—' and in an instant all was dark ! ' The true light or illuminating power within is not from without. The infinite ' I ' is the light of all that is. The Ego, the ' I ' in man, notwithstanding his finiteness of sense, is in his (man's) thought infinite, and this alone constitutes his moral and religious nature.

To know man as man, I need not have a sense-perception of every man : this is impossible ; but even if it were possible, I could only know him externally according to the flesh, not internally according to the spirit. Sight is finite, insight in infinite. To know the real nature of man I need only know myself : but such knowledge is great. The finite spirit of man, though in thought infinite and concrete, is, in a sense, only partial and abstract. It is infinite and concrete because it knows well that the full meaning of All means the totality of Being, and that is an infinite thought. Thus man has a better knowledge of infinite thought as such than of any of the finite spheres of Being. It is not easy to make this distinction clear, yet this is the case with our knowledge of every finite object around us, even with those of which we may have the fullest knowledge. This seems to say that I know and do not know : that my knowledge is infinite and not infinite : finite and not finite. Yet I know ' the all ' (the whole) of a dog, or of a watch, as well as I know the total All. The whole of a dog or a watch is there present to sense-perception, and yet there is much in both that I only know in part, not in its absolute concreteness of detail. So in this I have no more a full knowledge of the finite than of the infinite in its absolute total concreteness. The total-all is not present to sense-perception, and never can be : this total ' all ' is only present, and can only be present, to super-sensible thought, to reason-vision, to the intuitive understanding, to the infinite reflection in the light of the infinite I, whose seat and manifestation is in the finite Spirit. Supersensible or reason-thought overlaps and includes All and every object in the most universal sense of the term ' All.'

As there is much detail in the finite unknown by man, so there is much in the infinite unknown by him. Nevertheless, it is only because he in his thought is infinite that he knows that he does not know ; were man's thought not infinite, he could only, like the animal, not know that he did not know. This explains the seemingly contradictory expression of Paul when he speaks of ' knowing the love of Christ which passeth knowledge.' He recognized the absolute fullness and perfection of the love of God. He knew the love of God as supreme reality; he knew that he knew it; yet he knew that 'it passeth knowledge,' and so he knew that he did not know. This involves no real contradiction. Paul knew that none was involved: his intellectual vision was too clear and full for him to allow himself to be lost in a sort of intellectual puzzle-box. A candid thinker will readily see and admit that a thing may be known as a whole, and yet he may also as clearly see that a knowledge of all its properties and qualities admits of very varying degrees of fullness. This applies with great force to man's knowledge of God, but to argue from such premises the absolute unknowableness of God by man is the climax of absurdity: just as it would be to argue therefrom that man has no knowledge at all, though this is in the ultimate what any theory of agnosticism legitimately comes to. The term is a misuse of language, for, strictly, it denotes no knowledge.

We are here brought face to face with the question of the absolute certainty of the truth of human knowledge of any subject or object whatever. Can man be sure that his knowledge is true or false? Or as my four-year-old grandson said to his father, 'How do you know when you are sure?' This is one of the deepest questions in philosophy, and one that enters deeply into all the interests of human life, whether of morals, politics, physical science or religion. The confounding of truth with error in any department of knowledge cannot but seriously affect the general welfare of mankind, which can only be promoted by truth, and which must always be perverted or destroyed by error. A man's knowledge may be in part a knowledge of error, but in part a knowledge of truth. We must admit that knowledge of error is knowledge, just as a knowledge of truth is knowledge. There is, however, a wide difference between knowing that truth is truth, and that error is error, and in thinking and believing that error is truth. Error is not truth, even though millions of persons may regard many gross errors to be truth. It is not only a fact that many believe error to be truth, but also that many believe truth to be error. From this confusion of thought and belief arise much conflict, strife and bitter persecution, not only in religious, but in scientific and political circles. Thus we see a man may feel sure he is right when he is wrong, but he may also be sure he is right when he is right, that is, he may be sure that his knowledge is truth. How then, or from whence, does his true, as opposed to his false, assurance arise ?

We have already stated that logic is the science of truth, reason and thought ; it is essentially speculative philosophy. The term speculative means to see—that is, to see the whole as whole, not merely in fragments. This is reason-vision, and is therefore exactly the opposite of mere guessing, conjecture or hypothesis. It has no place for mere opinion any more than has mathematics. Speculative philosophy, then, is the absolute unity and movement of intuition in the logical evolution of thought, which together constitute one absolute concrete process. It is not mere abstract reason or an empty reflection.

The ' I ' as thought is at once intuitive, reflective, and logical. As intuitive it is its own light, seeing and knowing itself in its own light, for there is nothing beyond or outside of it, therefore no light can come into it from without. As intuitive it is the perceptive understanding seeking for a full knowledge of every particular in the universal, which is already present in the universal Ego, for, as Hegel says, ' Every man is a whole world of ideas buried in the night of the Ego.' Or, as Kant says, ' The whole is sooner than the parts.' It is a divine prerogative of man to have the infinite light which knows that he does not know. Intellectual intuition is the ground of all certainty of man's knowledge ; it is given to him in the light of intuitive thought to be sure that he knows with an undoubting certainty, and likewise to be equally sure that he does not know. Kant clearly apprehended the meaning of the intuitive understanding of God, but he did not see that an intuitive understanding belongs to man's thought; yet if Kant had not possessed an intuitive understanding, he could not have known that such an understanding must belong to God.

Thought is reflective as well as intuitive. Reflection cannot be a mere abstract identity, but must possess difference in identity—something and another, each possessing a light in and through which the one is reflected into the other. Thought, then, is reflection in itself, and reflection in its other : each is other in and to the other, without which essential relation, reflective thought is impossible. This involves the necessary co-existence of particulars in thought as the absolute universal. A universality without particularity would be a truthless abstraction of which nothing could be known. Thought is in reality nothing but Kant's unknown-thing-in-itself which contains all the particularity of the universe, or the total universality of Being—All that is—for thought in itself overlaps and includes in its absolute concreteness the infinite reflection of all-that-is. To deny the reality of reflection as a fact in human thought would be absurd, and to limit the sphere of reflection is impossible, for thought, and so reflection, is in every direction infinite and beyond all limitations. Intuition and reflection are both essential elements in logical thought : and it is only in and through the logical principle of the syllogism of necessity that intuitive and reflective thought can be saved from wandering endlessly in the ever-changing vagaries and images of a vain imagination, in which a picture-loving fancy delights to range without control.

Logic is the principle in thought that, like a bridle, guides the mind steadily and carefully in its search after truth, or to a knowledge of its own self. Intuition, however, is the eye of thought which alone gives full assurance that, in its ceaseless activity, it is strictly logical : for logic, as the science of truth, is a strait and narrow way. Intuitive reflection, however, without logic would possess no more certainty, so far as a correct knowledge of truth is concerned, than the mere chance movements in the varying pictures in a kaleidoscope. Sure or certain knowledge in man cannot be a mere question of memory ; indeed, man's memory often fails, even in important matters. Mere memory lifts man no higher than the animal, which is limited to a superficial knowledge of the fleeting matters of sense. To mere memory sense-knowledge, space and time are finite ; but in reason-knowledge they are infinite and always present to thought as an absolute infinity. Thought and space are in infinite relation to all that is. In sense-certainty of space there is, moreover, a sort of spectral illusion. The telescope seems to contract space into a smaller dimension when bringing distant objects into view, while the microscope seems to extend the dimension of space very considerably in ordinary sense-points ; but reason assures us there is no such contraction or expansion of space, and that space and our knowledge thereof stand in necessary relation to objects in thought.

With time there is an apparent difference. It is in itself in thought a mere after-one-another-ness of objects in space. Yet space and time are in necessary relation and identity in difference. Time is always now : but *now* has no meaning apart from an infinite *past* and an infinite *future*, of which man, however, has a certain knowledge. Mere memory does not give this knowledge of infinite time : it is in man, and is proof of the identity of Divine and Human thought. Memory-knowledge begins at birth, but reason-thought or knowledge is one with eternity.

Man in one sense is but of yesterday—created finite spirit, but in his thought as infinite he is uncreated, eternal, immortal. He alone in this world is the only being that can think the infinite. As already noted, the reason and ground of the fact that man as a finite being is in thought infinite, is that man, in so far as his thought contains the thought of absolute totality of being, is made intellectually in the image of God, and because the infinite thought of God is one with the thought of man—not merely side by side, but in essential unity. At the same time, there is an essential identity and difference between the universal self-consciousness of man and the universal self-consciousness of God. The self-consciousness of man is infinite, because he has in him the thought of all that is : and this is real knowledge, not fancy, or mere hypothesis.

The self-consciousnes of God is omniscience, and consists not only in the knowledge of the whole as whole, but of the whole in its infinite particularity. God, as Creator, knows all in all its detail : man knows all, but in its detail only in a very limited degree ; thus for him to know God he must first seek to know himself, for in the identity of infinite thought in God and man is the oneness essentially of man with God. It is vain to seek to enter the heart and love of God without knowing Him in His infinite thought, and the comprehension of the infinite love of God is as certainly a matter of the intellect as knowing that twice two are four. It has been asserted by a university professor that ' our experience is wider than our thought, and we possess objects in other ways than by intellectual apprehension ; our moral and religious life appeals to other powers.' If man in thought is infinite, then, nothing can be wider than thought, and all objects are necessarily unavoidably in intellectual apprehension, for the simple reason that *thought overlaps and pervades all that is.* A moral and religious life is only possible to a being who is in thought infinite, and thought itself is in the intellect. To affirm of anything that it is wider than thought or intellect is an ignoring of what intellect or thought is. The lack of loving thought in man alone clouds his intellectual vision, and prevents him knowing God and His works in their true light. The love of God in Christ is the intellectual eye-salve God has sent into the world to anoint man's mental vision, so that all men may see God and His universe in all their glory.

Paul felt assured that the Spirit of God revealed the things of God to the spirit of man, just as it is a matter of everyday experience that the spirit of one man imparts his thoughts to the spirit of another. Purity, love and holiness, the supreme conditions of a sound philosophy, are the Bible conditions of knowing God in His truth. Only sin and the absence of these moral qualities have prevented man from seeing the idea of the world, of God and of self, which are at once and for ever in man in their absolute unity and identity of thought. Only in the permanent idea of God in man is any form of religion in the world possible or actual. To quote again from Stirling: ' " God," says Hegel, " is essentially self-conscious, and it is only when man has realized himself into union with God; only then has he realized his true freewill." ' Paul says, ' Where the Spirit of the Lord is, there is liberty '; and again, ' He that is joined to the Lord is one spirit.' It must be remembered that this oneness of God and man can be understood in two senses; a thought-unity and a moral-unity. The latter, that of love, man may lose, by becoming full of evil and erroneous thoughts which control and dominate his moral character; but the thought-unity man cannot lose, because in God he ' lives, moves and has his being.' This substantial unity of God, Christ and man can only be logically found in a proper and satisfactory conception of the Ego.

In a sound philosophy unity is manifested in difference, most clearly revealed in the relation of father and son, for they are in their true and substantial nature one—an Ego in the unity of self-consciousness. Thus in self-consciousness, whether as father or son, man possesses ' the image of God,' and is in the most perfect identity with ' God, the Father of the spirits of all flesh.' Man, because he is in thought and spirit infinite, is, even in his bodily form, the highest in ' kind.' So far as he is flesh, he is mortal, but as a self-conscious spirit, in thought infinite and immortal, he is one with God, ' Who only hath immortality.' Christ as a man was the first to comprehend and reveal this great truth in its clearness, fullness and glory, hence He declared, ' I and My Father are one.'

The supreme Godhead of Christ is not here our

chief point (among Christians at least this is a doctrine universally admitted), but that these words when properly understood teach 'the substantial relation' of 'the unity of the divine and human nature.' The Jews reproached Christ for claiming to be God : this they regarded as blasphemy, and for that reason they sought to kill Him, and at last crucified Him. They sought to stone Him 'because,' they said, ' Thou, being a man, makest Thyself God.' Christ took this occasion to shed a new light on the words, ' I said ye are Gods,' the real meaning of which they had never seen. In this phrase the persons named as Gods were those ' to whom the Word of the Lord came,' that is, to the ' holy men of old, who wrote as they were moved by the Holy Spirit.' Christ in effect said, These men were named Gods, and you admit your scriptures do not blaspheme : then why do you say that I, ' whom the Father hath sanctified and sent into the world,' blaspheme because I said, ' I am the Son of God,' for if they are Gods, so am I ? It is quite clear that this great claim on the part of Christ was the one great offence in their eyes for which they crucified Him. They said, ' We have a law, and by our law He ought to die, because He made Himself the Son of God.' This was to them ' the stone of stumbling and rock of offence.' In the Psalm it is added, ' all of you are children of the Most High.' This teaches that the human relationship of Father and son is in all cases divine, and that God as Creator is the Father of all men, and all men essentially partakers of the divine nature. This agrees with the words in Psalm viii. : ' Thou hast made him (man) a little lower than God, and made him to have dominion over the works of Thy hands.' In the Epistle to the Hebrews the nature of man and of Christ are identified, just as both are identified with the nature of God the Father. The very words used to express the divine nature of man are used to express the divine nature of Christ. The only difference is that in the Psalm the words are, ' a little lower than God,' while in the Epistle they are ' a little lower than the angels.' The Bible, however, teaches that the angels intellectually are moral beings, knowing good and evil, and as such are also sons of God. Of course, the existence and nature of angels are not to us matters of direct experience in the same way as the existence of men, or of Christ as a man in the flesh. The fact of man ' being made a little lower than the angels ' renders it not less a great philosophical truth that God is the eternal Father of Christ and of all other men, and that the teaching of the Bible and the teaching of logical philosophy are in perfect agreement, in and through which we rise from the human Ego, or I, to the Ego of God the Father and of Christ.

The teaching of Christ and of the Scriptures generally on the nature of man, and of a possible conscious knowledge of his high relation to God in love, is of very vital importance, in its bearing on the Christian religion, as the Religion of Reason, and also on the rational solidarity of the Human Race. When Christ said, ' In that day ye shall know that I am *in* My Father, and ye *in* Me, and I *in* you,' He said in effect, ' this unity and oneness is already a fact, though as yet you do not know it as such ; it has not become to you a matter of conscious experience ; but ye shall know it.' Much of his teaching expressed the reality of this oneness very clearly, but the disciples, while He was with them, were too blind to understand it. He said, I must first leave you, and I will send My Spirit and the Spirit of My Father upon you, then shall you all know that we are all one, even as I and my Father are one. Just before His ascension He said, ' I ascend to My Father and your Father, to My God and your God.' They did not see that the words, ' your Father,' meant a deep, essential, spiritual relation to God. This meaning, however, soon came to them at the Pentecost in a great, glowing, conscious experience, and the full assurance of the great doctrine of the Witness of the Spirit, which entered so largely into the teaching and experience of the early Christian Church. Still, in reference to this truth, as a logical doctrine, the early disciples and the Church generally had much to learn.

The apostles Paul and John, but especially Paul, seemed to have penetrated most deeply into what was truly implied by all this. Paul reveals to us a little of his deeper insight in his address at Athens. He quotes approvingly the words of one of the Greek poets, ' For we are all His offspring.' Here is a recognition of the Fatherhood of God and the sonship of man, which mean much more than a mere feeling of active goodwill in a parent's desire to ' give good gifts to his children.' It points to the spiritual relation between God and man in thought, since it is through that relationship that Paul reasons from what they know of the intellectual nature of man to the nature of God. ' For as much then as we are the offspring of God, we ought not to think that the Godhead is like unto gold, or silver, or stone graven by art and man's device.' You must admit that man as a thinking rational being is much superior to gold, silver, or stone, therefore you cannot think God to be inferior to him (man), but rather much superior. So Paul reasoned with them. The vital point is, that men being the children, or offspring of God, there must be an identity of nature between God and man.

The conception of God as Father was not at all new. Malachi said, ' Have we not all one Father ? hath not one God created us ? ' Here he connects Creator and Father in one Person, and it is very certain that he saw that their Father meant the same kind of nature as God their Creator ; and Isaiah says, ' Doubtless Thou art our Father, though Abraham be ignorant of us, and Israel acknowledge us not ; Thou, O Lord, art our Father, our Redeemer ; Thy name is from everlasting.' In the book of Numbers, God is named ' the Father of the Spirits of all flesh.' Those words certainly expressed a vital union between God and man, and meant that God was more to them than a being *beyond,* or somewhere in a region far above them as a mere onlooker ; besides, there are references to the Spirit of God being a comfort, strength and joy to them, and also statements that God dwells in the humble and contrite heart.

Among the benighted heathen, in spite of their idol worship, there is a dim conception of a great Spirit being somehow in close connexion with men, and mysteriously controlling the material objects around them. This perception has its seat in man's spirit, and science cannot destroy it, but rather tends to show that spirit and thought are at the root of all things, as their formative matter and power.

No mere analysis in chemistry can show what matter is as an object of sense-perception. The words of the prophet still hold their ground in human reason, ' He hath made the earth by His power, he hath established the world by His wisdom, and hath stretched out the heaven by His understanding.' ' Who coverest Thyself with light as with a garment ' ; ' that stretcheth out the heavens as a curtain, and spreadeth them out as a tent to *dwell* in.' 'Thou sendest forth Thy spirit, they are created, and Thou renewest the face of the earth.' 'There is a spirit in man, the inspiration of the Almighty giveth Him understanding.' Touching the unity of the Divine and human, Christ, on different occasions, seems to have put the question, 'If David in spirit called Him Lord, how is He then his son ? ' He revealed to them a new and unexpected light in these words, and in other expressions from their own scriptures, bearing on this same doctrine of the identity of divine and human nature, and also on the question of the Trinity in unity. That Christ was both David's son and Lord, is the essence of Christianity and philosophy.

Hegel considers that the definition of God in what is called Deism, is a false view of God, whereas we have in Christianity, in which God is known as the Trinity, the rational notion of God. The real point here is that there could not be the relation of Father in time unless God is an Eternal Father of an Eternal Son. And why ?—because God could not be an Eternal Creator unless He was an Eternal Father creating the universe in and through the generation of an Eternal Son in His own image, an eternal incarnation ; without a world God could not be God, He would only be an empty, void abstraction. To be God, He must be both Eternal Creator and Eternal Father. This is the teaching both of the Bible and of logical philosophy. The relation of Father and Son is a matter of general rational experience in time ; and in this relation the identity of man with the eternal nature of God is proved from the nature of the Ego. As Hegel says, ' the Son is a necessary element in the true being of God.' This is how Christ, as man, is both ' David's son ' and ' David's Lord ' ; and how Christ is 'Everlasting Father'; 'Immanuel—God with us.'

What is called 'the mystery of godliness, God manifested in the flesh,' is, with Paul, in *perfect* analogy with the mystery concerning Christ and the Church, parents and children, husband and wife. They are substantially all one flesh and spirit. He says, ' We are members of his body, of his flesh, and of his bones.' ' For this cause shall a man leave his father and mother, and shall cleave unto his wife, and they two shall be one flesh. This is a great mystery : but I speak concerning Christ and the Church.' For the Church is the Bride, the Lamb's wife. Paul tells us, ' He that is joined to the Lord is one spirit,' just as ' there is one Lord, one faith, one baptism, one God and Father of all, who is above all, and through all, and in you all.' Adam is called ' the son of God ': thus God is at once his Creator and Father.

Of course, we are not taught that all men are one with God in the spirit of love and truth. Men may have ' their understandings darkened, being alienated from the life of God through the ignorance that is in them.' The Jews claimed to be both the children of God and of Abraham. According to their natural birth, they were still as rational moral beings the children of God and of Abraham, but in righteousness and holiness of faith and truth, they were spiritually children of neither. In this latter sense, Christ told them, ' Ye are of your father the devil, and the lusts of your father ye will do.' In one sense He no more denied that they were children of God, than children of Abraham, yet he said, ' If ye were the children of Abraham, ye would do the works of Abraham.' On this ground Paul demands that men ' put off the old man with his deeds and put on the new man, which is renewed in knowledge after the image of Him that created him.' Thus, though man in his intellectual nature is a moral being ' in the image of God,' he may be immoral in his character and require a great moral change of disposition ; only a moral being can become immoral, for only a moral agent can know God. If man's eye is evil, his whole body is full of darkness, but if it is single, he is full of light.

The key for the right understanding of the nature of man, as related in the three first chapters of Genesis, is found in the nature of the Ego, because man is an Ego. Men, being the sons of God by creation, are capable of receiving the Spirit of His Son, which is the spirit of love, into their hearts, crying, ' Abba, Father,' and of being restored to God's moral image of truth and love, for ' he that dwelleth in love, dwelleth in God, and God in him, for God is love.' Herein we see that love is the identity of thought and feeling, subject and object, God, Christ, and man, and likewise the absolute nature of Christ as God-man, a fuller exposition of which is given in the next chapter.

It will be seen that the exposition of the intellectual nature of man and Christ in their essential relation to God rest to a great extent on the same logical process. The chief difference is this : as ' without a world, God is not God ' (for without a world God could not be Eternal Creator), so without ' an Eternal Son ' God could not be Eternal Father, nor Creator and Father in time, because the very idea of eternal creation rests on the logical threefold unity of the Godhead in three Persons, Father, Son, Spirit. Viewed otherwise, God would be only an empty, truthless abstraction. An abstract God is no God. In Christianity God is known as concrete Spirit, not as a Being outside of the world and outside of self-consciousness. As Spirit He is actual self-consciousness in man's spirit.

CHAPTER IX

CHRIST—THE GOD-MAN

WE take it for granted that no one refuses to believe that Christ was really and truly a man. He claimed to be in His personality essentially and absolutely one with God, as God-man. The great question, then, is, How can Christ as God-man be presented as a logically demonstrated truth ? The knowledge of this can only be realized in the human consciousness by a proper understanding of the personality of Christ as God's eternal Son.

The greatest, deepest and most comprehensive problem in philosophy is, What is Personality ? We have already stated that if this can be logically and satisfactorily answered we are furnished with a key whereby all other mysteries can be ultimately unlocked. A mystery is not something which is, in its nature, unknowable ; it is only a mystery to man so long as it is unknown to him. When properly explained and brought into the light of the intuitive, reflective and logical understanding, then it ceases to be a mystery. It is well known that human thought has discovered and brought to the clear light of the human understanding many of the once-hidden mysteries of nature. We are told in the Bible that the deepest mystery of Christianity itself, the mystery of God, of the Father, and of Christ, was hidden for ages and generations, but ' is now made manifest to the saints by the holy apostles and prophets '; and we are further told that this mystery is revealed in and through the manhood of Jesus Christ, our Lord ; Christ, as man, was the first to see and disclose this mystery—the mystery of Godlikeness in man. This vision and disclosure of the unity of God and man was, according to Hegel, first introduced into man's consciousness by Christ. Hegel says, ' In the Christian religion, however, this is peculiar, that *this person of Christ*, His character to be the Son of God, does itself belong to the nature of God. Were Christ for Christians only a teacher, like Pythagoras, Socrates, or Columbus, then there were no universal message, no revelation, no instruction respecting the nature of God, in regard to which alone we desire instruction.'

The prophets had an approximate vision of the glory of God, and the glory of man, but it was only in and through Christ the full glory was revealed. Christ clearly teaches that the glory of both God and man can only be seen in and through a conscious fellowship with God, in and through Himself—the Son of God—the divine Logos—whom Paul names ' the first-born of every creature in heaven and earth.' Paul says, ' We have received the Spirit of God, that we might know the things that are freely given to us of God,' and ' No man can say that Jesus is Lord, but by the Holy Ghost.'

Christ explained the secret of how this conscious unity between God and man can be realized to be in ' love ' when He said, ' If a man love Me, he will keep My words, and My Father will love him, and We will come unto him, and make Our abode with him.' Also, ' In that day ye shall know that I am in My Father, and ye in Me, and I in you.' Here Christ teaches that there can be no true love where there is no true knowledge, nor a true knowledge of God and of Christ in His divine nature without love—the love of God in man. Love and true knowledge are simply and essentially difference in identity, but knowledge without love is tainted with error, corruption and poison. Christ further teaches in the above words that the threefold unity—God, Christ, Man—can and must be known by Love, and that only by such knowledge can man have complete salvation : so he again says, ' This is life eternal, that they might know Thee the only true God, and Jesus Christ whom Thou hast sent " ; also, ' He that hath seen Me hath seen the Father.' To see Christ truly is to know Him in His divine nature as one with the Father, for seeing is knowing, and knowing, seeing. Loving thought is the best thought, and God is the best. God could not be God were He not in Himself absolutely and essentially loving thought. Man can only attain to the perfection of his being in conscious fellowship with God in and through loving thought ; and therein is realized the perfect personality of Christ.

The mystery of love is the mystery of thought, for there is no love without thought. To know what love is, at its deepest and best, is to know thought at its deepest and best ; this can only be known when thought sees itself to be perfect love ; and this, we say again, is ' the mystery of God, and of the Father and Christ,' for ' God is love.'

> Thy thoughts are love, and Jesus is
> The loving voice they find ;
> His love lights up the vast abyss
> Of the Eternal Mind.

Paul says, ' I pray that your love may abound more and more in knowledge and in all judgment.' Love increases as true knowledge increases, by thought sounding and comprehending its own depth and fullness, and so it comes to be filled with all the fullness of God, ' the fullness of Him that filleth all in all,' ' which is Christ in you, the hope of glory.' The great concern of Christ in prayer was, ' that the love wherewith Thou hast loved Me may be in them, and I in them,' ' that the world may *know* that Thou hast sent Me, and hast loved them, as Thou hast loved Me.' These are pregnant words, as are the following : ' O Father, glorify thou Me with Thine own self, with the glory I had with Thee before the world was,' ' and the glory which Thou gavest Me, I have given them ; that they may be one, *even* as We are one ; I *in* them, and Thou in Me, that they may be perfect in one.'

Now, what is the glory in the Father, in Christ, and in those who are one with Them ? The words of Hegel will help us to an understanding of them : ' The pure essentialities are the pure thoughts ; Spirit thinking its own inner being, and this matter of content is God as He is in His eternal essence.' In Christ, then, is the perfect personality of God—the God-man. We further ask, What is the love of Christ ? The love of Christ is the manifestation of the thoughts of Christ in His sinless, suffering life and death. He knew the Truth because He knew God, and He knew that all men are the offspring of God. His thoughts so burned within Him that ' the zeal of God's house ate Him up,' for they filled Him with the intensest compassion for men in their blind sinfulness. His love compelled Him to rebuke them strongly. There was no other way to save them. He knew that in their blindness they would seek to kill Him ; yet His love was such that He was prepared to die for them, or as He said, ' to lay down His life for them.' His love was dying love ; but above all, there was an element in it such as the world has never seen before or since. He did not die as a patriot for His country, nor as a martyr for science, nor as a great teacher like Socrates, nor even as a great philanthropist. In one sense He suffered in consequence of His teaching and miracles, but He only suffered for these because of their bearing on the proof of His claim to be the Son of God ; His claim that in His substantial nature He was one with God. That this young carpenter from Nazareth, in flesh and blood to all appearance of the same nature as any other man, should claim to be one with God, seemed in the eyes of the Jews to be the most audacious and blasphemous claim that had ever been made ; such as none of their great prophets had dared to make. ' To love thy neighbour as thyself' was an old commandment with which they were quite familiar ; but Christ said, ' A new commandment I give unto you.' What can it be ? He said, ' That ye love one another *as* I have loved you,' and that is ' to lay down My life ' for you. No love can be greater or go to a more extreme point than to die for another. Christ's love in dying for men was not a blind dying-love, but a clear, full-seeing love in the clear light of God, in Whom is no darkness at all. The lack in men of this love as manifested in Christ, making Him to be the light of the world, prevented them from seeing their oneness with God. The disciples could not see His meaning until after His crucifixion, resurrection and ascension had revealed Him in a fuller light, and until after the extraordinary light flashed upon them by the Spirit at the Pentecost. While He was with them He had to say, ' I have many things to say unto you, but ye cannot bear them now.' Speaking to the Jews, He said : ' I know you, that ye have not the love of God in you.' With Christ, love is the true light of the intellect, the eye of the understanding ; so he says, ' He that loveth Me shall be loved of My Father, and I will love him, and will manifest Myself to him.' Without love, 'Ye neither know Me, nor My Father : if ye had known Me, ye should have known My Father also.' These are great and deep sayings, and need to be deeply pondered, otherwise neither sound philosophy nor sound science is possible. Herein alone is true, pure Religion.

When Hegel came to study and to write his sketch of the Life of Christ, he saw with absolute clearness that Christ was the Ego of Kant and Fichte which they had failed to see : and we cannot but think that whatever light came to Hegel through the study of the writings of these men respecting the Ego, the most glorious inspiration thereon came to him when he saw in the light of the New Testament the God-man in the Person of Christ. Whatever time he came to see that Christ was the true God-man, he must have cried out to himself, Why this is the Ego of Kant and Fichte (and what is Ego but that which makes man to be in the image of God ?), and if this can be worked out in a true, logical system of thought, then the goal of philosophy is at once and for ever attained, and the kingdom of God will have come to men in its fullness and glory, in both reason and faith ! The philosophy of the Ego thus becomes the means to reconcile Christianity to philosophy itself—to reconcile reason, faith and science.

It is a great point with agnostics, and with many so-called Christian Agnostics who belong to the school of Dean Mansel and Sir W. Hamilton, and indeed with theologians generally, that man, being finite, cannot comprehend the infinite, and yet some of these profess to believe in the supreme Godhead of Christ. They fail to see that if man, as a spirit, is not in thought infinite, for the same reason Christ could not be infinite in thought, could not be the God-man,

nor, in any true sense, the Divine One. Further, our
Higher Critics, appearing to see this defect in the
common mode of reasoning, in order to reconcile
many of the apparent difficulties and discrepancies
of the Bible, are obliged to take the position that
Christ was not free from error in His teaching, and
that, so far, He conformed to the errors of His times.
This must be so if man in his thought is not infinite,
for Christ, as a man, was finite in one sense just as
other men are finite ; yet if Christ were one with the
Father, the idea of the infinite Godhead must have
been in Him. There is no more difficulty in conceiving
the idea of the infinite in man as man than in conceiving the idea of the Godhead in Christ—for He, too, was
man. But just as He was the Son of Man, He was also
the Son of God, as certainly as all men are at once
both sons of men and sons of God. It is only in
and through the philosophy of the Ego, that which
Dr. Stirling calls the I-Me, that the difference in the
identity of God, Christ and Man can be logically
explained, for man can and does know himself as
infinite in thought, and equally and just as certainly
man can know Christ and God as infinite. If anyone
declare it absurd to say man can comprehend the
infinite, then we affirm it is equally absurd to say he
can fully comprehend the finite, and this lands us into
the glaring absurdity that we can know nothing at all.
This is the climax of the Absurdity of Agnosticism.

Christianity clearly recognizes that Jesus was really
and truly man. As a man, He was born of a woman
like other men, and grew in bodily stature from
infancy to manhood : intellectually He ' increased in
wisdom and in favour with God and man.' ' He
waxed strong in spirit, filled with wisdom : and the
grace of God was upon Him.' Like other men he was
' a little lower than the angels,' ' in all things it behoved

Him to be made like unto His brethren.' ' Both He that sanctifieth and they who are sanctified are all of one, for which cause He is not ashamed to call them brethren.' ' Forasmuch, then, as the children are partakers of flesh and blood, He also Himself took part of the same.' As a man He died, and as a man He rose from the dead, as a man He was seen alive after His passion and ascended to heaven. Now, since as a man He waxed strong in spirit and increased in wisdom like other men, how did He come to know himself to be one with the Father, and to be the first to attain this knowledge ? He knew the greatness and glory of man as no man before or since has ever known it. He knew Himself and He knew God with a clearness and fullness of vision never otherwise attained by any man. No poet, philosopher, prophet, seer, or righteous man ever realized in human form such transcendent knowledge of the unspeakable glory of the Eternal Father and Creator of all things visible and invisible ; in and through this Christ has received ' a Name above every name.' Christ as man in the flesh was, in a manner, a new creation, but on His divine side He was the uncreated eternal Son of the eternal Father, ' by whom also He made the worlds,' and as such He was ' the brightness of the Father's glory and the express image of His person.' As a man, Christ's love of the Father was perfect, therefore His intellectual vision was never dim. He said, ' I do nothing of Myself ; but as the Father hath taught Me, I do these things. And He that hath sent Me is with Me ; the Father hath not left Me alone, for I do *always* those things that please Him, that the world may know that I love the Father.' ' I have kept My Father's commandment and abide in His love.' ' I proceeded forth and came from God, neither came I of Myself, but He sent Me.'

If, then, Christ was the first man to see and declare the identity of divine and human thought, and to know Himself as one with the Father, the next question is, How and why was it that He was the first ? The answer is : First, because of His sinlessness, and secondly, because of the means taken by the Divine Father to preserve in sinlessness His growth in moral and spiritual purity, simultaneously with His increase in wisdom and understanding. Christ was sinless. He never had the sense of personal guilt arising from violating the moral law of God. Guilt brings spiritual darkness : Christ's vision of God, of Truth, was never dimmed. He said, ' Which of you convinceth Me of sin ? ' ' For I do always those things which please Him.' His sinlessness was not the mere innocence of the playful lamb, rather it was strong virtue, growing ever stronger in overcoming temptation, and battling against sin and error. He boldly declared, ' The pure in heart shall see God.' The single eye is the sinless eye ; the evil eye ' loves darkness rather than light,' because it desires to conceal its evil thoughts and deeds. The way of truth with Christ is, If any man will do the will of God, he shall know whether the doctrine be of God. Purity of thought, then, is the absolute necessity in seeking and acquiring a true knowledge of God, Nature and man. So because of the absolute moral and spiritual purity of Christ, He possessed and was the first to possess the clear, certain, intuitive and rational knowledge of God and man in their essential and substantial identity. He boldly insisted on the same condition in all men which He himself possessed. He knew that He possessed the true knowledge of God and that He had come to impart that knowledge to all who would believe in Him and receive the word which He had received from the Father. It was to this knowledge Christ referred when He said, ' All things are delivered unto Me of My Father,' for He immediately adds, ' and no man knoweth the Son but the Father, neither knoweth any man the Father save the Son.' This does not mean that no man had the idea of God before the appearance of Christ, for such thought belongs essentially to the thought of man ; but He refers to the knowledge of the essential identity of the Divine and Human Self-consciousness in thought, which He alone was the first to possess. Then he adds, ' and to whomsoever the Son will reveal Him.' Here, then, we have the great revelation of the substantial one-ness of thought in God and man introduced into human consciousness by Christ. It is the knowledge ' hid from the wise and prudent, but revealed unto babes.'

The real and true qualifying power which made Christ as man to be the first to realize intuitively and rationally the absolute identity of the Divine and human thought in man, was His miraculous conception by the Holy Spirit. It is evidently this to which He refers when He speaks of Himself as the one, and only one, whom the Father had so sanctified and sent into the world. To maintain that an ineradicable taint of sin belongs to our nature, not only makes the sin-lessness of Christ impossible, but renders it for ever impossible for man to be purified from all sin. What-ever may be the general hereditary tendency to evil, this was entirely removed by the miraculous concep-tion and birth of Christ. Such a birth was only needed once and involved no change in the general law of fatherhood and motherhood.

With reference to miracles, we need here only affirm that their possibility is not in the slightest degree contrary either to pure reason or to the general laws of nature. The miraculous birth of Christ was an important act of the Father's, used as a means of securing from His birth the perfect growth and development of His manhood in all moral and spiritual purity, excellence and truth. Christ was enabled to say with a perfectly clear consciousness, ' I am the Truth,' ' I am the light of the world,' ' As I hear, I judge,' and ' The word which ye hear is not Mine, but the Father's which sent Me.'

To say that Christ, because of His miraculous birth, is not and cannot be a perfect pattern to us, is a view approaching the absurd. Yet the miraculous birth of Christ is unique, and so far, is to be distinguished from the ordinary creation of a man in human history. In many respects, however, He is not intended to be our example. The chief purpose of His mission was to reveal the identity of the Divine and human nature, and to show how man can attain perfect love. This done, His mission on earth was ended. He is an example, as a revelation of the perfect love of God, in human thought, so that ' he that dwells in love dwells in God, and God in him.' Peter explains clearly in two sentences how Christ is meant to be our example : ' For even hereunto were ye called : because Christ also suffered for us, leaving us an example, that we should follow His steps ' ; ' For as much then as Christ hath suffered for us in the flesh, arm yourselves likewise with the same mind.' John expresses the same idea, ' Hereby perceive we the love of God, because He laid down His life for us : and we ought to lay down our lives for the brethren.' ' As He is, so are we in this world.' The same principle, touching the nature and manifestation of the love of God in .Christ, runs all through the teaching of Paul, but the following quotations from his writings will suffice : ' That I may know Him and the power of His resurrection, and the fellowship of His sufferings, being made conformable to His death.'

' Who now rejoice in my sufferings for you, and fill up that which is behind of the afflictions of Christ in my flesh, for His body's sake, which is the Church.'

The mission and work of Christ was to reveal the truth to man. He said, ' He that hath sent Me is true ; and I speak to the world the things which I have heard of Him,' ' the truth which I have heard of God.' He makes it clear that the salvation of man can only be attained by knowing the Truth ; therefore he says, ' If ye continue in My word, then are you My disciples indeed, and ye shall know the truth, and the truth shall make you free,' and, ' If the Son shall make you free, ye shall be free indeed.' He said to His disciples, ' The world hateth Me because I testify of it that the works thereof are evil.' ' If the world hate you, ye know that it hated Me before it hated you.' ' If they have persecuted Me, they will also persecute you : if they have kept My saying, they will keep yours also.' ' I have chosen you and ordained you that ye should go and bring forth fruit, and that your fruit should remain.' ' Ye shall be betrayed both by parents and brethren, and kinsfolk, and friends, and some of you shall they cause to be put to death, and ye shall be hated of all men for My name's sake.' ' He that taketh not his cross, and followeth not after Me, is not worthy of Me.' The cross of Christ is the cross of all His followers, and on no precept does He more insist than on ' He that findeth his life shall lose it, and he that loseth his life for My sake shall find it.'

The one central truth of Christ's teaching is, ' I and My Father are one,' ' I am in the Father and the Father in Me.' ' At that day ye shall know that I am in the Father, and ye in Me, and I in you.' The words of Paul contain the same truth, ' He that is joined to the Lord is one Spirit.' All other Christian teaching converges in this foundation truth, which is also embodied in the gospels of Matthew and Luke : 'All things are delivered unto Me of My Father : and no man knoweth the Son but the Father, and who the Father is but the Son, and he to whom the Son will reveal Him.' To give to all men the true knowledge of the Father and Son is the reason why Jesus came into this world. Such knowledge is eternal life. The word *reveal* expresses the purpose of His life, death and resurrection. When Jesus said, ' In that day ye shall know,' He meant clear, certain, genuine knowledge—not mere hypothesis or vague fancy : hypothesis alone has no saving virtue in it : food, to nourish, must be bread, not stone, or picture-bread. The philosophy of the Ego alone explains how Christ could say, ' I and My Father are one, ' My Father is greater than I.' The exposition of the Ego is the exposition of God, and equally it is the exposition of Christ—' Immanuel, God with us.'

In connexion with Hegel's *Life of Jesus* and its important bearing on the love and sinlessness of Christ, Dr. Stirling remarks : ' The person of Christ would seem to have entered into the very inmost thought of Hegel.' ' So Hegel is not contented with himself till he has written for himself a whole life of Christ.' Hegel, as we learn here, saw the absolute idea of love in Christ as the God-man. What for Hegel was proper and peculiar in the fate of Christ was ' His elevation above all fate, the sin of sinlessness.' This agrees with Paul when he said, ' He (God) hath made Him to be sin for us, who knew no sin, that we might be made the righteousness of God in Him.' John also says ' Herein is our love made perfect, that we may have boldness in the day of judgment : because as He is, so are we in this world.'

Loving-thought is the highest, deepest, and truest reason-thought, so he who has not realized in himself the love of God in Christ, has not attained to the deepest and fullest reason-thought, which in its truth is logical thought. So far as self-conscious thought is concerned, man is fundamentally one with God, but as far as he does not think and live in love, he does not truly know God, and so does not think and live in the truth and is not one with God, for God, who is both love and thought, is in the highest sense the Truth. It is only thus that, according to Peter, ' We are made partakers of the Divine nature,' and according to Paul can be ' filled with all the fullness of God,' and be ' renewed in knowledge after the image of Him that created us.' This is also ' the mystery of God, and of the Father, and of Christ, in whom are hid all the treasures of wisdom and knowledge.' To know this mystery is ' to know the truth as it is in Jesus,' and this, further, is to know the truth in its absolute relativity. An essential quality of the person of Christ is expressed by Paul when he states that Christ ' is the image of the invisible God, the first-born of every creature.' He also speaks of Him as Creator : ' For by Him were all things created that are in heaven, and that are in earth, visible and invisible, whether thrones, or dominions, or principalities, or powers : all things were created by Him and for Him, and He is before all things, and by Him all things consist.' John declares that Christ was the Logos that was with God and was God, and ' that all things were made by Him '—by the Ego. As a Son, Christ is called both Lord and God, for as a Son it is said of Him, ' Thy throne, O God, is for ever and ever.' As a Son he is the source of light and understanding to all men. In this reference the words of John are remarkably clear : ' We know that the Son of God (the eternal Logos) is come, and hath given us an understanding that we may know Him that is true : and we are in Him that is true, even in His Son Jesus Christ. This is the true God and eternal life.' This life is in His Son.

Thus the eternal Son of God, as the source of all life, light, understanding, wisdom, power, and love, became ' in the fullness of time,' by a miraculous conception and birth, the divine Son of Man, ' born of a woman, born under the law,' that men might receive the spiritual consciousness of a divine sonship which has been lost through sin. Christ is both Son of God and Son of Man in time, just as certainly as all other men are sons of God and sons of men in time, but the rationale of both rests on the rationale of the eternal Son of an eternal Father. Christ as the eternal Son of God, and as Son of God and Son of Man in the flesh, is in both respects unique, and is thus differentiated from mankind in general. So Christ (the God-man), Man, and Nature, have each in their difference their absolute inseparable unity, and essential identity in God, who is the one living, eternal, immortal, personal self-conscious Spirit of the universe. The religion of Christ as a system of pure reason must in its universal nature embrace in its fullness the fullness of Him that fills all in all, for as reason, as thought, as Spirit, He cannot be limited to His human manifestation in the flesh. So in this light Paul declares, ' Though we have known Christ after the flesh, yet now henceforth know we Him no more.' The true knowledge of Christ is according to the Spirit, for it is only in thought, in spirit and in truth that He is all in all, or can fill all in all : because He is Ego, or I.

Christ, however, in His divine and human nature, in His all-embracing reason-thought, must be seen to be the spirit of love, for reason devoid of love is not true reason. True love, it must be added, cannot deviate a hair's-breadth from eternal truth, either theoretically or practically. This was the fate of Christ, His ' sin of sinlessness ' ; He necessarily felt the pain and agony of sin. It was the fate of His sinless personality to lay the axe of truth to every tree of error. He said, ' Every plant which My Heavenly Father hath not planted shall be rooted up.' Every blow He struck at sin so reacted on Him that He was necessarily made to bear the intense suffering which belongs to the nature of sin. The only way for any man to avoid suffering for the sake of others, and so to avoid bearing the Cross of Christ, is to shrink from reproving and condemning sin and error in others. The goodness and love of Christ could not allow him to take such a stand in relation to sin, so He ' resisted unto blood, striving against sin.' This is how Christ ' bore our sins in His own body on the tree.'

Though the appearance of Christ in the flesh soon passed out of the range of sense-perception, it was an absolutely necessary manifestation, because the darkening and bewildering influence of sin in the human understanding prevented man from realizing his true greatness and dignity, and his identity in and with the divine self-consciousness. It was in this appearance in the flesh that the apostles ' beheld His glory, the glory as of the only-begotten of the Father, full of grace and truth.' The mystery of perfect godliness can alone be seen in God manifested in the flesh, or as otherwise expressed ' in the face of Jesus Christ.' As man, it was the unalloyed and perfect love of God in Christ that enabled Him to see in perfect clearness of vision, that though a man, ' I and My Father are one,' and that the same right and privilege belonged to, and might be possessed by, all men : ' That they all may be one, as Thou, Father, art in Me, and I in Thee, that they also may be one in Us ' : ' That they may be perfect in one, even as We are one.'

On this question of divine and human identity the gospels and epistles are in perfect accord. It was the general sense of this consciousness in the Early Church which made its members so strong in boldly preaching the gospel and in their endurance in its defence. We are afraid that the great power and value of love as the essential element of true thought in clearing the intellectual vision is only recognized to a very limited extent. We cannot be too much impressed with the fact that Christ was, in the highest sense, ' holy, harmless, and separate from sinners, and guile was never found in His mouth.'   We need to remember that it was *holy men* who ' spake as they were moved by the *Holy* Ghost.'   Even in pagan Greece it was, without doubt, a high moral principle that lay at the root of the intellectual greatness of Socrates, Plato, and Aristotle.   This was the case also with Augustine, Anselm, Wycliffe, Luther, George Fox, Knox, Wesley and Hugh Bourne.   But in the perfect clearness of intellectual vision in the knowledge of God which holy love gives, Christ, as the Son of Man, had in all things the pre-eminence.   He makes no mistakes in judgment.   He judged not according to appearance, but always judged righteous judgment.   He also makes perfectly clear in His teaching the possibility of all men ultimately attaining to the same true and righteous judgment, if they will, as Paul says, ' honestly renounce the hidden things of dishonesty, not walking in craftiness, not handling the word of God deceitfully, but by manifestation of the truth commending themselves to every man's conscience in the sight of God.'   Christ makes no allowance for error on

the grounds, now much advanced, that a difference
of opinion is necessary. He condemned in His disciples all lack of a right understanding, whether in
word or deed. Paul also insisted upon all ' being
perfectly joined together in the same mind and in
the same judgment.' Not that all were expected at
the same time to be equal in knowledge : but he
insisted that ' if in anything ye be otherwise minded,
God shall reveal even this unto you.' Let us first
be sure our knowledge is truth before declaring it as
such. All men are required to speak the truth in
love, for let every man be assured that if he does not
do so he has neither attained the truth as it is in Jesus,
nor is in the way of truth, for Thought only attains
to its highest when it attains to the fullness of perfect
love ; though reason-thought is the fundamental and
substantial element of love.

Now, although the great truths of the Christian
Religion can be reduced to and presented in the form
of a genuine logical philosophy, yet neither the
prophets, nor Christ, nor the Apostles give to us these
truths in this form. It does not follow, however,
that the writers of the Bible were not sound logical
reasoners. The general form of the writings themselves forbid such a supposition. The writers were
great and good men who grasped with marvellous
clearness the secret root of things, and saw that
neither individuals nor nations could become truly
great without a true knowledge of God and the
practice of righteousness. But the Christian Religion
had yet to wait many centuries for its presentation
in the form of a logical system of philosophy. The
form of logical thought comes to us by way of ancient
Greece, for by the Greek philosophers, thought was
first given a logical form, that is—the form of a syllogism. I know of no writer who has stated this point

so clearly as Dr. Stirling in the words already quoted. He there tells us that Socrates first discovered the abstract Notion, and that Aristotle completed it into the Abstract Logic ; that Kant first discovered the Concrete Notion, and Hegel completed it into the Concrete Logic. These statements give us volumes in a nutshell. Hegel saw that if philosophy as a rational explanation of the totality of Being could not be reduced to a genuine logical concrete syllogism or a connected system of syllogisms, philosophy was nothing but an empty and worthless name. But he saw that the Ego being thought in its absolute fullness, embracing every particular in all that is, was properly another name for God, and the logical science was the science of God ; that man as a spirit is infinite in thought, as such is Ego and essentially one with God, and that therefore logic is also the science of Man ; that Christ is Ego and that the science of the Ego is equally the science of Christ ; that externally, Nature was, in a sense, unsubstantial and transient in its existence, and that therefore its essence, its substantial nature, could only be found in the Ego, God, its Creator. Consequently we cannot have a true science of Nature apart from the science of God ; that in fact and in reality the essence of universal gravitation is thought ; that thought is essentially a process and as such is a system of categories, the many of which can all be developed dialectically from the unity of self-consciousness, that is, from the Ego, and, finally, he saw that Being was the most abstract, or poorest, notion in the Ego itself, and this, when correctly seen into, involved the notion of Becoming which implicitly contained not only the notion of changeableness, but also the notion of objective creation. Therefore matter is only another name for quality and quantity in external sensible existence ; and further, thought, form and matter exist in such necessary and essential relation to each other that the one cannot be without the other. Thus the categories of thought in their subjective relation are seen to be essentially the real matter of thought—since the matter and the form of thought are equally universal—for the categories in the process of thought are all seen, in the light of intuitive thought, to be the substantial elements of thought, of self-consciousness.   Thus with Hegel, Ego, Thought, God, Christ and Nature were in absolute unity in the logical system of the categories.   Self-consciousness, then, is the Absolute and Infinite—the logical development of the Concrete Notion.   It is the substantial Nature of the Ego, of God, of Christ the God-man, and of man, for Christ was not only sinless but was absolutely free from all error in His teaching.   God in His love is perfect, therefore Christ in His love was perfect : the mission of Christ is to bring man as man into the perfect realization and enjoyment of the love of God.   As ' perfect love casteth out fear,' so it is only in and through the knowledge of God that man can attain to the full perfection of his nature, and in the words of Paul, ' be filled with all the fullness of God,' just as ' in Christ dwelleth all the fullness of the Godhead.'   ' Our life is hid with Christ in God.'   Then, since the philosophy of the Ego is the philosophy of man and God, it is the philosophy of Christ as the perfect God-man, and of Christianity.   As Christ in the supreme Divinity of His Person is the eternal Creator, so this philosophy will be found to be the philosophy of Nature.   Consequently, there is no doctrine so important as the God-manhood of Christ.

CHAPTER X

EGO—THE WITNESS OF THE SPIRIT

EGO alone gives the true science of the Witness of the Spirit as taught by Christ and His apostles. It is the I-Me-I.

In the highest sense God is Ego, because Ego is absolute Thought, the First and the Last, Absolute Reason, and infinite self-consciousness. Whatever can be predicated of the Ego can be predicated of God, and whatever can be predicated of God can be predicated of the Ego. The predicate always expresses the substantial nature of the subject. When God says, 'I am that I am,' He begins and ends with 'I'; that is, He begins and ends with the absolute unity of Being and Ego (I *am*). Thought is light; it shines in and through All that is. In it 'the eternal power and Godhead are clearly seen.' It is eternal and infinite and so omnipresent, which are also essential elements of human Thought. The Divine Thought (self-consciousness) is love, in which alone man can have a true saving knowledge and experience of God and His Christ. 'For he that loveth not knoweth not God,' for ' God is love.' There is an important sense in which God's thought dwells in all men, even while they do not yet reciprocate God's love.

Hegel very distinctly and clearly recognizes that ' man is a finite spirit, yet at the same time that he is in thought infinite,' and therefore can only think and know God as infinite Love. With Hegel, God is Truth and Love. To know God is to know the truth in Love, and to know what love is, is the same as to know what God is. In the highest sense the pure heart is one with Love in the love of God. With the pure God shows Himself as pure Love, wherein He makes man to know wisdom and understanding in his inward part, which is essentially the witness of His Spirit in man's spirit. This witness is at once thought, feeling, and knowledge.

All feeling is one with knowledge. This is true of all sense-feeling such as sweetness, bitterness, pain, cold, heat, roughness, smoothness, etc. Much knowledge comes through feeling, and yet all feeling is in thought and consciousness, for without consciousness feeling is impossible. Love, joy, peace, consolation, are feelings, and yet they are constituent elements of thought and knowledge in man's spirit. These latter feelings are of a higher spiritual quality than the former. They both, however, have their seat in the Ego and are universal and necessary functions of thought at once subjective and objective. Kant names feelings subjective judgments of sense-perception, to distinguish them from judgments of experience. The judgments of sensation and feeling he holds are only subjectively valid, whereas judgments of experience, in addition to what is given in feeling, require special notions *à priori* generated in the understanding to make them objectively valid; it is the *à priori* notion that makes such judgments universal and necessary. As a matter of fact, there is no particular feeling experienced in human thought that does not contain the elements of universality and necessity. So Kant's distinction falls to the ground. All feeling is a matter of conscious thought, especially in the higher feelings of love, joy and peace, though men may have bad as well as good feelings. But Man only truly knows God when he knows and feels that God is love. If to man, because his thought is only finite (as maintained by many), God is unknown and unknowable, then plainly, love, which is the witness of God's Spirit in man's spirit, is impossible. The Bible from beginning to end teaches that a real and increasing knowledge of the love of God is possible, and is in part actual in all men. If any system of philosophy teaches what is called Agnosticism concerning man's knowledge of God, it is not only at variance with the teaching of the Bible but in direct opposition to the teaching of man's own thought, for all men know what love is. To call a man an agnostic because his knowledge is not as full and perfect as God's, is a total perversion of human thought : it is a bowing of the knee to the image of Baal—to a false philosophy. Thus man contradicts his own thought, his own true reason. However strange and forbidding such an attitude of thought towards itself, it is nevertheless a fact in common human experience ; it is just as strange that men should lie and steal, knowing well that such acts are morally wrong ; or that even educated men, because of some secret bias, should hate the light and love darkness rather than light, calling good evil and evil good. That such is the case is everywhere well known. In human experience there is a mingling of good and evil, light and darkness, which not only may, but does, secretly form a bias which may unwittingly, unless great care is exercised, lead men into the plausible way of error. Men may, however, love the good and hate evil, and walk in the light of God which shines in all men, for the manifestation of the Spirit is given to every man to profit withal.

The Witness of the Spirit of God in man's spirit

is the most fundamental of all the doctrines of the Bible as also of the teaching of Pure Reason. It is no more logically true that twice one are two, than that logically True Reason is True Wisdom, that True Wisdom is True or Perfect Love, and that Perfect Love is God, in whom love, wisdom and reason are one. Or, reverse-wise, perfect love is perfect wisdom, and perfect wisdom is perfect reason. Or again, logically true faith is one with love (this is the faith which justifies from all unrighteousness), true hope is one with love—it is the hope which cannot end in disappointment—it maketh not ashamed, because the heart is filled with love by the Spirit of God. Love is the bond of perfection between man and God, wherein man is joined to the Lord in one Spirit. In this absolute unity man has a real genuine experiential knowledge of the infinite absolute God, the Creator of the universe, however ignorant otherwise (as a babe in Christ) he may be. Love is the secret ' hid from the wise and prudent, but revealed unto babes.' It is the *Secret* of the Logical System of the Philosophy of Hegel and Stirling, which is at once theoretical, experiential, practical—in the unity of Intellect, Emotion, Will. It is the very essence of Christianity; the inward light of the Spirit wherein Jesus is revealed as both Lord and Christ. ' If ye abide in Me and My words abide in you, ye shall ask what ye will, and it shall be done unto you.' ' If a man love Me, he will keep My words, and My Father will love him, and We will come unto him, and make Our abode with him.' ' At that time ye *shall* know that I am in My Father, and ye in Me, and I in you.' Here is knowledge in a threefold unity, a unity of theoretical and practical experience. It is not only a belief that Jesus is Lord, but a knowledge of God the Father and His eternal

only-begotten Son by the Spirit. All men, as
personal spirits, have one and the same substantial
nature, because God is the eternal Father of the
spirits of all flesh, and consequently the eternal
Father of the one eternal Son, by whom all things
were and are created. The eternal Son as one in
Spirit with the eternal Father, is the eternal incarnation of the eternal Son, ' the image of the invisible
God, the first-born of every creature, made of a
woman, made under the law, to redeem them that
were under the law, that we might receive the
adoption of sons, who by sin had been alienated
from the life of God.' Herein is the loss of the true
spiritual sonship and heirship of God. ' But because ye are sons—the offspring of God—God hath
sent forth the Spirit of His Son into your hearts
crying, Abba, Father.' ' Wherefore (by the Spirit
of Love) thou art no more a servant, but a son,
and if a son, then an heir of God through Christ.'
This change is made when ' the love of God is shed
abroad in our hearts by the Holy Ghost.' ' For
as many as are led by the Spirit of God, they are the
sons of God.' ' Ye have not received the spirit of
bondage—the spirit of fear—but ye have received
the Spirit of adoption whereby we cry, Abba,
Father ; the Spirit Himself beareth witness with
our spirit that we are the children of God, . . . heirs
of God and joint heirs with Christ, if so be that
we suffer with Him, that we may be also glorified
together.' This witness of the Spirit is the inward
assurance of God that our sins are forgiven.
' Then being made free from sin, ye become servants
of God, servants of righteousness, ye have your fruit
unto holiness,' ' wherein ye are made to rejoice with
joy unspeakable and full of glory.' ' The fruit
of the Spirit is love, joy, peace,' ' the peace which

passeth all understanding.' There is consolation
in Christ, fellowship in the Spirit (the Spirit is the
Comforter), comfort in the enjoyment of love
through the Spirit.

Christ says, ' Ask and receive, that your joy may
be full ' : also, ' These things have I spoken unto
you that My joy might remain in you, and that
your joy might be full.' In the Old Testament it is
written, ' The joy of the Lord is our strength ';
frequent mention is made of the shining of God's
face in men ; the light of God's countenance shining
within them ; the Psalmist says, ' The Lord is my
light and my salvation,' ' Take not Thy Holy Spirit
from me,' ' Restore unto me the joy of Thy salvation,
and uphold me with Thy free Spirit.' It cannot
well be doubted that these and like forms of speech
denote a conscious experience of the spiritual
presence of God, such as cannot be realized in any
other form of religion. The experiential knowledge
of God is in perfect accord with logical philosophy.
This experience is denied in Kant's system of
philosophy. It separates entirely the theoretical
from the practical reason, though logically theory,
practice and experience are essentially one. Ego
is at once thought, truth and love in *true* knowledge : for the activity of the one is the activity of
the other. Thought without love is not true thought.
In God, thought and love are one, so man is only
true to himself when his thought and love are one.

Fundamentally true reason and true faith are
one, and signify spiritual insight, intellectual insight.
They constitute the unity of thought, knowledge,
and experience in the identity of the divine and
human nature in one spirit, for therein God dwells
in man and man dwells in God. It is mere superstition and is one with slavish fear to think of God

as an object outside and beyond human thought and consciousness. Hegel says : ' God in the Christian Religion is known as Love, wherein the Idea of God is divested of all strangeness, and God as an object of fear is overcome, (man) becomes one with God in His Son and in His redemption, puts off the old Adam and knows God as his true and essential self.' He here gives the Witness of the Spirit in its real philosophical import. ' He that dwelleth in Love, dwelleth in God, and God in him. Herein is our love made perfect.' ' There is no fear in love : perfect love casteth out fear : because fear hath torment,' so ' he that feareth is not made perfect in love.' ' He that loveth God, loveth his brother also.' ' Hereby we know that He (God) abideth in us, by the Spirit which He hath given us.' Love, then, is not a mere feeling outside of reason-thought. It is knowledge. Paul says, ' God hath not given us the spirit of fear : but of power, and of love, and of a sound mind,' ' in faith and love which is in Christ Jesus.' Thus the Witness of the Spirit is not only the supreme doctrine of Christianity, but has been in every age the fundamental problem of philosophy. No philosopher has stated it more distinctly than Hegel.

The Spirit is the essential being of all existence, whose special manifestation is thought, life, feeling, love and knowledge in the finite spirit of man, and therefore is the notion of the absolute Concrete Idea. In the cognition of love, man in feeling rises to the perfection of union and fellowship with God in the Spirit, in which he knows even as he is known, wherein 'abideth faith, hope, love : the greatest of which is love.' It is the bond of perfection. It is the mightiest passion of which man is capable : at once the power of God and the wisdom of God. It is the living soul of concrete logic, the full assurance, the Witness of the Spirit. He who understands this properly has got to the core of things and is strong, while the man of mere general knowledge is weak. To know the doctrine of the Witness of the Spirit is to know the depth of the Godhead, and is the passion of the Spirit, without which, as Hegel says, nothing great can be accomplished. It is the power in the apparently poor, weak, and despised things of the world which confounds and brings to naught the things which in the eyes of the world appear to be mighty. The Spirit of God in man is the power which crucifies the lusts of the flesh and the lusts of the spirit, and perfects him in holiness in the fear of God.

There have been five periods in the history of the Christian Church when the doctrine of the Witness of the Spirit was held and spread forth with more or less clearness and fervour.

The first period was during the first two and a half centuries after the crucifixion of the Lord Jesus. Christian zeal and enthusiasm has never been manifested with a stronger and more intelligent conscious force than during those years. Never were more subtle and gigantic obstacles and difficulties met with and overcome. The Roman Empire, East and West, was practically conquered in the name of the crucified Christ—the people were turned from the worship of dumb idols to the one true living God. The causes of the after declension in morals and theological doctrines do not here concern us.

The second period began with Luther and the great Reformation in Germany, England, and France. With Luther the special doctrine of Justification by Faith meant the Witness of the Spirit of God in man, the knowledge of sins forgiven, and the consciousness of sonship and heirship of God through Christ, and it was accompanied with great insight into the things of the Spirit of God, and the divine side of man and nature. Luther lived and fought for the truth as it is in Jesus with the firm assurance that Jesus as the living Christ dwelt in him as the one energizing power; his one living source of true light, to guide, direct, and control him in all he did, whether preaching, writing, or translating the Bible. A new light had entered his soul, and moved him as by an irresistible impulse to face and force down all opposition. Naturally, because of his surroundings, and the kind of work imperatively laid upon him, there arose on all sides the most conflicting forces, moral, social, political and religious. Wycliff, Jerome, John Huss and many others had done much in creating a widespread dissatisfaction with the general corruption then prevailing in the Church. In this work Calvin, Knox and Zwingli became mighty co-operators, each in his respective sphere. Around each there soon arose a mighty host of efficient co-workers. The Reformation in the Lutheran and Reformed Churches was very great and radical, and was effected by the fuller comprehension of the central doctrine of the Witness of the Spirit, properly called the inner light of the Spirit, opening and illuminating the eyes of the understanding to the deep meaning of the inspired book, the Bible, and at the same time showing the necessity of the individual right of private judgment, which no external Church authority can or ought to try to take away, or attempt to destroy. Every person must think, reason, judge and believe for himself at the risk of losing his own soul. The injunction is, 'let every man prove his own work,' and 'work out your *own* salvation.'

The Reformation in France was almost entirely

destroyed by the sword, in England it was very much damaged by the unchristian conduct and autocratic ambitions of its sovereigns and selfish nobles, and only saved from utter ruin by the Puritan Nonconformists of the sixteenth and seventeenth centuries, though in the end the Anglican Episcopal Catholicism with its unscriptural dogmas largely triumphed, and became the State Church, exercising complete control over the universities and national education. In Scotland and North Germany the Reformation doctrines obtained to a great extent the general consent of the people and the rulers of their different State governments, and through them gained general control of national education, the influence of which is powerfully and beneficially felt to this day. The relapses, reverses and cross-currents of thought must be passed over, for our chief concern is with the fact that the great leaders of the Reformation were men who had obtained a fair measure of the light of the Spirit, refusing to be led by a benighted visible Church, a Church fallen from its high estate, and which had become steeped in the wisdom of this world, which is foolishness with God.

With the early Reformers there was a general prevailing perception, more or less clear, that the inner light of the Spirit, reason and the revelation of the Bible were in some important sense one, though the written Word as a divine oracle was rightly regarded as more reliable than Reason, as Reason was then understood. Fierce conflicting controversies, however, arose on these points ; great political strife was also thereby engendered. Germany in particular became the theatre and centre of long, desolating wars. The Catholic Church used all its power to crush the spreading spirit of the Reformation. Under these circumstances the real voice of the Divine Spirit came to be less and less distinctly recognized. For nearly two centuries the Catholic Church used all its social and political influence to overwhelm the Reformation in England and Scotland. In Germany it was not unnatural that a strong party (the Pietists and Moravians) should arise, which strove to give more prominence to religious feeling, to the spirit of love, joy, and peace in the heart than to what, in part, had become a somewhat dead, formal dogmatism of a soulless or heartless belief.

As yet the real nature of pure reason had not been grasped—that is, that thought, reason, religious feeling, love and peace are essentially one. To see that true reason-thought is love, and that true love is reason-thought, was a step further. The first Reformers saw this identity more closely than the later. A sort of quasi-mathematical and mechanical definition of Christian doctrine came much into vogue. This evidently came about because of the belief that only mathematics could give certainty. As yet the deep spiritual nature of Logic was unknown. Nevertheless, a striving for certainty of thought in relation to God was the common aim, which in one form or another is still a strong element in the German mind. The Germans are strongly averse to their religious thinking being done by proxy, but in general, physical and mathematical sciences were more studied and better known in the seventeenth century than the science of Spirit, or the Science of Logic, which is the science of sciences. Much was done which helped to show the necessity for acquiring a better insight into this Queen of the sciences.

We must not overlook the important part played by the Puritans and Covenanters of England and Scotland during this second period, for their deep insight into the nature, work, and manifestation of the Spirit was of the greatest value. They were the life and soul of true religion in the seventeenth century. The only drawback in their great work was that their illogical view of predestination, election, and reprobation, gave in part a hard aspect to their otherwise fine achievements. To them, however, belongs the credit of being the chief cause in securing national and religious freedom from the bondage of a corrupt Church and a narrow-minded oligarchy. They had a clear and decided belief in the Divine Sovereignty over all things great and small; of justification by faith alone; of the need and possibility of obtaining Spiritual illumination; and they believed that the sacerdotal teaching of the Church should be destroyed root and branch. They were clear as to the need of attaining the assurance of grace and salvation in this life, and the duty of all to seek for this assurance by the Spirit. Their view of ' effectual calling ' partially limited the power of the human will, but they held that the *will* is renewed in conversion. The Covenanters effectually reformed the Church in Scotland : this the Puritans failed to do in England, and the sacerdotal Prayer Book of the Episcopal Church triumphed over State Government. They, however, prevented the re-establishment of the Roman Papal Church as the State Church in England. In after years, however, the Puritans lost much of their previous clear knowledge concerning the inward testimony of the Spirit, while from the time of the passing of the Acts of Uniformity the religious life of the Established Church gradually sank to the lowest level. This is only what could have been expected in view of the unscriptural doctrines then forced upon all its ministers, which led to the expulsion of two thousand of the best and most highly educated of them. When the doctrines then enforced are duly considered, it will be seen that they destroy at the root, and render totally unnecessary, the individual personal witness of the Spirit in the heart. The doctrines are so linked together that they form a chain so forged that each link is of no value apart from the other. The two main links, however, are Priestly Absolution and Baptismal Regeneration : the other links form parts of the chain, so that if one is admitted as necessary to salvation, the others are equally necessary. Once men put themselves in the hands of the priest, then all else follows. The links in the chain are joined together thus, first, the preacher or minister is changed into a priest; second, baptismal regeneration takes the place of a change of heart by the Spirit through personal faith in the Lord Jesus Christ, for the child is taught to believe and say, ' In my baptism, wherein I was made a member of Christ, a child of God, and an inheritor of the kingdom of heaven ' ; then afterwards, the Bishop is required to say and believe at their confirmation, ' Almighty and everlasting God, who has vouchsafed to regenerate these thy servants by water and the Holy Ghost, and hast given unto them the forgiveness of all their sins.' Third, touching Priestly Absolution, the Prayer Book reads that God ' hath given power and commandment to His ministers to declare and pronounce to His people, being penitent, the Absolution and Remission of their sins,' and ' by His authority committed to me, I absolve thee from all thy sins in the name of the Father, and of the Son, and of the Holy Ghost.' Here the priest is made the medium for the forgiveness of sins, and the people are thus taught, that instead of going direct to God in prayer and faith, for pardon and the assurance of the Spirit's witness in their hearts, the only assurance they need or can have, is to rely on the word of a man who presumes to bestow pardon when he himself may have no sure evidence that his own sins are forgiven. The apostles knew by the Spirit that their sins were forgiven, and they taught all to seek forgiveness in the way they themselves had obtained it. There is no evidence that any apostle ever professed to forgive sin in the name or by the authority of God. Then, most monstrous of all these unscriptural doctrines, the Episcopal Established Church of England claims, and has got the claim confirmed and sanctioned by an Act of Parliament which remains in full force to this day, that no minister is properly called by the Spirit to preach the gospel unless ordained by a Bishop, and for this reason, according to English law, he cannot be allowed to preach in any of its churches. In many English churches the confessional is set up, and the doctrine of the Mass as a continual sacrifice of Christ has supplanted the Lord's table. Many people make much to-do about the wearing of what are called priestly garments, but do little in seeking to purge the Prayer Book from false doctrine. The priests know full well that it is saturated with sacerdotalism and that legally their position is safe. Such doctrines set aside the grand saving doctrine of the witness of the Spirit and set up an illogical, unspiritual doctrine in its place. The same is the case with the Roman Catholic Church. It claims most illogically to be spiritual, and the only channel of the Spirit : and because the spiritual is recognized to be higher than the temporal power, it claims the right to govern kings and civil governments. No doubt it is reasonable to expect the Church of Christ to be more spiritual than ungodly, unspiritual State governments, though some kings and rulers have been more spiritual than the head or heads of the Church : but because both State and Church governments are divine institutions, it is the duty of all alike to possess and be governed by the immediate sense of God's spirit in them. This, unfortunately, is seldom the case. Since the Reformation, the Church and State have alternately, by a spirit of fear, coerced each other into adopting false principles of government. Indeed, the Anglican and Roman Catholic Churches are essentially one in doctrine ; the chief difference between them is, that the pope is recognized as the head of the one and the king as the head of the other. In deference to the clergy, the king and parliament, under the delusion of the cry of ' no bishop, no king,' caused these doctrines to be the fundamental principles of the laws of the nation. So far, the country and the constitution of the State still rest on an unsound foundation. These two Churches, in consequence, form the great barrier against the adoption of a national system of education in England ; and that, too, in the name of conscience. (Yet conscience, as generally understood, is quite unreliable.) This shows how little the members of these Churches, men of science, .politicians, philosophers, and the nation at large, understand the true nature of logic as the science of thought, the philosophy, i.e., the Christian or Biblical doctrine, of the Spirit. This doctrine is almost universally excluded from the science of logic ; yet the science of thought necessarily includes the Spirit of Truth (self-consciousness, Ego, Reason), which constitutes its universal scientific element. Error is simply the false negative side of thought, while the true negative of thought is the free positive self-activity of Spirit—all in all. Nothing exists apart from the spirit of thought, which is at once wisdom, truth, love. If this were generally understood, a radical reconstruction of the constitution of Churches and States would immediately follow, and the new heaven and the new earth would then appear.

To no one in modern times do we owe so much as to George Fox, the Quaker, the Founder of the Society of Friends, for the great doctrine of the inner light and witness of the Spirit and its indwelling power in man. As far as I can learn, he was in no way indebted for the light to a previous study of philosophy and logic. However, apart from such study, he was none the less endowed with great intuitive and reflective powers of thought, and was able to reason logically. It came to him as a great yet simple revelation, that God, the omnipresent Spirit, who inspired the prophets and apostles who wrote the Bible, was there and then present always to inspire, to teach, to enlighten and to fill the true believer with the same power, and to guide him into all truth : and that God in His love willed that all men should be saved. Consequently, he came to see, as he says, that, ' Though he read of Christ and God, he knew Them only from the presence of a like Spirit manifested in his own.' This is the very heart, soul and spirit of the philosophy of Hegel. It says much for the new clear inner light Fox had now received that, while working away at his leather, he felt so constrained by an overpowering sense of love and sympathy for men, that in order to preach the gospel of freedom from everything not of God, he devoted himself to a life of indescribable toil, hardship, and suffering. Concerning the inner light, Barclay, one of his chief followers and exponents, writes thus : ' God hath placed His Spirit in every man to inform him of his duty and to enable him to do it.'

This idea lifted John Bright (a member of the Society of Friends) into a spiritual atmosphere, in which he dwelt alone in the House of Commons, and which made him its brightest ornament. Another Quaker, the poet Whittier, thus expresses himself : ' I have an unshaken faith in the one distinctive doctrine of Quakerism—the light within—the immanence of the Divine Spirit.' His (Whittier's) faith in Christ not only meant ' a faith in the historical manifestation of Divine love to humanity, but in His living presence in the heart open to receive Him.' Some of the aberrations of Fox and of other persons who have at any time professed to be possessors of this inner light and testimony of God's Spirit, require no notice, for they do not invalidate its truth.

That the Puritans generally recognized, though not so fully as George Fox, the value of the witness of God's Spirit, is seen in the words of their great poet, Milton :—

> ' And chiefly thou, O Spirit ! that dost prefer
> Before all temples the upright heart and pure,
> Instruct me, for Thou know'st ' ;—
> ' What in me is dark,
> Illumine ! what is low, raise and support ! '

and again, in Bunyan's illustration in the *Pilgrim's Progress* of the loss and recovery of the roll. Without undervaluing the importance of the teaching and spiritual experience of the Puritans and Reformers, we hold that Fox and the early members of the Society of Friends raised this doctrine of the Spirit to a higher and clearer level of experience than had hitherto been realized since the early years of the Christian era. Fox and his immediate associates became not only a great power in England, but also in America and many parts of Europe. One can see, in some measure, their influence on Kant, Fichte and other German philosophers, as well as on Schleier-

macher and other German theologians. Whether
it had any direct influence on Hegel through the
Pietists and Moravians, is not known with certainty,
though it seems highly probable. Be this as it
may, it is the cardinal doctrine and principle of Hegel's
philosophy from first to last.

After studying the life of George Fox and discern-
ing in some measure the greatness of the man, one
ceases to be surprised that Carlyle should have
given to this shoemaker, who had made for himself a
suit of leather, such a prominent place in his philosophy of clothes. He there makes some remarks
one could only expect from a Carlyle. ' The most
remarkable incident in modern history, perhaps, is
George Fox's making to himself a suit of leather.
This man to whom the Divine Idea of the Universe
manifests itself. Sitting at his stall, this youth, a
living Spirit, with an antique inspired VOLUME,
discerns its celestial home. Amid his boring and
hammering came splendours and terrors. The temple
of immensity wherein as man he had been sent
to minister, was full of holy mystery to him. The
clergy of the neighbourhood whom he consulted,
advised him to drink and dance with the girls. The
ordained interpreters were the blind leaders of the
blind, though girt-on their surplices and cassock
aprons. Fox turned from them, with tears and
sacred scorn, back to his leather-parings and his
Bible. That spirit would not be buried under
encumbrances. Through long days and nights of silent
agony it struggled and wrestled with a man's force, to
be free, and emerged into the light of Heaven. That
Leicester shoe-shop, had men known it, was a holier
place than any Vatican or Loretto "shrine." He
said to himself, " Only meditation and devout prayer
to God can ferry me across to the Land of Light,

I will to the woods, wild-berries feed me, and for clothes cannot I stiteh myself one perennial suit of leather ! " Let some living Angelo or Rosa, with seeing eye and understanding heart, picture George Fox on that morning, when he spreads out his cutting-board for the last time, and cuts cowhides by some unwonted patterns, and stitches them together into one continuous all-including Case, the farewell service of his awl. Stitch away, thou noble Fox : every prick of that little instrument is pricking into the heart of slavery, and world-worship, and the Mammon-god. There is in broad Europe one free man, and thou art he ! '

Carlyle asks, ' Why in a discussion on the Perfectibility of Society reproduce now Fox's perennial suit ? ' We see it was because it had some relation to the Divine Idea of the world, because it is connected closely with Fox's great insight concerning the Witness of the Spirit. Hegel's insight into the Spirit of the Universe was the conception of the ideas of Milton, Fox, and Carlyle. The great and far-reaching results of the labours of Fox will never be fully estimated. He must be estimated by one doctrine, and that alone, for it alone made him the burning and shining light that he was.

The fourth period is especially associated with John Wesley, and through it the doctrine of the Witness of the Spirit has obtained a permanent place in the Christian Church, as also have the hymns of his brother Charles. From early childhood he manifested a strong religious devotion. At college he was an earnest student of the Holy Scriptures, and at the same time gave considerable attention to what he names Natural Philosophy. He studied many metaphysical books, but attached the greatest value to a knowledge of the science of logic as a means of obtaining a satisfactory insight into the real and permanent nature of Christianity. To a lady, who made inquiries of him as to a course of Christian Theology, he wrote telling her, that for a true knowledge of Christianity an acquaintance with logic was most important (' really worth all the rest,' he says), and he adds that when near, and convenient, he would be willing to aid her in the study thereof. At the same time he strongly recommended the study of Whitby's *Metaphysics*, Bishop Browne on the *Nature, Procedure and Limits of Human Understanding*, Locke's *Essay on the Human Understanding*, and Malebranche's *Search after Truth*. This latter book must have opened Wesley's mind to the value of philosophy more fully than anything else. It must have affected greatly his general study and his study of the Bible in particular. It had also a great influence on Kant. Malebranche says: ' The essence of the soul is thought,' ' We see all things in God,' ' God is the place of spirits,' ' The soul has the Notion of the Infinite and Universal,' ' We find in our consciousness, sensations and pure thoughts. God is the Truth, therefore in seeing the Truth we see God,' ' This union in the Word of God, and our will with his Love makes us in the image and likeness of God.' There can be no doubt Wesley had deeply pondered the rich spiritual reasoning of this book, which must have helped him ultimately to grasp with such clearness and fullness the Witness of the Spirit as taught in the Bible. He had been startled by the direct question being put to him, ' Does the Spirit of God bear witness with your spirit that you are a child of God ? ' This question he had never put to himself. It somewhat surprised and confounded him. His study of logic and metaphysics helped him to appreciate the vital reality of the question at its true value. For about two years he gave the subject his undivided attention and study. His eyes were opened to see the nature of true saving faith as never before. He says : ' An assurance was given me, that He had taken away my sins, even mine, and saved me from the law of sin and death.' It was a new discovery. Although he had previously been prayerful and devout, the new light caused his spiritual life to burst into a mighty inextinguishable flame. As with Paul, the love of Christ which constrained him was not a mere feeling devoid of rational knowledge : it was thought that burned. The Witness of the Spirit with Wesley was an intellectual logical apprehension of the spiritual nature of God as the universal Spirit of the universe, therefore he did not regard human reason as something separate and distinct from Divine Reason. With the leading followers of Wesley, reason was limited to a very narrow sphere or province, chiefly to obtaining a knowledge of the doctrines directly bearing on human salvation, to miracles and prophecy, and other collateral external evidences of the authenticity and divine authority of the Bible as the Word of God, along with a limited exposition of its doctrines and moral precepts. Few Methodists have ever logically grasped the nature of assurance through the Spirit as Wesley did, and fewer still know how he came to realize it. They only know that he was aided thereto by some Moravians. True, the Witness of the Spirit became the main doctrine in the Methodists' creed and experience, but it lost most of its real logical depth and became a mere dogmatic opinion, held with more or less firmness of conviction, based on Wesley's own words, and on several widely-quoted words of Scripture bearing on this doctrine.

The words already quoted from Malebranche are most valuable in indicating the quality of Wesley's philosophy, but many of the statements of Wesley are quite as important in showing the high estimate in which he held the science of Reason, or the science of Logic, in giving stability in Christian experience. He shows clearly in his sermon on Divine Providence that he saw how the general includes the particular and the particular includes the universal, the genus the species and the species the genus, and the absolute whole the parts and the parts the absolute whole, for he adds, ' If there be no parts there can be no whole.' He saw that ' great ' and ' small ' are merely relative terms. With him the relative did not exclude the Absolute, as with some of our short-sighted moderns. He speaks of the infinite wisdom and power of God, though it is not easy to see whether he regards the term general as meaning the absolute whole as infinite. His view of Reason, however, was far in advance of his time. It was diametrically opposed to the Auflärung of the eighteenth century, falsely called the ' Age of Reason.' In proof of Wesley's estimate of Reason, I quote the following from Hagenbach : ' He (Wesley) spoke prominently of the use of reason in religion. " There are many," he said, "who decry the use of reason in religion ; but I by no means agree with them. I rather find in the Holy Scripture that our Lord and His apostles always went to work in a reasonable way. The greatest reasoner was Paul, who laid down the law for all Christians : Be not children in understanding ; howbeit in malice be ye children, but in understanding be men. But the grounds must be true and right from which to draw conclusions, for it is impossible to deduce the truth from false premises.' " Here, he does not tell us how we obtain a knowledge of the difference between true and false premises, but he elsewhere tells us that ' The faculty of the soul which includes these three operations of the mind (simple apprehension, judgment, and discourse), I term reason, the progress of the mind from one judgment to another.' In regard to Reason, Wisdom, and the Providence of God, Wesley and Hegel are substantially one. ' Divine Wisdom,' says Hegel, ' i.e. Reason, is one and the same in the *great* as in the *little*; and we must not imagine God to be too weak to exercise His wisdom on the grand scale,' and ' Divine Providence presides over the events of the world.' Wesley says : ' When you depreciate Reason, you must not imagine you are doing God service.' Then he adds : ' God made you in His own image : a Spirit like Himself : a Spirit endued with understanding : without which . . . (man) could not be a moral agent, any more than a tree or stone.' He is least satisfactory when he declares reason cannot produce faith, hope, love : yet without these reason is not reason, or is false reason, just as God without reason, faithfulness, and love would not be God. It was reason which gave him his clear knowledge of the Witness of the Spirit, for he gave the subject a long, earnest study, in and through which he attained a reasoned faith. In reason, he made a close approach to the logical assurance of faith in the Spirit's witness attained by Hegel. In some respects he was much superior to Hegel, in others he was much inferior. If Hegel and Wesley could have been blended into one person, such a person would have been near the stature of the apostle Paul. At any rate, it only requires the logical philosophy of the Spirit as unfolded by Hegel infused into that of Wesley, or Wesley's into that of Hegel, to have a philosophy of the Spirit as nearly perfect as is possible.

15

Hegel says much calculated to satisfy the most fervent Methodist. Wesley's spiritual insight as teacher and leader was very great, but the Wesleyan Church has lost much of his spirit, which cannot be recovered until its professors and tutors are thoroughly imbued with the logical philosophy of Hegel. The great difficulties now in the way of its recovery are, the wide prevalence of an unspiritual science, agnosticism and evolution by natural selection, and an illogical and unscientific criticism of the Bible. For the most part, the logical basis and secret of the Witness of the Spirit are unknown, so this doctrine retains little more than a sort of pragmatic value, having ceased to be a real conscious experience of Reason.

This brings us to the fifth and last period of the strong realization and power of the Witness of the Spirit as manifested in the origin and early growth of the Primitive Methodist Church. The real secret of its origin and rapid extension is due more to this great and vital doctrine than to any other cause, the deep and clear apprehension of which belongs almost entirely to Hugh Bourne, the real Founder of the Church. As was the case with Fox, there is no evidence that he had ever studied logic or any metaphysical book, ancient or modern. He had received little ordinary day-school and no college education : yet it may safely be said if there had been no Hugh Bourne the Primitive Methodist Church would have had no existence. He was the centre of the great spiritual awakening of the first decade of the nineteenth century. The beginning of Primitive Methodism was unknown to all the other Churches of England, and for a long time it was generally regarded with a feeling approaching disgust. It was looked upon as a wild, boisterous religious fanaticism due to a number of poor, ignorant enthusiasts. Even the Wesleyan Church failed to see its deep significance, and during forty, fifty or more years looked askance at its progress with a feeling not unmixed with jealousy. The Wesleyans were generally much annoyed at the name. They thought the old body had worked well, and therefore they conceived that nothing more could be expected or required of them than to move on the old lines, although they had really left those lines, having abandoned open-air preaching. Their leading ministers, though holding Wesley in the highest esteem and veneration and accepting his special teaching, yet failed to see this doctrine with Wesley's eyes, and so the Church sank, and instead of being great evangelists, they only became distinguished as popular preachers and great administrators. In a word, they became too much mere pragmatic writers, historians and legalistic rulers of their Church. For this deviation from the logical position of Wesley they suffered a serious loss immediately after his death, and took such action on several occasions that they continued to suffer great loss for at least seventy years. They still suffer—and for very much the same reason—an inward spiritual decline. They have nearly a million Sunday-school scholars, and yet they report a decrease in Church members. In the eighteenth century Wesley was without an equal as a philosopher and evangelist. This union of a sound philosophy with the spirit of the Gospel made him to be the mighty power he was. It is doubtful whether a greater spirit than his has lived since the days of the apostles. But for the lack of philosophic insight in the leaders of Wesleyan Methodism, and the entrance of a pragmatic spirit as a subordinate cause, it is highly probable that Primitive Methodism would not have arisen. For this new state of things the chief secret must be sought, and can only be found, in Hugh Bourne.

In intellectual capacity Hugh Bourne was a greater man than any of his biographers have conceived him to be. Be that as it may, he, like Fox, without scholastic or college training realized a clearer vision of the universal presence of God as the living personal Spirit of the universe than any of his contemporaries. This is the supreme fact of his life. The further question is, What was it that otherwise contributed to make him to be what he ultimately became? It is deeply to be regretted that this question has seldom been asked or made the subject of serious study, whilst everything odd, eccentric or quaint about him, or anything calculated to excite a smile, with a shade of pity at his supposed ignorance, as if he were quite behind this age of enlightenment, has been well noted and oft repeated. It seems to have been assumed that the less we inquired into and knew of his early beginning, the more to our credit, and that to know of his apparent weaknesses only adds to God's glory in doing so great a work with such a weak instrument. Such a notion is fraught with evil consequences, and misrepresents the full essential quality required of God's workmen. There are men who can disparage his knowledge and attainments, who in comparison are mere children, not possessing a tithe of his knowledge. One thing is certain—he was an earnest student all his days.

Hugh Bourne was born on April 3, 1772, a year and five months after the birth of Hegel. I put these two names together to show that at that time, in widely separated quarters, many persons were longing for a fuller knowledge of God and greater certainty in the doctrines pertaining to the Christian life. In deep longing for God they were so far alike. In other respects they differed much, yet the one aim of both was to help in ushering in the kingdom of God in its truth and glory. The farm where Hugh Bourne was born was situated in a sequestered and unattractive spot in Stafford-shire, a district affording no facilities for education; favourable, however, for meditation. When four or five years of age, great thoughts of God filled his mind; he thought even then that God was an eternal Being who had created all things in heaven and earth, and that He was everywhere present. When quite a boy he committed to memory the morning and evening prayers of the Prayer Book, the ' Te Deum ' and the Litany. Having no means of gaining an education, his mother was his teacher. He attended for a short time two village schools, but, chiefly by the aid of his mother, he soon mastered the ' Three R's.' Hegel's opportunities for gaining a good education were most excellent, so that in his twelfth year he had learned the Wolfian definitions of the so-called ' Idea clara,' and in his fourteenth, all the various figures and rules of the syllogism, and could always repeat them from memory. At school he was a quiet, steady lad, simple and naïve, but took eagerly to his books, and ' liked to walk with his seniors.' In his social relations he was ever strictly moral and conscientious; while religion and the purity of the marriage relation were to him the prime principles of the State. Hugh Bourne, near the close of his seventh year, commenced a course of constant reading and study of the Word of God. He seems to have felt more the need of Divine help in order to do right than did Hegel; this he earnestly sought, but his sorrow of heart kept increasing. For twenty years he had an alternating experience of doubt and sorrow, now dreading damnation, which he felt he deserved, and now hoping for the salvation of God. He was most exercised about the nature of faith in the Lord Jesus Christ to the saving of his soul and the realizing of the consciousness of pardon and peace with God. He was anxious to find some one to give him the kind of instruction he most needed, but found none. He had yet to endure many wearisome days, nights, months, and years. At the same time Hegel was plunging into and studying the deep problems of the Philosophy of Spirit. During three years from the spring of 1793 to 1796 he was specially studying the philosophy of Kant and writing for himself a life of Christ. He, too, had his pain and agony in endeavouring to reconcile reason and faith in a logical system of philosophy. At the time of Bourne's conversion, in 1799, Hegel was completing the first sketch of his system, and in 1807, the year of the first great English camp-meeting at Mow Cop, appeared the first great work of Hegel, the *Phœnomenologie des Geistes*. During this period and for many years, in Germany, there was a deep and widespread ferment in the study of the Spirit (in the realm of Pure Reason); in England there was going on a great spiritual Revival, which in forty or fifty years spread more or less deeply into every nook and corner of the land. Of this great spiritual awakening Hugh Bourne was the central and moving spirit.

By trade he was a carpenter and millwright, and was often required to assist in various kinds of engineering work. At times he was engaged in work on his father's farm. He became practically acquainted with certain mechanical arts, for he had early devoted himself to various branches of science and to their application to wind, water and steam. He obtained a fair knowledge of hydrostatics, hydraul-

ics, pneumatics and optics. He gained his learning
often by the midnight lamp after a hard day's toil.
About this time he applied himself to the study of
the Hebrew, Greek and Latin languages. We find
him studying Greek in the hayfield. Some members
of the Society of Friends lent him several books,
which he diligently perused. Before his conversion,
among other religious books, he read Alleine's *Alarm*,
Baxter's *Call to the Unconverted*, and Wesley's
Sermon on the Trinity. This latter relieved his
mind of many difficulties which had long oppressed
him. His conversion, as we have said, took place 'in
the year 1799. It was while reading Fletcher's
Letters on the Manifestation of the Son of God,
that he then ' believed with his heart unto righteousness, and with his mouth made confession unto
salvation.' He says : ' My sins were taken away in
an instant : I was filled with all joy and peace in
believing. I never knew or thought anyone could
in this world have such a foretaste of heaven. In
an instant I felt I loved God with all my heart,
mind, soul and strength. I felt I loved all mankind
and a desire that all might be saved. Life, light,
liberty, flowed in upon my soul, and such rapturous
joy that I could scarcely tell whether in the body or
not. The burden and guilt of my sin was gone. I
could call Jesus Lord by the Holy Ghost. I now
received the spirit of adoption and felt the Spirit of
God bearing witness with my spirit that I was a
child of God. I was as if brought into a new world :
creation wore a new aspect, the Scriptures were
opened to me, and I read the Bible with new eyes.'
Not long afterwards he became somewhat despondent,
evidently by reason of asking himself questions
about the reality and soundness of the nature of his
new experience, but soon afterwards he attended a

meeting of the Quakers at Leek. While one of them was speaking on the point which bore directly on his passing experience, he had his doubts and fears in relation to faith cleared up, and the Lord restored unto him the joy of His salvation. This brought him a good deal into the company of some of the members of the Society of Friends. These, too, lent him works of the most eminent of their persuasion, which he greatly prized, and which enabled him to understand much more fully the things of the Spirit. Here we see how reason helped him into a full and abiding assurance of the invisible things of God, which he never again lost. About this time he joined the Methodist Church. His reading now became more confined to the Wesleyan Magazines, Wesley's *Sermons and Notes on the New Testament*, Fletcher's *Checks*, and the Bible. He says : ' By earnest prayer and diligent study I obtained a more comprehensive knowledge of the Scriptures, Christian experience and the doctrines of Christ.' He was led to see the great importance of always preaching ' the possibility of a full, free, and present salvation.'

In the year 1801, Hugh Bourne was made a trustee of one of the Wesleyan chapels, a class-leader and a local preacher. He preached his first sermon on July 12, 1801, yet, strange to say, the Wesleyans never put his name on the plan as a recognized preacher : but having become a local preacher, he now began to study more assiduously Hebrew and Greek, feeling more than ever the necessity of knowing the original languages in which God's Book was written, and from various accounts, he gained a fair proficiency therein. In 1808, however, he was expelled from the Methodist Society for no other offence than because he persisted in favouring and holding camp-meetings in the neighbourhood of the Potteries, when and wherever possible.   He saw that they were productive of much good.   Many sinners, some of them very notorious, had by means of these meetings been converted.   The Conference decided that they were likely to be productive of considerable mischief, and disclaimed all connexion with them. Bourne had been a member from June, 1799, to June, 1808, had been a preacher for nearly seven years without having his name on the plan.   The first class of the Primitive Methodist Church was formed March, 1810, so for nearly two years he was not a member of any Church, having no desire to form a new Church.   The natural desire for Christian union and fellowship forced the formation of the first class, hence the origin of this new Church and a new name.

Thus we see its origin did not spring from any great agitation arising concerning a reform of Church polity or a dispute of a doctrinal character.   It arose entirely from a clear restoration of a belief in the Witness of the Spirit and the forgiveness of sins. Men are prone to think such knowledge is impossible or a delusion.   Wesley's father denied the possibility of attaining to a knowledge of the forgiveness of sins, and even treated the idea with sarcasm.   Priestly absolution seems to mere sense so much easier : though in the nature of things lacking absolute certainty, and affording encouragement to sinful deeds.

From the time of the conversion of Bourne, 1799 to 1810, a great spiritual fire began to burn and spread in the neighbourhood of Harriseahead, Burslem, Bemersley and Tunstall, out of which sprang Primitive Methodism, a Church now numbering 212,000 members.   The philosophy of the history of this Church has yet to be written.   As yet we have only, or chiefly, a more or less connected chain of facts unphilosophically strung together. It may, however, be confidently asserted that, taking it all in all, as a special Christian influence for good, the rise and progress of this Church is without a parallel in the history of the Christian Church. For upwards of half a century its one all-dominating doctrine was the need of consciously realizing the inward witness of the Spirit, assuring peace with God and the certainty of sins forgiven. The question always asked was, Have you obtained peace with God ? The new converts immediately became mighty in prayer, and in making confession of faith unto salvation. The shy and timid were made strong. They rejoiced greatly in God their Saviour. Their passion for prayer was intense ; it was the spiritual atmophere in which they lived, moved, and had their being. The presence of the Spirit caused them to shout aloud for joy. While Bourne lived it was the chief theme of his preaching. We find in his *Ecclesiastical History* it was the golden thread he sought from first to last. He called this work ' The Chain of Piety.' It begins with Adam and Eve and concludes with Susanna and John Wesley.

Unlike Wesley, he was not, apparently, a student of logical and metaphysical philosophy, but he was a sincere student of the things of God, and so, we maintain, in the best and truest sense of the word a Christian philosopher. It is very doubtful whether any Primitive Methodist has ever had such a full, clear insight and experience of the Spirit's witness as that possessed by Hugh Bourne. William Clowes, the co-founder, ranks next in this experience, and we think he did more in proclaiming it abroad far and wide. Wherever he went he was like a flaming fire. As with the Wesleyans, the character of the hymns they sang had much influence in the spread of the

Gospel. It was little short of a calamity that when, some years later, the Primitive Methodists revised their hymn-book, they should leave out some of these hymns, such as the following :—

> 'Lift up your hearts, Immanuel's friends,
> And taste the pleasures Jesus sends ;
> Let nothing cause you to delay,
> But hasten on the good old way.

> 'O good old way, how sweet thou art !
> May none of us from thee depart,
> But may our actions always say,
> We're marching on the good old way.'

> 'Come, saints and sinners, hear me tell
> The wonders of Immanuel,
> Who saved me from a burning hell,
> And brought my soul with Him to dwell
> And gave me heavenly union,'

with several others of like tone, all denoting a conscious enjoyment of and fellowship with God in His Spirit. Great stress, too, was laid in preaching on the boundless love of God to vilest sinners. It is a great error to think that their chief topic was the torments of hell. Their chief aim was to make good Christians, and that meant to be filled with the love of God in all wisdom and spiritual understanding. They taught that he that loved God loved his brother also, and as God was holy, so ought they to be holy in all manner of conversation and conduct. There is no doctrine that gives such a real substantial assurance, or such a stirring and uplifting influence, as the inner light of the Spirit, or that secures such effectual prayer. The early Primitive Methodists were mighty in believing prayer. They believed that the kingdom of heaven ' suffereth violence, and the violent take it by force.' Christ certainly urged the necessity of persistent prayer, that ' men ought always to pray and not to faint,' which explains the words 'This kind goeth not out but by prayer and fasting.' They certainly obtained extraordinary answers to their prayers. There is evidently a spiritual element in wireless telegraphy when rightly understood, for it is in some sense independent of electricity. It reveals the essential spiritual nature of the universe. Is it said, wireless telegraphy is only physical mechanism ? We say such a statement is unwarranted and unscientific, as unscientific as to assert that universal gravitation is only physical. Of course, prayer may be extolled to the disparagement of earnest study and preaching of the Word, just as preaching may be extolled to the disparagement of prayer. Jesus Himself both prayed and preached : so the early Primitive Methodists both preached and prayed with a vengeance, and by such means they went on from conquering to conquer. At the beginning they had such a passion for prayer that it culminated in a whole day's praying at Mow Cop, and finally in the origin of the Church and its rapid extension. The Spirit's witness became in them a mighty flame which spread rapidly in every direction : it was the chief cause of the success both of the Primitive and Wesleyan Churches. No activity in other directions can supply the lack of this conscious presence of the Spirit. It is the absolutely supreme principle of Christian Faith, and is at the same time the absolute goal of philosophy, consequently mere assent and consent is not faith, but superstition. When properly understood, the Witness of the Spirit is seen to be the ontological Idea and Being of God of Anselm : it is the solution of Kant's problem, How are synthetic judgments *à priori* possible ? Paul expresses the synthetic judgments thus : ' He that is joined to the Lord is one spirit ' : ' Ye are the temple of the living God, as God hath said, I will dwell in you ' : or in the words of John, ' He that dwelleth in love, dwelleth in God, for God is love.' So the most perfect knowledge is the knowledge of the spirit of love. It is the intuition of the Holy One, which enables men in full assurance to say, ' Truly our fellowship is with the Father, and with His Son Jesus Christ,' ' The same anointing teacheth you all things, and is truth,' ' And hereby we know that we are of the truth and shall assure our hearts before Him.' It is the Begriff and Ego of Hegel, wherein love is one with thought in man in the identity of human and Divine thought. Only so do we and can we properly know God. This is logical thought, judgment, reason, faith, at its deepest and truest, for without love, man's understanding or intellectual power is darkened.

Now, just as there was a decline in the inner light of the Divine Spirit in the early Christian era, in the Lutheran and Reformed Churches after Luther's death, in after years among the Puritans and Covenanters, as also among the Quakers after Fox, in the Wesleyan Church after Wesley's death, so there has been a most serious decline among the Primitive Methodists since the death of Bourne and Clowes. The cause of the decline among the Primitives has been much the same as among the Wesleyans. Both alike have had popular preachers and able administrators, but in both Churches there is a painful lack of deep insight into and experience of the vital doctrine of the Witness of the Spirit. Wesley, in his study of logic and metaphysics, was far in advance of any evangelist of the seventeenth and eighteenth centuries. As a philosopher he was not inferior to Wycliff and Luther, probably even their superior. In this sense the Wesleyan ministers have seriously failed to tread in his steps : so also the ministers of the other Methodist Churches have equally failed,

The decline of the Primitive Methodist Church is however, mainly due to the teaching of Mansel's *Lectures on the Limits of Religious Thought*, Darwin's *Origin of Species by Natural Selection*, and such books as the *Essays and Reviews*, Bishop Colenso's and many others relating to the higher criticism of the Bible. Mansel's book, however, had by far the most damaging effect on the quality of its spiritual life, for if man cannot have a genuine logical knowledge of God, how can he have the Witness of His Spirit in his heart ? And if man's knowledge of God cannot stand the test of a logical examination, how is the Bible likely to stand the false logical test of Mansel ? Besides, we have now not only Mansel, but also Spencer, Darwin, Huxley and others attacking our knowledge of the Personality of God and man, the three latter especially from the physical, blindly disregarding the true logical and metaphysical side. Spencer reduces our knowledge of God to an unknowableness, and puts in the place of God ' An Infinite and Eternal Energy.' Hamilton in part destroyed the real value of logic by his quantification of the predicate, and Mill still further by defining logic as the science for the estimation of evidence—not the science of reason-thought. Besides, Mill's doctrine of liberty is not that of true liberty. Like Kant, he saw the defect in the four figures of the syllogism, and like Kant, he failed to see how to remedy it : so a false logic came to reign supreme. Hegel and Stirling have been largely ignored as unintelligible, though by these two men we are furnished with a real conerete logic of being, thought, and Spirit, in which the figures of the syllogism are reduced to a grand intelligible rational triplicity of thought. Therein we have a real logical knowledge of God in thought and feeling, since the feeling of love penetrates to the depth of the Godhead (for love is the true and perfect light of God), just as we have a real logical knowledge of physics in thought and in sense-feeling. Together they form an absolute concrete logic of the totality of Being. The Philosophy of Spirit is at once the Immanence and Transcendence of God in self-consciousness.

It is difficult for the present generation to realize the general excitement caused by the appearance in 1858 of Mansel's book and the effect it had on the deeper nature of religious thought for many years afterwards. Many ministers and laymen of the Primitive Methodist Church wrote able articles in defence and praise of the book, the purport of which may be expressed in some words of Kant : ' To abolish knowledge to make room for belief.' An able Biblical expositor, a Primitive Methodist, said publicly,. after reading Mansel's book : ' I am now convinced I shall never truly know God,' and ' I now see as I never saw before the weakness and feebleness of man's intellectual capacity.' These views spread rapidly, and are now all but universally accepted. To say we cannot know the Infinite, has a very humble look, but, as Hegel says, ' such humility does not count for much,' for ' the object of Logic is to know God as the truth.' Hegel's logic is a difficult subject to master : it is much easier to write novels with petty finite aims, which only require one to indulge in plausible and well-arranged flights of a vivid imagination. The novelist tells us that the poet attains to a thorough knowledge of the Truth by one intuitive flash of pure genius, while the metaphysical logician resembles a man with a lantern, groping in the dark, seeking to find the foundations of the universe. The knowledge of God in Spirit and in Truth is not thus easily attained. Of course, those who hold the views of Mansel, viz. that on account of the limits of human thought a logical theology is impossible, urgently recommend the study of the Bible, the Life of Christ, and the Fatherhood of God, overlooking the fact that if we cannot logically know God, we cannot know Christ as the God-man or understand the great truths of the Bible. Those who advocated such views little thought they were preparing the way for the decline of deep spiritual life and power in the Churches, and least of all did the ministers of the Primitive Methodist Church think so.

That there has been a great spiritual decline in the Primitive Methodist Church cannot be doubted. One proof of this is revealed by the fact that in 1897 it had twelve fewer circuit pledged ministers in active work in the British Isles than in 1877. During the first fifty years of the Church's existence the circuits believed in calling out new ministers, and the membership increased by leaps and bounds. It is worthy of note that the two first ministers were chiefly supported by four persons, poor men, each contributing five shillings a week. During the second fifty years much unsatisfactory legislation was adopted, which greatly retarded the progressive growth of the Church.

Another proof of its spiritual decline is that, although it has nearly half a million Sunday scholars, it yet reports either a decrease or only a very small increase of Church members. Its administrators have in a quiet way abrogated, with the general consent of the Church, the law recognizing the Sunday-school as the Catechumen Department of the Church which made easy the adoption of a system for the training of teachers as leaders—for a knowledge of vital Christian doctrine is quite as necessary for Sunday-school teachers as for preachers—thus fitting them for official standing in the Church.   Teachers and preachers who are unable to explain to their scholars and hearers the Witness of the Spirit are unfit to be either teachers or preachers.   Until scholars are taught this doctrine, Sunday-schools *must be a failure.*

Every year about a hundred thousand scholars must leave and be added to the Wesleyan Sunday-schools, and about forty-six thousand leave and be added to the Primitive Methodist Sunday-schools. If five out of every hundred of those who leave were retained as members, this would yield to the Wesleyans a yearly addition of twenty thousand and to the Primitives nine thousand : thus ninety per cent. of the scholars who yearly leave these schools never become members of the Church—that is, nine out of every ten of those who leave the Sunday-school are entirely lost to the Church.   This it is not difficult to see if we remember that nearly the whole population of England has passed and is passing through one Sunday-school or another.   And what is a fact in relation to these two Churches is equally true of all the other Nonconformist Churches.   The present failure in the working of the Sunday-schools is strong evidence of the general superficial knowledge and experience of the Witness of the Spirit.   Like Samson, the Church now and again shakes itself and says, ' I will go out as aforetime,' but ' it wists not that its power has departed from it,' and then makes all kind of excuses for its failure.

When a true logical experience of the Witness of the Spirit declines, the most fantastical doctrinal illusions and delusions take its place.   Men hew out to themselves broken cisterns, wherein the water of life is lost.   Apart from a true knowledge of the Witness of the Spirit a true knowledge of morality and religion is impossible, because without such knowledge morality and religion take the form,

16

almost invariably, of mere legal enactments in both Church and State. When a man's sense of right and wrong is no higher than what is legal, his moral and Christian character is very low, for justice without mercy is not justice. Without the knowledge of God's Spirit in the heart, all manner of conflicting views concerning God, religion and morals prevail. Yet all the while the Bible everywhere implies and teaches that all men think the Being of God as Spirit, Creator, Eternal, Infinite, All-wise, Almighty, Holy and Good. In an important sense, to think is to know, but such knowledge may be very superficial; or to use a form of speech not uncommon, it may be in part abstract, or in part be made up of gross contradictions. On the other hand, if men do not love God, Christ says, they know not God. In this sense men without love are a living lie. The Bible teaches that love is the supreme principle of all knowledge, because ' God is love.' If men do not love God, they not only deny their own true being, but the real Being of God. So Christ said : ' I love the Father,' ' and if I should say I know Him not, I shall be a liar like unto you.' Again He says : ' He that loveth me shall be loved of My Father, and I will love him, and will manifest Myself to him,' ' and We will come unto him and make our abode with him.' Such knowledge is absolutely Concrete. As in part already stated, in these sayings we have the identity of the subjective and objective ontological Idea of the Being of God, which Anselm was the first to annunciate ; and also the secret of Kant's synthetic judgments *à priori* of which he was in quest. It is also Hegel's logical exposition of the doctrine of the Ego, the infinite absolute personality of God manifested in the finite spirit of man, and is none other than the witness of God's Spirit in man's spirit, as also the manifestation to man of God in Nature as its Creator. In the light of the Spirit we see that Christianity is the unity of Faith and Reason—the unity of the Immanence and Transcendence of God—God in man and man in God. The Ego in its logical nature is a trinity in unity—the Fatherhood of God, the sonship of man, in the unity of God's Holy Spirit, which is the true logical doctrine of the Witness of the Spirit. So ' when this earthly house of our tabernacle is dissolved, we have a building of God, a house not made with hands, eternal in the heavens.' ' He that hath wrought for us this self-same thing is God, who hath given unto us the *earnest* of the Spirit in our hearts.' So John says, ' I saw no temple therein : for the Lord God Almighty and the Lamb are the temple of it.' The Spirit is the warp and woof of the web of the universe, which Hegel in his logical philosophy undertook to unfold in all its detail.

When the Witness of the Spirit fails to be properly realized in the Christian Church, the people inclined to religion naturally attach themselves to a sacerdotal or priestly Church, where the priest is accepted as a sort of mediator, and great reliance is placed in the efficacy of external ordinances, baptism, Holy Communion, and especially in priestly confession and absolution. The rest become sceptical on matters pertaining to God. The reasoning and teaching of Mansel and Newman, though differing in some important respects, practically led to a priestly Church, for the Witness of the Spirit had no place in their teaching. There was no absolute certainty in their religious belief, yet both thought they were doing God service. They both accepted the teaching of the Prayer Book. The influence of both has been very great. The one has intensified the sacerdotalism of the Episcopal English State Church, and the other has had an enormous indirect influence in inoculating the Nonconformist Churches with what has come to be called Agnosticism. It is, to a greater extent than is generally recognized, the secret cause of the arrested progress of the Free Churches. Mansel's teaching, being regarded by the High Church Party as a form of atheism, the Oxford Movement was thus strengthened, and the Church of England gained a hold of the nation it had not hitherto possessed. It greatly aided in the spread of evolution and gave a new direction to Biblical criticism. Henceforth creeds and the study of systematic theology came everywhere to be spoken against. The doctrine of the Witness of the Spirit came to be gradually ignored, as it was said it tended to a morbid introspection and interfered with spiritual enjoyment. If the conscious presence of the Spirit of God in the heart is in any degree ignored, spiritual decline in the Churches becomes inevitable. Their numerical strength will only be retained, if retained at all, through the family tie and the social friendships of the members.

It is remarkable how little colleges and universities do in promoting and developing spiritual life. They are often the source from whence originates gross error. We do not mean by this to disparage these institutions, but they can never fulfil their proper vocation if the Witness of the Spirit is allowed to occupy a subordinate position in philosophy and religion. It is impossible to reconcile the real recognized experience of the Witness of the Spirit in a full, present salvation in this life, so clearly taught in the Bible, with the theories of Agnosticism and Evolution. The Bible teaches the necessity of ' *growth* in grace and in the knowledge of our Lord Jesus Christ,' but it is utterly absurd to confound such ' growth ' with these two theories.

CHAPTER XI

NATURE—EVOLUTION OR CREATION?

THE fact of the existence of matter, in all its numerous forms and variations, and of self-conscious thought itself, is universally admitted, and cannot be rationally denied.

It is, however, not sufficient for man—a born metaphysician—whose nature is thinking-reason, simply to know these facts; his great requirement is an explanation of them. Burke said, 'One fact is worth a thousand arguments'; we say, One fact explained is worth a thousand unexplained.

The business of philosophy is to explain: to give a logical explanation even of existence. To philosophize is to explain what are known merely as 'bare facts.' A man's knowledge of facts will be greater or less according to the extent of his observations. Such knowledge, however, is only superficial, but it must not be regarded as mere assumption. To assume is not to philosophize: assumption is no more than mere guessing, conjecture, or opinion. When we attempt to explain facts by assumptions we have become false to reason, false to philosophy.

Only the most superficial observer can fail to see, on reflection, that everything is connected in an essential relation with every other thing throughout the infinite totality of Being. The inorganic and organic worlds exist in a unity involving a close and essential relation. Universal being is a concrete whole consisting of infinite particulars, and man by his very nature is compelled to ask for an explanation of the reason and cause of all these things, even of the cause of existence or the secret of life itself.

It is often declared, at the present time, that the secret of the universe is not to be found in the philosophy of creative power, wisdom and design essentially inherent in the nature of thought itself, but rather in an evolution under the blind guidance of ' natural selection.' We are compelled to ask, Evolution from what ? for evolution cannot begin from nothing, from an absolute void. Even agnostic evolutionists must admit existence in manifold forms as a present fact. From what did this stupendous universe, with its astonishing varieties and wonderful harmonies, evolve ? Did it evolve from matter without thought ? Was it from matter in a state of fire-mist, or from matter in an invisible, infinitely diffused gas, or from matter in the shape of atoms and molecules ? If thought has to seek, as from its very nature it is compelled to do, an intelligible cause for the start in the process of evolution, all these are utterly unintelligible beginnings. However much time, as part of infinite time, be allowed for the evolutionary processes an intelligible cause is still demanded as a reason for the start. But why should we wander aimlessly back into the infinite past, or grub and dissect in protoplasmic cell-germs, molecules or atoms for an intelligible cause, when each man himself is in possession of thought whose absolute nature is infinite and constitutes the very highest and greatest glory man's nature can possibly possess, either here or hereafter ? Since thought is, why could it not always have been ? As for matter, as Dr. Stirling says, ' There are particulars in existence, each for itself and as such; but matter, as matter, does not exist; it *is*, but it is only a universal of thought, an entity in the intellect.' ' The atom itself was but a thing of thought, and sensibly in existence nowhere.'

Matter as matter gives not in any way an intelligible explanation of the origin of the universe, or of thought. We cannot but regard with the greatest astonishment the fact that educated men should, so willingly and readily, without apparently much scruple, believe that thought may spring from matter, and yet be quite shocked to think or suppose that matter may spring from, or be created by, thought. It is a known fact that thought can comprehend and explain matter in its qualities as it exists in innumerable states and uses, while no one supposes that matter can, in the same way, comprehend thought, or give an intelligible explanation of its nature, operations and powers.

Yet it must be either that matter creates or blindly gives birth to thought, or that thought creates matter. We hold it is irrational to contend that matter gives birth to thought; reason rather compels the belief that thought creates matter in all its infinite manifold forms and qualities, and so compels the disbelief that thought in any way springs from or has been created out of matter, as mere matter.

A logical philosophy demands a deeper unity and identity in nature than can be found either in matter or even in gravitation, and this can only be found in Thought. Thought as thought cannot but be regarded as superior to matter as matter, and it must also be acknowledged that the latter derives all its value from the former. Indeed, the universe is nothing but a stupendous system of ideas. It does not follow that this universal bond of unity is in every different object in its externality identically the same ; here, as elsewhere, there is difference in identity, and identity in difference. Potential and Active Energy possess identity in their difference, for the entire doctrine of ' the transformation and conservation of energy ' implies the principle of identity in difference and difference in identity. Form, matter, force and thought are all difference in identity, but thought is the eternally necessary, essential and intelligible bond of unity between matter and form ; gravitation apart from thought at its root is unintelligible. To say with the agnostic that force is unknowable, or with a certain class of theologians, that it is merely an inscrutable mystery, is to cease to reason ; yea, it means that man turns his back upon himself, upon his own essential spirit. This was not Paul's attitude, for he tells us that ' the Spirit searcheth all things, yea, the depth of the Godhead or the deep things of God.' (If Paul did not mean here the Spirit of God vitally and essentially in man's spirit, then the words are totally misleading, for the Spirit, in the sense of omniscience, has no need to search.) ' The Spirit of God in man reveals to man the things that are freely given to us of God,' for ' the manifestation of the Spirit is given to every man.' Reason in man cannot fully and finally renounce itself. Man may by indifference to some extent stultify the action of his own nature, but the question of the ' What ' perpetually returns. What is it that gives unity to the differents ? What is gravitation ? What is matter in which gravitation is said to inhere ? We cannot stop at merely asking questions ; reason demands answers : it is the still, small voice, which may for the moment be stifled by the din of mere clamour, þut never fails to reassert its divine prerogative to reign supreme. In other words, it demands a satisfactory answer of itself to itself. Merely to say that universal gravitation is an unknown force in nature, and that it thus implies a universal relation and gives a universal bond in and throughout nature, is not a sufficient answer to the question of what is the principle or element of identity in differents. Force, gravitation and matter are each in themselves differents, yet there is that in each and all which constitutes in them an all-pervading identity, but this element is in no sense a mere object of sense-perception. It is not, however, any the less on that account real and rational ; even matter, not to mention gravitation, of which the materialist asks so much, is nowhere as such visible to sense-perception. Matter and gravitation are differents, but the one is nowhere without the other ; thus being essentially one, so Nature is essentially spirit, of which it is the external manifestation. Spirit, thought, is deeper than a mere universal ether. The introduction of a supposed ether does not give any nearer approach to an intelligible solution of the problem of existence, for it is only a supposed finer matter. The solution can nowhere be found but in the subjective and objective unity of thought itself as manifested in Man. Reason leads to and compels belief in the reality of an invisible gravitation, and it equally compels a rational belief in an invisible reason in invisible thought as the life of All, in All that is.

A thoroughgoing evolutionist loses himself in the mere multiplicity of detail in nature and man, for to him there is no intelligible living bond of union. He cannot find the universal bond by merely looking at external nature, any more than he can find the living bond in dissecting the carcass of an animal, or in the decayed stem and branches of a tree. The bond can only be found in universal self-consciousness, the Ego.

The secret of this infinitely variegated universe is

identity. What is this ? Can it be known ? Hegel
asserts that it can, and names it the Notion—the
Concrete notion. Dr. Stirling names it Thought,
the living Absolute Thought between and within the
I and Me. (He says also that Thought is the Absolute
Ratio wherein God and man are one. So through
Christ we have access by one Spirit—one universal
Thought—unto the Father.) This is the same as the
' synthetic judgment ' of which Kant is in search :
or his question in reality is, How can we be sure that
matter and notion, though different, can be in essential
unity or identity ? He must find the apodictic
certainty of the unity of matter and mind, otherwise
the element of necessity between effect and cause
cannot be found, and Hume's problem remains
unsolved. In the synthetic judgment it must be
shown that notion as internal, and matter as external,
form in their unity one concrete notion of difference
in identity which must exist throughout all space
and time. If matter and spirit have not an identity
in human thought, then we have no ground for thinking that matter is in unity or identity, or in essential
relation with the Divine Ego, Thought or Spirit, and
so, as a necessary consequence, it will follow that God
cannot be Creator, but only an Architect. Existence,
thought, reason, philosophy, religion, all rest ultimately
on this principle of identity in difference : all proof
is founded on it. In the necessary relation between
cause and effect, this principle of identity must be
found, otherwise causation, creation, growth and all
improvement will for ever remain without an intelligible, scientific explanation. If there is not an
intelligible rational principle of identity in this relation, then there is an absolute break in the continuity
of existence ; no necessary connection exists anywhere,
and reason, as reason, is not : all is mere haphazard.

There is no worse sign of the superficial thought of the present age than the general attention given exclusively to materialism and physical science, and this is especially noticeable when contrasted with the way in which metaphysics, theology and logic are neglected, or even derided. This is evident even in theological writings and sermons. Thus a recent writer has endeavoured to show that it is not only evolution by natural law in the natural world, but also that natural law ruled in the Spiritual world. The deeper and truer conception of law is that it is spiritual throughout. In common speech, nowadays, nature is the supreme power, and the name God is put so much into the background that He has lost His proper place in the thoughts even of Christian men. The terms Nature, physical force, natural laws and laws of nature, have supplanted the terms spiritual world, spiritual law and spiritual power, which belong essentially to the nature of God and man.

Thought, reason, consciousness, idea, conscience, will and spirit constitute properly the invisible secret of the universe, in and through which alone all investigation can be carried on ; unfortunately, most men give almost exclusive attention to the external side of the world and man, in seeking a knowledge of the secret of the universe, instead of seeking it in the invisible and internal side of man, that is, in thought, reason and spirit.

A sound philosophy shows that material phenomena are the external manifestations of Thought, that is, of Spirit. Professor Tyndall, when strongly criticized for declaring that matter contains the promise and potency of every form of life and thought, was driven to say, he often wondered whether there was not an intelligence at the root of things. Many stumble at the thought of viewing Nature as the external form and manifestation of God—of Thought—but find apparently little difficulty in believing that thought may be evolved out of matter.

To say atoms, germs, whether vegetable, animal or human, explains nothing. Mere sense, at best, does not carry us very far in our knowledge of things. Many of our physicists offer us for knowledge mere assumptions, which they dignify with the noble name of science while at the same time regarding metaphysics with great contempt. Yet, beyond doubt, man's nature is metaphysical, spiritual.

Logical thought can give no intelligible ground for the evolution of the Ego (self-consciousness) out of the unconscious matter of nature or out of a dead universe. Thought, on the other hand, is essentially living and active, and, therefore, creative : and in its true nature is the secret of all causation. Thought implies process, and process implies creation and preservation—both a coming to be and a ceasing to be. This becoming can only be in the sphere of particularity, which is an essential element in thought, in the Ego, in existence in general, and thus creative thought manifests itself in the particularity of external nature. If thought cannot create matter, external nature, or the world, then it cannot objectify or manifest itself, and God cannot be Creator, cannot manifest Himself, cannot be God, for a God that cannot create is only an empty name.

The idea of God implies especially the idea of Creator, and this implies a creation. Hegel says : 'Without a world God could not be God' : this is so, for it would mean that God could not be Creator, nor an eternal Father. Creation may be said to be the crux of the whole matter, for the principle that solves the idea of creation equally solves the idea of preservation, and just as certainly solves the idea of the possibility and reality of miracles. Evolutionists surmount the difficulty as to the origin of all by saying evolution, and by pointing to modifications as proof that evolution is a fact. True, they admit it is only a hypothesis, ' a good working hypothesis,' but then, with them the idea of creation is also a hypothesis, and they say, evolution is by far the better hypothesis of the two.

As before, we may ask, Evolution from what ? Certainly not from matter alone. Our agnostic evolutionists tell us that no one knows what matter is, and they take refuge in what they call agnosticism. In this they only contradict themselves, for at the same time they are anxious to show that they possess more advanced knowledge than any idealist or theologian.

The idea of the evolution of thought from an infinitely diffused gas lacks every element of intelligibility : Ego, thought, self-consciousness, personality, is the only intelligible first. The thinking I (and there is no other I) denotes process, creation, and therefore matter is the essential external manifestation of the categories of Thought.

Thought alone has the potency of every form of matter and life, whether vegetable, animal or human. Man, being made in the image of God, is the end and aim of all creation. He is the microcosm of the Universe. The true idea, then, of creation by God is the manifestation of thought, of reason, of Himself, in material forms. How otherwise can God be rationally conceived as Creator ? Creation is God manifesting Himself, for He must appear, so He ' covereth Himself with light as with a garment, and stretcheth out the heavens as a curtain, and spreadeth them out as a tent to dwell in.'

Huxley, who is regarded as one of the leading scientists of more recent times, attempted to prove that protoplasm was the ' physical basis of life,' and thought, or rather, he tried to prove, that matter became protoplasm, and that by a process of evolution all forms of life and thought originated. He claimed, most emphatically, to proceed in all his investigations only on strictly scientific principles. When his protoplasmic theory of life fell to pieces under the irresistibly clear, logical criticism of Dr. Stirling, he took refuge in agnosticism with his four ignorances—ignorance of cause, ignorance of substance, ignorance of consciousness, and ignorance of externality. When he endeavoured to show how thought might be evolved out of matter—and that he endeavoured to do so cannot well be denied— he became lost.

Kant, in attempting to furnish a theory of the metaphysical construction of matter, began from an assumed matter, two assumed independent forces, and an assumed empty space between the atoms ; at the same time he assumed that some atoms were in contact, for he felt the difficulty of making the atoms act through empty space. Attraction emptied, repulsion filled, space. His fundamental error was that thought or notion was empty until supplied by sense-perception with matter from without, whereas, as Dr. Stirling points out, thought contains essentially both form and matter. ' A matterless form would vanish, and a formless matter never even be. Either, in fact, is but an element of the other. Both together are the concrete truth : as much an inside as an outside.' The work and the architect are there essentially together.

Hegel, with irresistible force, effectually demolished all these assumptions of Kant. Reason demonstrates

to man that the particular forms of matter, in objects
of sense-perception in external nature, are neither
more nor less than the external manifestations of an
infinite, universal, self-conscious, personal being,
which, in brief, is named by the single word—God.
Creator implies relation—nay, not only creation,
but existence, life, growth, progress, attraction, repulsion, cause, effect, thought, reason, personality, self-
consciousness are all impossible in thought and in
reality except in absolute relation. Relativity of
thought and knowledge involves relativity of existence,
for thought itself is existence, though it is much more
than mere existence. Much exists that is transitory ;
thought, however, in its real, rational nature is not
transitory, but permanent and eternal. The transitory and eternal, however, always stand in essential
relation. The principle of gravitation teaches us
that every finite, transitory object contains in it the
attractive and repulsive element of force, which is in
every other object in nature, so that the whole belongs
to every part, and every part belongs to the whole.
This inner unity is not open to sense-perception : it
is only seen in reason-vision : reason tells us that
every dust atom contains the principle of universal
gravitation, and at the same time, gravitation and
matter, each in their essential relation contain
universal thought. It is only in reason-thought
that the materialist can have the' conviction of universal gravitation, motion and matter. It follows
that reason-thought must be just as universal as
gravitation and matter, yea, more reasonably so,
in a sense, for reason-thought in man *consciously*
overlaps and includes in itself all matter and gravity,
otherwise no one could have the rational assurance
of their universality, which universality is generally
admitted. Reason proves that thought and matter

are co-existent in an essential relation. As there is no matter without gravity, which latter is absolutely invisible to sense, so there is nowhere any matter and gravity without reason, nor reason without thought ; reason-thought is the first and uncreated, while matter is just as essentially the created and vicarious representative of the first and uncreated.

Self-consciousness is the original unity of matter and form which contains all the lower forms of thought. Although Nature is the product of thought, it cannot, through its inherent weakness, take into itself the higher forms of self-conscious thought. In this sense Nature is mere externality, yet a necessary externality, for without externality internality could never be. Nature, then, must be a system of grades harmoniously blended together, and, as such, can only be the work of a supreme intelligence : these grades must co-exist, and not be evolved the one out of the other—the man out of the animal, the animal out of the vegetable, the vegetable out of the stone, and the stone out of—no one knows what. We need not wonder that the believer in the origin of species by natural selection, when hard pushed, should ex- claim, ' It is as absurd to inquire into the origin of life as into the origin of thought and matter.' But to know the ' origin ' is still the supreme requirement. ' Modification ' is a fact, but ' modification ' is not origin.

It is to the honour of Kant that, notwithstanding an apparently agnostic result of his philosophy, his transcendental logic furnishes the principles which, if logically carried out, will solve the problem of Hume, give the true principle of Biblical interpretation, and lead to a genuine knowledge of God, man, and Nature. The cause of Kant's failure was that in his system he held that thought and matter exist outside, and in some unexplained manner only alongside, of each other. This view implies that God is not omnipresent, but only fills up the voids between atoms and interstellar spaces. To quote Hegel's remarks as translated by Dr. Stirling: ' Kant says this proof (design) exhibits God only as an Architect, not as a Creator; it applies only to the contingency of forms, not to the substance. This quality, says Kant, is only form, and the agency at work were one only that dealt in form, not one that created matter. The distinction is of no account. *Production of form is utterly impossible without the production of matter.* Once we have Notion, we are far above the difference of form and matter; we know then that absolute form is something real ' (namely, the Ego). ' The content of this form is, the world is designful : particular designfulnesses concern us not ; Design is the Notion, not as in the finite things only—it is the absolute determination of the Notion, it is God's notion, God's quality. God is power, self-determination, and that is, He determines Himself—designfully.' In design, then, there is the absolute unity of thought and matter : either apart is impossible. Identity and difference—thought and matter—have their essential unity in the Ego, and so in the Ego there is an infinite diversity of causes and effects ; but the principle of universal identity as the centre and cause of all difference is in the absolute and universal Ego, ' the one identical I throughout all space and throughout all time.'

At the present time the majority of scientists regard the evolutionary theory or hypothesis as having ' outgrown the trammels of controversy, being now accepted as a principle '; they contend that ' even without Darwin, the theory would now be generally accepted '; yet it is ' a historical fact that the world has accepted evolution chiefly because of Darwin's Natural Selection.' Contributors to the debate on evolution are now expected to do no more than ' merely criticize, amplify or re-marshall Darwin's facts '; yet Darwin is still regarded as the founder or leader of modern evolutionists, and it is held that no single empirical law ' has as yet shown signs of taking rank as a *vera causa* comparable with the Darwinian principle of natural selection.' It is generally admitted that the Darwinian theory of evolution by natural selection is not scientifically established, for Darwin, in his reasonings, could get no further than to say: ' We cannot prove that a single species has changed '; ' nor can we prove that the supposed changes are beneficial '; ' nor can we explain why some species have changed and others have not.' Yet no other evolutionist, who may be supposed to have made an advance upon Darwin, can go one step beyond this!

The theory of Natural Selection, which Darwin calls his *deity*, is used by him to explain, if possible, the design which is apparent in Nature, without the necessity of recognizing a supreme creative intelligence. He declares: ' The old argument (for the existence of God) from design in Nature fails now that the law of natural selection has been discovered.' Even while he calls ' Natural Selection ' a law, he is afraid that it may be regarded as more than mere accident or chance : doubtless, because a law necessarily implies a lawgiver or maker. So he says: ' Neither of them (Lyell, Hooker) really understands what I mean by Natural Selection.' Professor Huxley makes this astonishing avowal: ' The teleology which supposes that the eye was made for enabling the animal to see, has undoubtedly received its death-blow.'

In spite of the rejection of the principle of design in nature, Darwin was compelled to say : ' Often and often a cold shudder has run through me, and I have asked myself whether I may not have devoted my life to a phantasy.' Well might he shudder, for his theory led him to doubt the existence of God—yet why the shudder, if he knew and believed that his theory was scientific, and why should that which he feared might be a mere phantasy, be named science by himself and others ? Does not the general and ready acceptance of such a theory on such unsubstantial grounds show that the last half-century was not a period guided by pure reason ? and the same superficial mode of thought still widely prevails !

Of course, the elimination of design does not quite satisfy the so-called *Christian evolutionists,* as this would dispense with the idea of an intelligence at the root of things, and so, among others, Dr. H. Drummond, in his *Ascent of Man,* endeavours to insert the principle of design. Evolution, with design in it, is not Darwin's theory, and yet without design evolution is pithless and sapless. If there is no design, then all must be mere chance, and as Dr. Stirling says, Darwinian evolution is ' an accident of an accident.' It was because Darwin's theory was believed to give the death-blow to design that its advocates were filled with exultation and with burning enthusiasm to promote its general diffusion. Is it not astonishing that the Christian world generally has regarded Darwin as a second Newton, even though he has proved nothing ? Newton proved much, but Darwin and many of his followers have been satisfied with mere plausibility. In most of the works dealing with evolution, the terms ' natural selection,' ' struggle for existence,' ' struggle for life,' ' survival of the fittest,' are used as if they stood for exact scientific

principles or laws, which they in no true sense
are. From the way in which the expression ' survival of the fittest ' is used, we might almost conclude
that the phrase embodies a principle as certain
as any in mathematics. If it were a scientific principle, then the fittest to survive would always survive, but this, even in human life, is rarely the
case. The best often ' go to the wall,' and the most
unfit to survive do survive. ' I returned and saw
under the sun that the race is not to the swift, nor
the battle to the strong, neither yet bread to the
wise, nor yet riches to men of understanding, nor
yet favour to men of skill : but time and chance
happeneth to all.' ' This is the true picture of the
contingency of all things.' It prevails in every department of Nature, in the mineral, vegetable and animal
worlds, and necessarily so. The accidental often
prevents the survival of the fittest : ignorance amongst
men often crushes the fittest to survive : selfishness
and partiality, in Church and State, are often able
to crush the best, and so cause the most unfit to
survive. This now popular phrase in no way harmonizes with the death of martyrs for the truth,
whether Christian, or martyrs, as there have been,
for what is named physical science. It is also in
direct opposition to Christ's teaching, ' He that would
save his life, shall lose it, but whosoever will lose his
life for My sake and the Gospel's, the same shall find
it.' What a taking and plausible word is ' fittest ' !
It would not have answered to have said ' best ' or
' strongest,' as the falsity of that is self-evident, but
' fittest ' imposes on the unwary and acts as a blind,
especially when associated with the variation everywhere occurring.

The Idea of existence implies change, variation ;
a changeless existence is unintelligible, for that would

imply no action, no motion, no thought. But though variation and even modification prevail everywhere, Darwin still had to say, 'We cannot prove that a single species has changed.' Huxley, also, tells us we are ignorant of the cause of variation. Now, one of the chief aims of Hegel and Dr. Stirling has been to explain causation, and if they have not done this, then their philosophy is an utter failure, so far as their attempt to restore a genuine Christian Faith is concerned.

Dr. Stirling (Annotations to his translation of Schwegler's *History of Philosophy*) says : ' Hegel enables us to regard Anaximander as the earliest Darwinian ; he conceives man to develop from a fish, etc. "Develop" (hervorgehen), says Hegel, " comes forward in recent times also : it is a mere after-one-another in time—a form, with which a man often believes himself to say something brilliant—but for all that, there is no necessity, no thought, no notion in it." Would not one think that Hegel had read Darwin ? '

We quote again from Hegel (Stirling's translation) : ' It has been an inept conception of earlier and later " Naturphilosophie " to regard the progression and transition of one natural form and sphere into a higher, as an outwardly actual production which, however, to be made clearer is relegated into the obscurity of the past. To Nature, externality—that is, to let the difference fall asunder and present themselves as neutral existences—is precisely proper ; the dialectic notion which guides the stages is the inner of the same. Thinking consideration must deny itself such nebulous, at bottom sensuous, conceptions, as in especial the so-called origin of the more highly developed animal organizations from the lower.' As Stirling remarks, ' This, written many years before the appearance of Mr. Darwin's book, reads like a critique on nothing else.'

Although Darwin said, ' It is mere rubbish, thinking at present of the origin of life : one might as well think of the origin of matter,' yet he remarked, 'I should like to see archebiosis (spontaneous generation) proved true, for it would be a discovery of transcendent importance.' ' If it could be proved to be true, this would be most important to us.' ' Spontaneous generation,' says Dr. Stirling, ' then, he cannot have, and creation he will not have, so there is nothing left him but his indefinite " appeared." To use " appeared " as Darwin did for beginning is utterly unscientific and proves nothing.'

Huxley regarded creation as an utter impossibility ; his language shows that he regarded evolution as all but absolutely certain, and that he thought the creation theory was only a fit subject for ridicule. The whole mode of reasoning adopted by these men is utterly unscientific, whether as regards evolution or creation. It is pure unreasoned dogmatism to call creation a hypothesis. Evolution begins with an assumed pure matter (which as such is nowhere known to exist), from which follows the development from the most imperfect to the most perfect forms, even to the highest forms of existence. On such a theory the perfect not only does not exist, but is for ever unattainable and unrealizable ; such a beginning is unthinkable except by a vain imagination. Creation begins with the perfect, with thought in and for itself ; thought does not begin with an assumption. By an assumption is meant a conception of something for the time unknown ; but thought is only thought as knowing itself existing, and what is already known cannot be assumed. Thought, as already stated, is necessarily active and self-creative ; so creation is not an assumption or a hypothesis, but a fact of reason, while evolution, as generally understood, is an assumption devoid of reason. Growth, improvement, is not evolution. The theory (of evolution) was, and is, only intended to stand for the origin of new species, and especially to set aside creation.

It is, of course, quite rational to think that matter exists in the forms of atoms, molecules, and germs ; atoms and molecules as elements in minerals, etc. ; germs, as essential to the generation or reproduction of living, organized beings, whether vegetable, animal or human. This, however, only bears upon reproduction or propagation of species, and not at all on the origin of species, for all forms of germs originate or are created in the species. It is certainly contrary to sense-perception and reason to think that germs are not continually originated or created, and also continually being lost, or perishing, in the life and death of the individuals which constitute the different species. The individual and the germ always co-exist, so evolution gives forth no light on an intelligible first. (Even Darwinian evolution must ultimately lead back to creation in some form or other.) Neither is there any light on a first from mere modification. Reason must have a first ; it is absolutely reasonless to say it is ' rubbish to inquire into the origin of matter and life.' Why, then, *Origin of Species* ? There must be a first which continues through all, and is therefore also the last. ' I am the beginning and the end ; the first and the last,' is sound science. As it is with germs so it must be with atoms and molecules, they are always coming to be and always ceasing to be, for without change and process all organic life in this world would cease, or rather, could not be. Even chemical research is tending to prove that atoms are continually being formed from one all-common matter or source, and that they are so far destructible. Because we cannot in sense-sight see atoms as the smallest particles of matter, come or cease to be, that is no proof that they are not being continually created just as certainly as germs are. Just as it is a matter of sense-certainty that flowers, fruit, etc., come to be and cease to be, so it is equally a matter of reason-certainty that atoms, molecules and germs come to be and cease to be. It is, however, only logical philosophy that can furnish demonstration here, as in all other departments of Nature and Spirit.

The microscope has extended the sphere of sense-perception, but only to show that the various germ-points cannot be thus distinguished one from the other, and that reason-thought only can prove that difference is, and must be, in them. We cannot but conclude that they are different in their nature, even though the microscope shows no difference to the eye of sense, since one germ grows into a cherry tree, another becomes an apple tree, another a fly, another a whale, and another a man ; environment alone cannot cause all the difference in the development. ' God giveth it a body as it hath pleased Him, and to every seed his own body.' I suppose even no physicist expects to see by sense-perception gravitation or consciousness, which belong to the sphere of reason and understanding ; in the same way it is impossible by mere sense-vision to distinguish between germ-points, as they may be termed. It is vain to try to confute us by declaring that we are not embryologists, for the study of embryology does not, and cannot, with the best instruments, go far enough. In spite of the parallelism which scientists state to exist between individual and ancestral development, extended knowledge has caused a 'reluctance to attach detailed importance to the embryological argument for evolution.'

The most superficial view of Nature forces home the conviction of creation and generation in time of new germs of life in the vegetable, animal, and human worlds—germs which, as such, were at one time non-existent, just as you and I, in our empirical being, once did not exist. It is of no use to cry evolution and to allege that all new germs are evolved from pre-existent germs and cells (by natural selection), for no theory of evolution can logically set aside the necessity and reality of creation, since it cannot be doubted that new germs do come into being. Indeed, this idea of a coming to be of what once did not exist in sensible form, involves the idea of absolute creation, and this is what the theory of evolution was thought, and even intended, to have set aside as incredible in the light of advancing science. Properly looked at, evolution is only another name for creation, and thereby, as a theory of existence, it annihilates itself and does not avoid the necessity of an intelligent Creator. To suppose that any theory of evolution can set aside the fact of direct creation is a mere freak of a vain imagination. Evolution creates nothing, yet creation is a self-evident fact of existence and reason, and cannot be successfully ignored by any mode of mere plausible reasoning. The prevalent idea of evolution does not mean growth and improvement. The idea of growth has always been familiar, but not the growth of man out of an animal.

Creation, however it may be explained, involves essentially the idea of a personal Creator. That which is created must possess the thought and mind of the Creator, and therefore must always be absolutely dependent on its Creator for its existence.

Consequently, the philosophy of the one can only be realized in and through the other, and therefore they cannot be properly regarded and treated as independent units, but as the absolute unity of the total whole of existence.

The statements of the Bible are in no way inconsistent with a sound philosophical treatment of this subject, but rather assist in the attainment of a genuine system of philosophy. Thus, ' All things were made by Him, and without Him was not anything made that was made.' ' He was in the world, and the world was made by Him.' Paul speaks of Christ as ' the image of the invisible God, the firstborn of every creature : for by Him were all things created that are in heaven, and that are in earth, visible and invisible, whether thrones or dominions, principalities or powers : all things were created by Him and for Him, and He is before all things, and by Him all things consist.'

We may note that if an opponent of the evolutionary theory quote any of Darwin's remarks, he is at once met with the answer, that the true theory of evolution has *now* outgrown Darwin ; yet with all present-day scientists and evolutionists he (Darwin) is regarded not only as a great scientist and philosopher, but has even been named a second and greater Newton (this we have already referred to in another connection), though with him design was nowhere, with Newton everywhere. As touching these claims, we summarize the following quotations from Darwin :—

' It is mere rubbish thinking at present of the origin of life : one might as well think of the origin of matter.'

' As to the origin of matter, I have never troubled myself about such insoluble questions.'

'The old argument from design in Nature . . . fails, now that the law of natural selection has been discovered.'

'I have long regretted that I truckled to public opinion, and used the pentateuchal term of creation, by which I really meant "appeared," by some *wholly unknown* process.'

The word 'truckled' revealed the peculiar moral working of Darwin's mind. With him there was no real God, nor any real design in Nature—his 'Deity' was 'Natural Selection,' yet he concludes the *Origin* with the words, 'There is grandeur in this view of life, its several powers having been originally breathed by the Creator into a few forms or into one,' which can only be considered as very misleading to his religious friends and readers. We see the same trait in dealing with the polar bear case. 'In North America the black bear was seen by Hearne, swimming for hours with widely-open mouth, thus catching, almost like a whale, insects in the water,' (*Origin of Species*, page 141). He writes to Lyell afterwards in reference to this : ' I do here show the first step by which conversion into a whale would be easy, would offer no difficulty.' He strikes the bear story out of the second edition of the *Origin* in deference to Lyell, but ' it goes to his heart ' to do so, and then he deliberately re-inserts it in the sixth edition. To give weight to this example, he calls Hearne ' an excellent observer.' To Hooker he exclaims, ' What a book a devil's chaplain might write on the clumsy, wasteful, blundering, low and horrible works of Nature.' Surely this is not ' the grandeur of the view of life breathed by the Creator into a few forms,' but rather agrees with Darwin's accidental evolution, not with true science. Are these the words of a sober scientist ? They can only be intended to disparage the idea of design, and of Nature as the work of an all-wise Creator. It cannot be that such a trifler with Nature could be a great scientist, much less a great philosopher. Some inadvertencies we can readily allow in really great men, but these statements of Darwin, when all they involve is reflected upon, render it hard to regard him as such, however generous and genial he may have been in his general intercourse with men.

There are many frank admissions seemingly not antagonistic to the orthodox theology of the Bible in the writings of Darwin apt to mislead the unwary, as also in many other writers who are endeavouring to square the teaching of the Bible and Christianity with the doctrine of Evolution.

Organic evolution necessarily falls back for its beginning on the Nebular Hypothesis of Kant, and that means with the physicists ' a primordial vapourous matter diffused through space,' so Darwin conceives ' from a single slight variation of accident and chance ' appeared ' a proteine compound,' then ' some single prototype,' then again ' four or five primordial forms.' All this contains no intelligible origin or beginning of anything. To try to conceive an eternal, inactive God existing in an infinite, universal gas, only makes the matter worse. The wisdom of the world (the wisdom ruling in Nature) is one with the wisdom of God, so even in the mythologies of Greece and Rome Minerva is conceived as springing full-armed from the Head of Jupiter. This shows that a gradual evolution of one form of organic matter out of another was to the Greeks and Romans unthinkable.

With origin or beginning, in the strict and true sense of the word, Darwin never troubled himself, for he said, ' It is mere rubbish thinking of the origin

of life,' etc. Then the words ' Natural Selection '
are ambiguous. Selection means choice, and natural
is as applicable to the *nature* and quality of consciousness as to the *nature* of flint, or any other physical
object. In reference to the former, what is properly
named supernatural is also natural. In one sense,
so-called natural selection is nothing more than mere
chemical affinity. But what could be more absurd
than to name the act of personal conscious choice,
chemical affinity ?—yet this is practically what
Darwin's Natural Selection amounts to. In reality,
the term Natural Selection might be applied to
personal conscious *choice* and *design*, because the act
of selection belongs to the *nature* of a person, but
not to the nature of stones and plants. Essentially
there is no natural selection, since all selection is
governed by the law of Spirit. Darwin, however,
supposed that with Newton the Law of Gravitation
was wholly physical in inorganic Nature, and wishing
to emulate Newton, he became ambitious to prove
that organic Nature was equally *physical*, and that
the latter was complementary to the former : all
was *physical* Selection. So his Deity was Natural
Selection. With Newton universal gravitation had
a clearly-expressed law, viz., that every particle
of matter attracts every other particle in inverse
proportion to the square of their distance. But
Darwin's so-called law of Natural Selection has
no real definite formula, mathematical or logical ;
his law is nothing but ' an accident of an accident,'
such as ' a bird may be born with 100th of an inch
longer beak than usual.' This is his favourite illustration ; this theory is, ' favourable variations would
tend to be preserved, and unfavourable ones to be
destroyed,' but of the causes of variation he says,
' we are profoundly ignorant.' He begins and ends

254 THE PHILOSOPHY OF SPIRIT

with accident, from which he derives what he falsely calls 'the struggle for existence,' and 'survival of the fittest,' and maintains there is 'no design now that the law of Natural Selection is discovered.' Huxley thinks that everything may 'work loose from everything else' : thus it is foolish to suppose the eye was made to see : it is all accident.

Some physicists—Lord Kelvin in particular—calculated that the world has existed for only one hundred million years, others, for three hundred millions, some come down to ten millions, and many are concerning themselves at present more about how long the universe will last than about its origin. Reason demands an eternal NOW. Little reflection is required to make it evident that an eternal past and an eternal future is an eternal NOW present in the thought of every human person. Eternity is duration without beginning and without end, and that is a clear, definite thought actually in man. To know Christ is to know the eternal and absolute God and Father of All. This is *eternal* life in man, which in its depth is the love of God in Christ. Divine and Human Reason are one. God, then, is the *eternal* beginning of all things.

Certainly human reason requires an *eternal NOW*, in fact, Reason is an eternal NOW, and demands an eternal creation, for inactive, processless Spirit is a contradiction of terms, though it implies a creation in harmony with itself. The universe is full of ideas—all in perfect agreement with Absolute and Infinite Reason, such as can only belong to the nature of an all-perfect God. Stirling expresses this thought in reference to geology in a very rational form : 'In these perpetual wearings down and heavings up, that seem really intimated there to go on, and round and round for ever, I had a most vivid picture of an eternal life even on the part of this little Earth of ours. Yet how, in their estimates that would describe or prescribe periods, our very best, whom we admire and honour *in excelsis*—differ ! They separate themselves, the one from the other, by millions and millions—by tens of millions—by hundreds of millions—of years : they might as well separate themselves by infinitude ! ' ' The repose of an eternal NOW is what our religion guarantees to us.'

Logically, evolution is origin from nothing, which is absurd. Creation is an eternal logical dialectical process of Spirit. It is in essence one with miracle, manifested in special acts as revealed in the philosophical history of the Bible, for, as already stated, the Bible is the most metaphysical book that was ever written, for, strictly, ' metaphysieal ' and ' spiritual ' are synonymous terms.

The logical dialectical process of Spirit just referred to is Hegel's logical, dialectic, immanent and transcendent process of the Ego, and is the body, soul and Spirit of his philosophy. I know of no one but Dr. James Hutchison Stirling, who has fully grasped this great principle in its deep significance. Professor James seems to scoff at it as if it had no intelligible meaning. Briefly, it signifies the self-activity and creative power of God, and is the key to the right understanding of the words of Christ, ' My father worketh hitherto, and I work.' It also explains what Hegel means by the Negation of the Negation, the creation of the world and Becoming, i.e. coming to be (origin), and ceasing to be (decease). With him Being is not an abstract Nothing, but the real creation of worlds. Some professed admirers of Hegel have endeavoured to show that his theory of Becoming is essentially one in principle with the modern theory or theories of evolution, and this amalgam they have dubbed Neo-Hegelianism. Nothing could be further from the truth. Hegel says : ' God be praised ! we can negate the abstract Nothing, and be landed in Being,' which becoming necessarily implies. Thus creation by a Creator is a genuine logical deduction from the fact of the infinite and absolute reality of human thought, as an irrefutable fact of human experience, from which all logical philosophy must begin. Many evolutionists confound evolution with the growth of plants and animals from germs, and also with the principle of the improvement of species. But growth and improvement of species belong essentially to the true idea of creation. If evolution were only used to signify growth, there were nothing to object to, but it is intended to denote the origin of species independent of any direct creative power, and especially the origin of man from the animal, and, in the ultimate, the origin of all the infinitely variegated universe from a supposed original vapour or gas diffused through space. Then, as Hegel says, ' in order to make it clearer it is relegated to a dim and distant past.' Although Darwin says, ' We cannot prove that a single species has changed,' yet he declares, ' *I cannot doubt* that during millions of generations individuals of a species will be born with some slight variation profitable to some part of its economy.' He further adds, ' Nor can we prove that the *supposed changes* are beneficial, which is the *groundwork* of the theory.' That is his whole reasoning for Natural Selection. Is it surprising that Carlyle should say of Darwin's theory, ' Wonderful to me as indicating the capricious stupidity of mankind—never could waste the least thought upon it.' The following quotations from *Sartor Resartus* show how much superior was

Carlyle's view of Nature to Darwin's : ' Nature is
one, and a living invisible whole : mankind, the
Image that reflects and creates Nature, without
which Nature were not.' ' We speak of the volume
of Nature : and truly a volume it is, whose author
and writer is God.' ' Is not God's universe a Symbol
of the Godlike ; is not immensity a temple ? ' ' What
are the laws of Nature ? To me, perhaps the rising
of one from the dead were no violation of these Laws,
but a confirmation. The Machine of the Universe
is fixed to move by unalterable rules. I, too, must
believe that the God " without variableness or shadow
of turning " does indeed never change. All things
wax and roll onwards ; Newton has learned to see
what Kepler saw ; but there is also a fresh heaven-
derived force in Newton ; he must mount to still
higher points of vision. So too the Hebrew Law-
giver is, in due time, followed by an apostle of the
Gentiles.' ' The real Being of whatever was, and
whatever is, and whatever will be, is even now and
for ever. Then sawest thou that this fair Universe
is in very deed the star-domed City of God ; that
through every star, through every grass-blade, and
most through every Living Soul, the glory of a present
God still beams. Nature is the Time-vesture of God,
and reveals Him to the wise.' ' Our highest Orpheus
walked in Judea, eighteen hundred years ago ; His
sphere-melody still flows, still sounds. We are spirits.
Whence ? Whither ? From God to God.'

CHAPTER XII

THE SPIRITUAL NATURE OF UNIVERSAL GRAVITATION

THE science of Nature in its unity with the science of thought may here be considered from another point of view. 'Gravitation,' says Hegel, 'is a profound thought': 'Regarded in the sphere of Reflexion, it has only the import of the result of an abstraction . . . not the import of the Idea explicated in its reality.' By Reflexion, Hegel evidently means that the nature of gravitation was not scientifically or logically explained. It was merely named a Force, without an explanation of the real nature of the Force. Then, to account for the varying velocities of the planets, in consequence of the variation of their distance from the sun, two supposed necessary forces, attraction and repulsion, were conjectured to belong, in some fashion, to what was named one force, viz. universal gravitation. These two forces were named respectively centripetal and centrifugal, one drawing to the centre and the other driving away from it; they were supposed to act independently, so that when one had spent itself, the other began to act in the opposite direction. Newton, the discoverer of what is called universal gravitation, has demonstrated mathematically its law, that 'all bodies attract and repel each other in inverse proportion to the square of their distance,' yet, the *nature* of the Force, so far as physical science is concerned, is still unexplained, and therefore still unknown : and, after all, *the nature of the force is the vital question.* To give it a name and leave it unexplained is certainly not scientific : true science explains and proves, yet mere mathematics cannot explain or tell what gravitation is. To say that it is a purely physical force is merely assumption ; mathematicians can only prove that the motion of the planets is in agreement with the mathematical formula, but not that the formula is deduced logically from the nature of the force, or the force from the formula. We certainly know as a matter of fact that force is something real and universal in Nature, but we only know this because human thought is universal and is in itself a real force or power. All force has its necessary relation and identity in the relation of ideas in the human Ego. We know nothing of a physical force separate from and independent of its essential relation in human thought, therefore the thought of universal gravitation can only be logically one with thought as the moving, guiding and directing power of the created universe. Consequently, all motion is one with the dialectic movement of the conscious power of the Ego, the universal intelligence and reason of the universe. The reign of law is not a blind reign ; intelligent design is the inner nature of everything, everywhere. If any one deny that man's thought is universal, he by his very denial denies himself, denies the universality of force, and universal gravitation ; for no one can rationally deny that the thought of gravitation is an essential element and fact of human thought : that is, if he thinks universal gravitation a fact, he thinks the infinite as spiritual. To know anything that is outside and independent of thought is impossible ;

indeed, such so-called knowledge is mere conjecture, and not true knowledge or science. But each man knows for himself that his own thought is a real power, is force itself, and is at one and the same time both attraction and repulsion. Thus he has no need to resort to conjecture or hypothesis, he has simply to explain logically the nature and action of his own thought, his own reason; therein he will find the explanation of the centripetal and centrifugal forces and of the motions of the heavenly bodies. But he must not confound his reason with his fancies.

Newton warned his followers to beware of metaphysics, but to his honour, as Hegel says, he disobeyed his own injunctions, for with Newton the vast infinity of space was the sensorium of the Deity. He says : ' God is one and the same always and everywhere ; Him we know by His qualities and attributes, and by final causes—final causes are always spiritual.' If it can be shown that Newton has said that the force of gravitation was wholly physical, then he contradicts himself, for he says : ' The whole of things created could have its origin only in the ideas and will of a necessarily existing Being.'

UNIVERSAL THOUGHT IS AT ONCE REPULSION AND ATTRACTION

As the science of concrete logic is grounded on the three functions or three moments of the Ego, so the centripetal and centrifugal forces are based thereon. As universal, the Ego embraces the totality of Nature ; as singular, it is the spirit of nature in its oneness, in the absolute centrality of all bodies in one ; as particular, every separate body has a specific gravity of its own in essential relation to its universal. The Ego is the dialectic power in matter as its essential activity, or it is universal gravitation manifesting itself in the movement of its various bodies. As one, it is the repulsion of one into many ones, because thought is many in one; as many ones it is the attraction of the many into one, because thought is one in many ones; only so are repulsion and attraction possible. There can be no repulsion without attraction, and no attraction without repulsion. If many were not one, and one were not many, there would be nothing to attract and repel. Sense-thought and reason-thought are, at bottom, one. Through sense I become aware of the many, and through reason I know that every object is a thought, and that every thought is in essential relation to one universal thought, in and through my own infinite, universal reason-thought. It is thus absurd to speak of universal gravitation if the term universal does not mean the veritable, infinite, Concrete Being and Thought of God including my own thought.

The laws of motion, as discovered by Kepler, were all real and metaphysical, and Newton's mathematical formula was sound and good, but if, as we have just remarked, he regarded gravitation as a mere physical force, his metaphysics was at fault and very misleading. It was a conjectured, hypothetical cause, the real nature of which was unexplained, and therefore unscientific. So far, then, his metaphysics was unsatisfactory, because the nature of the force was not logically deduced from the concrete nature of thought, that is from the Ego, which is the entire secret of the universe. Though far from Newton's intention and wish, yet this undoubtedly tends to eliminate God from philosophy and science, and also from the government of the world. It left the real relation of God to the world unknown. Any system of philosophy, or any theory of science, mathematical or otherwise, which ignores the existence of thought as an all-pervading, intelligent force in Nature is entirely false. It cannot but be admitted that what is named gravitation is as invisible to sense as conscious thought is; therefore, if the motion of objects proves the presence and reality of gravitation, it equally proves the presence and reality of thought. Further, to regard the starry heavens as the visible manifestation of a mere physical, universal gravitation most certainly falls very far short of being as logically intelligible and certain as the conception that the starry heavens is the visible manifestation of self-conscious reason-thought, that is, of God. Thought is a fact of man's conscious experience, while gravitation, as something merely material or physical, is not so, and as a matter of fact, the purely physical nowhere exists by itself. Apart from self-conscious reason, a rational system of reason is impossible, and therein alone is God known. The world is not governed by irrational thought, while to know what rational thought is, is to know God, for a God who in His being and essence is not self-conscious rational thought is not a God at all, and so is necessarily unknown. So, because thought cannot abstract its being from itself, or from existence in general, the thought of God's Being cannot be abstracted from the self-consciousness of man, or from universal existence.

THOUGHT IS AT ONCE EXTERNAL AND INTERNAL

Nature as the external side and manifestation of thought, or as a system of objective thought, is necessarily a mechanical system of particular bodies acting in essential relation to each other. No satellite, planet, sun, or star has an independent existence; every single body is, in its very nature, a part of and dependent on the whole. All the heavenly bodies are particular thoughts of the universal; each has a power of action, special and universal, according to its nature and mass. Every visible particular mass is a finite body of thought, and only in part a physical force, for internally it is spiritual and infinite in relation to all other bodies throughout universal space. This, according to Stirling, was the philosophical view of Kepler in reference to his three famous laws. Kepler says: 'The motion of the earth, which Copernicus had proved by mathematical reasons, I wanted to prove by physical, or if you prefer it, metaphysical.' He and Hegel were of one mind, they both ' sought to see in it a whole, a system, a *one of reason.*' His ' highest wish was to find within, the God whom he found everywhere without.' With him God was at once within and without, the universe was a system of thinking reason, and the Force was in its essence universal thought. It was only physical in so far as the physical was a real, external side of thought, and it was metaphysical in so far as self-consciousness was the internal side of thought. (Mathematically, it seems that Kepler was very much inferior to Newton.) Dr. Stirling says : ' Newton was undoubtedly by much the greatest physico-mathematical thinker that ever lived.'

NEWTON AND KEPLER

Newton's formula was, without doubt, a very great achievement and a distinct step in advance, but it may be questioned whether it was equal to the discovery of the three laws of Kepler. ' It is admitted that Newton's famous law of gravitation was derived from Kepler's laws.' It may be well to place them together in contrast. First, Newton's : ' Every particle of matter in the universe attracts every other particle with a force varying inversely as the square of the distance between them, and directly as the mass of the attracting particle.' Second, Kepler's: ' Every body moves in an elliptical orbit, the line joining it with the sun sweeps over equal areas in equal times and always in the proportion of the cubes of the distances to the squares of the times.' According to the law of reason it was, in a certain sense, a great advance in physical science to introduce the Idea of Force, but to explain the Force as physical only, instead of spiritual, was a backward movement as regards pure reason and Bible teaching, since the Bible teaches that God is the one universal spiritual power in Nature. The Idea of Force had really never been absent from men's minds, only now it was supposed to be a sort of rational physical force immediately present in Nature, not however as the direct manifestation of the spirtual presence of God, but rather as a Power in matter independent of the direct control of God, or rather, tending to render a belief in Him unnecessary.

RELIGION IS AT ONCE REASON AND THOUGHT

As yet, neither the nature of matter, nor its relation to Spirit, nor the logic of thought in its essential quality and relation to both matter and spirit, had been philosophically explored. Hence arose the old antagonism between reason and faith. Religion was named faith, and Reason became mere free thinking; nay, worse, religion and faith became identical with superstition, fraud, oppression, licentiousness and the grossest tyranny under the name of Christianity. So faith was not faith, religion was not religion, and reason was not reason; yea, Christianity was not Christianity; all four became falsely named. Kant's Copernican Metaphysic in his transcendental logic was the first dim recognition that the Idea of Force in nature was spiritual—was thought (this was logically completed by Hegel and Stirling); for Kant's idea that objects must conform to thought, and not thought to objects, implies necessarily that the force is spiritual.

EXTENSION AND INTENSION EQUALLY UNIVERSAL IN THE EGO

We have stated that sense-thought and reason-thought are, at bottom, one ; and that one is Ego, the middle term, which unites and comprehends the two in one. Time, space and matter are nothing but three external elements of thought in concrete unity, and, at the same time, they are manifestations of inner living thought. We know nothing of space as merely abstract ; it is only known in the concrete unity of light, darkness, colour, air, and material extension in sense-thought in its unity with self-conscious reason-thought, and that because Ego is the infinite and absolute concrete notion—the term of both greatest extension and greatest intension. Externality and internality are everywhere in absolute identity in thought. Time is its absolute activity and is the eternal now, while space is the everywhere-presence of thought ; for time and space are a unity of difference and identity in the absolute Ego ; and the finite times and finite spaces are determined by the motions of the particular bodies of the Ego. Light is the most immaterial form of matter, and most closely approximates to the conscious form of thought, since light possesses neither gravity or weight. It is the great revealer of Nature, thus ' God is light, and in Him is no darkness.' It is sound philosophy to say that 'God clothes Himself in light.' Air and water are external media of smell, taste and sound, in the three forms of sense-thought in man. Heat

is a state of matter as a mode of motion pertaining
to the general mechanism of Nature, for universal
Nature is in a constant state of action and re-action.
The forming and dissolving of bodies is in constant
process. Elasticity is inherent in all material bodies.
Centripetal and centrifugal action express more
definitely the free motion of the heavenly bodies,
but the secret and source of all movement, and of
repulsion and attraction in thought, can only be
found in the logical dialectic of the Ego; or as Dr.
Stirling says: 'The virtue within is the necessity
of reason; the virtue without is the necessity of its
own contingency.'

EGO IN THOUGHT—AT ONCE INTUITIVE, REFLECTIVE,
LOGICAL

A universal that is not the concrete infinite of
thought is not in truth universal, for I can only have
a true conception of the universal because my thought
is itself infinite. My only immediate sure knowledge
of the infinite is the knowledge of my own thought
and being. Of universal gravitation as something
merely physical, I have no knowledge either by
sense-perception or by reason-thought. The knowledge of my thought's own self is based on intuition,
reflection and logical reason, and is infinite because
the Infinite I is in thought essentially identical with
the Finite I.

In spite of the special influence of the doctrines of
the Reformation, ever since what is currently named
the resurrection of the sciences, exclusive attention
to and scientific research into the so-called forces
of Nature, chemical, physical, electrical, and the forces
of gravity have largely pushed God and religious
thought aside, or into a region supposed to be beyond
the sphere of human thought. Indeed, the name
Nature has largely supplanted that of God.

MAN KNOWS THE INFINITE

Such a view of Nature overlooks the fact that *all that is*, is an essential, infinite, universal, connective tissue of thought, which is the logical necessity contained in the very Idea and Being of God, and that is equally the same logical necessity and dialectic substance of man's own thought and reason. I know what universal thought *is*, even in its infinite particularity, because it is actually present in my individual self-consciousness, but I do not know in the least what universal gravitation or any other force is, if it is assumed to be something separate and distinct from the essence of conscious reason-thought ; for I can form no conception of what such something is. If possible, it is more vague and empty than Kant's fiction of an unknown thing in itself. I know what reason-thought in a book is, and equally well what reason-thought in Nature or in any work of Art is, but I also know with equal certainty that neither the book nor Nature, nor the work of Art, is conscious of the reason-thought that is inherent in it ; and I am quite sure that neither the one nor the other created itself. Such creations are necessarily the work of self-conscious persons who are in thought infinite. The book is the work of a man made in the image of God, but I know that birds and bees, etc., are not persons, however skilfully their work may be done. The thought of birds, bees and ants is very limited ; it is not infinite, like the thought of man. Nature, however, is not the work of man, but of God, and as much excels the work of man as man's work excels that of bees and ants, yet the element of reason pervades all, and is manifest even in trees and stones. Sense-thought in man is finite, like sense-thought in animals ; it is limited on all sides; but reason in animals is limited to sense-objects, while reason-thought in man in infinite, unlimited on all sides. This proves that Nature being in all its details the manifestation of the thought of God, universal gravitation must be in its essence spiritual.

THE PHYSICAL IS ESSENTIALLY SPIRITUAL

This agrees with the philosophy of Paul, for he says: ' The invisible things of God are clearly seen (in the things that are made), because that which may be known of God is manifest in them (that is, in man's intellect), for God hath shewed it to them.' Thus man's intellectual capacity exalts him infinitely above all other created things. He, the Christian philosopher, sees in his own intellect the things of God in the things that are made—' even His eternal power and Godhead.' If I cannot know God's thoughts (in nature), I cannot know God, just as I only know a man when I know his thoughts, and as I only know any object when I know the thoughts it contains. The inorganic world is petrified thought. A rational existence necessarily requires a boundless variety in essential relation. The inorganic world is the lowest form of external thought and matter, to which the animal and vegetable worlds are related, and wherein each is dependent on the other.

Quality, as quality, is infinite; yet in this infinite quality everything has a specific quality of its own, for all things are only what they are by their own special and universal quality. So the various bodies constituting external nature possess in different degrees a repelling and attracting force according to their own peculiar and specific quality. It matters little, except for convenient and intelligent use, whether the connecting force be named cohesion, attraction, or gravitation ; the real power is thought. It is the same power working in all bodies in different degrees according to their density and vitality, whether on the earth, or in the free movement of the heavenly bodies. 'Freedom is, consequently, the truth of necessity,' and the truth of substance is the Ego. Apart from the inherent design in the various bodies, and the different degrees of density, of cohesion or adhesion, [all have a particular utility as well as a general utility for the life of plants and animals ; these qualities are in every case the thoughts of God addressed to man. To deny that the various objects and forces in heaven and earth are God's thoughts, is worse than to deny that a watch is the thought of a man. In both cases, the invisible things of God and man are clearly seen in the things that are made, for thinking-reason is evident in both forms of work. The material of the watch is God's thought, its make or special design is man's thought : both are spiritual.

NATURE—THE VOICE OF GOD

When the forces of Nature are properly understood, they are all seen to be spiritual. Nature in its infinite variety is the voice of God speaking in manifold tones to its foster-child, the soul of man, 'day unto day uttering speech, night unto night showing knowledge,' 'their sound has gone out into all the earth, and their words to the end of the world.' 'Blessed is the people that know the joyful sound, they shall walk in the light of God's countenance.' Sometimes this voice of God sounds somewhat harsh and terrible, so that even a Moses fears and quakes. 'His voice maketh the earth to tremble, that the nations may tremble at His presence.' The grand old Hebrew prophets were excellent interpreters of the voice of God in and through Nature. Their intellectual vision was not perverted and blinded by a false science or by a false philosophy. With them, what are now called the forces of nature, were regarded as the manifestations of God, either of His favour or of His displeasure, or as a means of discipline and instruction in righteousness. It is now said that the progress made in scientific knowledge has altered all that, so that God, if there be a God, is only·a helpless or indifferent spectator; He has nothing whatever to do with earthquakes or pestilent diseases. When Luke records that Jesus said, 'The same day that Lot went out of Sodom, it rained fire and brimstone from heaven, and destroyed them all,' we are asked to believe that this is a mistaken record, or that Jesus accommodated His statements to popular beliefs, and that the record in Genesis about Sodom is false. It cannot, however, be proved that Sodom was not destroyed in the manner and for the reason stated in Genesis. The only reason for disbelief concerning it all is, that it is declared to be contrary to the established principles of science. As a matter of fact, such bold statements are not science at all, and have no better, if even as good, a basis to rest on as the Ptolemaic theory of astronomy. The accepted principles of this so-called modern science are derived from a false philosophy built on a spurious logic. It may be that there have been greater sinners than those who dwelt in Sodom (Christ Himself said as much), or than those Galileans whom Pilate slew, or than those upon whom the Tower of Siloam fell; or it may often occur that in great calamities the most excellent perish with the worst, but all this does not prove that Nature is not under God's immediate control, nor does it prove that there are not, or never have been, special direct acts of God as manifestations of His righteous judgments against sin. Indeed, a true philosophy of Nature proves the contrary, namely, that every act of nature is an act of God in the unity and harmony of a universal reason, in which necessity, *contingency* and *freedom* are perfectly blended. (Christ never taught that God did not in special acts directly punish sinners.) Any view of the universal and permanent reign of law in nature which regards it as impossible, or as unscientific for God to perform any special action out of the ordinary course of nature, is contrary to sound reason, and is therefore not scientific, because such a view excludes rational necessity, contingency and freedom, whereas these are essential elements of true reason. Even if this kind of modern science admits the existence of God, it relegates Him to some unknown sphere, which is an absurd conception. Persons who hold such views are deaf to the voice of God in Nature and in their own soul. This was the case with the bulk of the Jewish nation at the time of Christ; and it is the case with millions of professed Christians at the present time. While showing much zeal of a kind, they have eyes but see not, ears but hear not, hearts that do not understand; they know not the voice of reason, nor the true voice of Nature. To all such can strictly be applied the words which Paul addressed to the Jewish nation, ' They that dwell in Jerusalem and their rulers knew Him (Jesus) not, nor yet the voices of the prophets.' The Christian religion is more that what is named Christian Socialism and moral duties, it is God in nature, God in man—the life of God in man. The prophets knew the voice of God, but the rulers and the mass of the people did not, so they crucified Christ, as the so-called Christian world is doing to-day.

THE VOICE OF CHRIST IS THE VOICE OF GOD

The voice of Christ was pre-eminently the voice of God, in a fuller sense than that of any of the prophets, even Moses, though in all these the voice of God was speaking. Christ's voice, in all His miracles, was the voice of God in Nature, for Nature obeyed Christ's voice. He boldly declared, ' Ye neither know Me nor My Father ; If ye had known Me, ye should have known My Father also ; if God were your Father, ye would love Me, for he that is of God, heareth God's words.' With the prophets, God was a real presence everywhere ; so the impossibility of miracles never entered their thought, nor the idea that a miracle as a special act of God in Nature was contrary to reason or to the perfect law of God ; neither did they see the impossibility of a miraculous inspiration and vision in the inner logical consciousness of man, such as is recorded as having been given to Moses, Elisha, Daniel, Isaiah, Jeremiah, Peter, Paul, etc. They never imagined that God could not be a Person, or could merely be a kind of universal unconscious reason pervading Nature ; they never supposed that Nature could exist apart from God as its Creator, even though they had not, in one sense, reached a philosophical explanation of the relation of God to His works.

It is certainly contrary to reason to try to explain away the miraculous visions and inspirations of the Bible on the two baseless assumptions that there is no God, and to say that this inspiration can only be regarded as an exaggerated and Oriental mode of speech. The old Hebrew prophets not only heard the special miraculous voice of God in them, but they heard and understood that voice speaking in the manifold operations of Nature.

NATURE SO FAR SPIRITUAL

To speak of the forces of nature may be proper and convenient, if such usage is not made to imply that these forces are merely physical mechanism. It is impossible that Nature in its form and content can be the created workmanship of God without it being a real and substantial expression of God's thought, and therefore, [so far, spiritual. No man can find a single object within the range of his senses that is not full of thoughts and ideas. Apart from thought, Nature is nothing ; but since the objects are there as matters of fact, they are there as thoughts, ideas, categories, middle terms of syllogisms ; on the one side external and finite, on the other, internal and infinite. No matter in what form Being and Thought may be presented, they are a unity, and at bottom, one, manifested in infinite difference, in infinite variety —both one and many—in their action crossing and re-crossing boundlessly in every direction. The voice of Nature is manifesting itself in infinite variety of voices, notes and tones, yet none without a definite signification, all blending freely in glorious moral harmony. The painful jarring discords that prevail are caused by men refusing to hear the voice that speaks to them on all sides from heaven and earth. What thought is, contains the whole secret of universal gravitation.

KANT, THE ORIGINATOR OF MODERN GERMAN PHILOSOPHY

The principle of what is properly named German philosophy had its origin in Kant's attempt to solve what is called the ' Problem of Hume,' viz. What is the universal and necessary principle in the essential unity of cause and effect ? Kant stated the problem thus : ' How are synthetic judgments à *priori* possible ? ' We must, however, more fully expound and criticize Kant's theory of the system of pure reason. Such criticism is necessary in order to see clearly the spiritual nature of the philosophy of Hegel and Stirling.

We have stated that, in reality, German philosophy had its origin with Kant, and that what we may name his Copernican metaphysic, as grounded in his transcendental logic, was the first dim recognition or suggestion that the real idea of force in Nature was spiritual, was thought, was Ego. He must in part have come to see that this was the case, even in mathematics and physical science. At any rate, he held that both possessed synthetical judgments à *priori* as principles which were named transcendental, and therefore were in essential relation to the transcendental unity of self-consciousness, ' for otherwise,' he said, ' they *could not be thought*, and would be *nothing for me*."

How he came to his New Conception of Metaphysics

He says : ' A new light must have flashed on the mind of the first man who demonstrated the properties of the isosceles triangle,' and saw that he ' must not attribute to the object any other properties than those which necessarily followed from that which he had placed in the object himself.' This discovery ' determined for all time the path which this science must follow.' So Kant considered ' a light broke upon all natural philosophers ' when ' Gallei experimented with balls,' ' Torricelli with air,' and ' Stahl with metals.' Then, in like manner, he seems to have held that a new light flashed on the mind of Copernicus when he said to himself,

' Instead of looking for the explanation of the celestial movements by assuming that the heavenly bodies are revolving round the spectator, I will assume, contrary to the apparent testimony of the senses, that the spectator revolves, and, so far, regard the stars as being at rest.' He had long pondered on the question, though the new thought which flashed on his mind was the old idea of Pythagoras, the Grecian philosopher, who lived five centuries before Christ. With Pythagoras it was, however, only a guess, though based on the fitness of things. Up to that time all attempts to reduce the movements of the sun, moon, planets and stars to a system such as reason demanded, had failed, because based on the supposition that all moved round the earth. But if the earth really revolved on its axis and also moved round the sun, though this was contrary to what the senses seemed to warrant, then all the demands of reason would be fully met.

This discovery, along with its exposition, demolished for ever the Ptolemaic theory of Astronomy, which theory shows how the evidence of the senses may be misinterpreted by a false method of reasoning. The error was not due to the senses, but to a defective conception of the true nature of reason.

METAPHYSICS OF PHYSICS

In all ages men have more or less reasoned falsely through a lack of a true metaphysic of physics and of sense-objects in general. This lack became especially manifest in the reasoning of Hume, concerning the ' tie ' between cause and effect. If this ' tie,' as he held, could not be known, neither could the universal *bond* of nature be known. This seemed to involve the total overthrow, not only of metaphysics as a science, but also of the physical sciences ; but

Kant was firmly convinced that ' metaphysics must be considered as an actual science, and if not as a science, then as a natural capability.' He says: ' To all men, as soon as reason has advanced to speculation, a metaphysic of some kind has always been and always will be.' He had become assured that metaphysics could be demonstrated to be a science as truly as any mathematical or physical science.

As a speculative science, the sure scientific method of metaphysics was unknown, or lay buried in the writings of Aristotle. A new light apparently flashed on the mind of Kant in relation to the science of metaphysics. This happy thought was that there seemed to be some analogy between the power or force by which the earth and the other planets constantly move round the sun and thought, as the universal formative and ruling power of all objects in Nature. Universal gravitation seemed to be the only explanation required by reason of the apparent movements of the heavenly bodies, so Kant asked himself, ' Why should not the science of logical thought (the I think) furnish the proper ground of the categories, and, at the same time, be the power that ' prescribes laws à priori to Nature ? ' An explanation of Nature and of the general laws of motion would then be fundamentally metaphysical without in any way excluding the physical and mathematical.

METAPHYSICAL GRAVITATION

He also asks, Why has metaphysics not hitherto found the sure path of science ? He replies, because it has been assumed that our cognition must conform to the objects which surround us. Let us assume, on the contrary, that the objects must conform to our cognition, and thought will then be the universal centre and quality of gravitation. Thus Kant virtually proposed to do for metaphysics, the science of reason, thought, or The Ego, or if you will, the science of Nature, what Copernicus had done for the science of astronomy. (It will be noticed, however, that Kant viewed mathematics, physics (or natural philosophy), logic and metaphysics, as four absolutely independent sciences, nay, independent existences.) Be this as it may, he suggested a universal metaphysical gravitation as the essential nature or basis of a universal physical gravitation, and in his way endeavoured to give it a logical basis. He did not, however, carry out this grand conception of a metaphysic of Nature to its logical issue. He failed to do so because he held that a system of pure reason could not be considered necessarily a doctrine, or an 'organon' of reason, or a complete system of philosophy. He divided Logic, the science of Thought, into general and transcendental logic, but they were both false because he failed to see that the science of metaphysics is neither more nor less than the science of concrete logical thought, in other words, the universal science of Concrete Logic. He says, ' Logic advanced in a sure course from the earliest times,' while metaphysics, he declares, ' has remained in a vacillating condition'; again, ' metaphysics, a purely speculative science, occupies a completely isolated position,' and ' is entirely independent of the teachings of experience.' The fact is, no science is independent of experience, and every particular experience involves the universality of reason-thought in all matters of sense. The particular contains the universal and the universal the particular. Thus with Kant, metaphysics is isolated at once from physics, mathematics, and sound logic, so from the standpoint of his critical philosophy, the problem of ' How are *à priori* synthetic judgments possible ? ' remains unsolved, since from his stand-point such judgments are not possible, either for mathematics, physics or logic.

IMPERFECT CONCEPTION OF CATEGORIES

Kant conceived that he could show ' How are synthetic judgments à priori possible ? ' by his Trans-cendental Logic, his Schematism of the categories, and his Transcendental Synthesis of Imagination. By ' synthetic judgment,' he meant the conjunction of the objects of sense-perception and the empty notions or categories of the understanding. This he failed to do. Further, his attempt to make the notions of time and space the all-connecting links of Nature, only made his failure more glaring. For-tunately for the interests of a sound logical philo-sophy, thought, reason, idea, Ego, spirit, are not so empty, void, or barren of all matter and content as Kant represents, for they are each and all ' the fullness of Him that filleth all in all,' and contain, therefore, the entire system of the à priori synthetic judgments. In this, their true light, they are well-known things in themselves, and not Kant's merely supposed unknown things in themselves. Metaphysical is only another name, in the Biblical sense, for what is in its essential truth spiritual. The mathematical infinite is in its truth the metaphysical infinite. Here, then, on the ground of a sound logical philosophy, we have the basis of the metaphysics of physics, and the metaphysics of mathematics. Logic, then, is the ground-science of all the sciences.

To contend that objects must conform to cognition, is not enough, and does not meet the demands of logical philosophy. Creation or external Nature is an absolute free necessity of the logic of reason-thought in its relation to transitory thought or transitory objects. The only rational beginning of the world must be in thought. As before noted, many appear shocked at the conception of matter being created by thought, but have no difficulty in believing that thought may be evolved from matter. Thought as a first, is the only logical demand of thought itself, while only a thinker can be a creator. ' Thought is the spore of philosophy.'

THOUGHT NOT A HYPOTHESIS

Astronomy as a physical science became something approaching to a universal science under the influence of mathematics and the unknown force called universal gravitation. With a school of self-styled advanced thinkers, God, or an eternal, universal, self-conscious being, became a mere hypothesis, of which Laplace is reported to have said he had no need. No man can have a true conception of science who discards a belief in the existence of God. Gravitation and matter were treated as one in absolute unity without considering their reality in necessary relation to Spirit and thought, which latter were regarded as belonging to the barren field of metaphysics. Reflexion on sense-objects apart from their relation to spirit, could never have given of itself the idea of universal gravitation, or of an ' Infinite and Eternal Energy.' The phrase ' Infinite and Eternal Energy ' would be unmeaning but for the fact that thought is necessarily an infinite Personality : this is Immanuel, God with us.

Since thought, then, is the only known universal, can Spirit and matter, contrary in this case also to what the senses seem to warrant, be equally cognized as one in the unity of thought ? that is, in the unity of the Ego, which Kant names, Die reine Apperception, die ursprüngliche Apperception, and die transcendentale Einheit des Selbstbewusstseins ?　(Pure apperception, original apperception, the transcendental unity of self-consciousness.)　In whatever way Kant named the Ego, his treatment of it was defective. He, consequently, failed to explain, How synthetic judgments à priori are possible, for, all through his philosophy, in spite of the conjunctions of the manifold objects of sense, of their unity in the categories, and of their ultimate unity in the Ego, they are all treated by him as if absolutely separate from and independent of thought.　Thus, his transcendental synthesis of imagination, with sense-perception on one side and the categories as purely intellectual notions on the other, is a mere fiction of the imagination, and not a logical deduction.

THOUGHT NOT A MERE MECHANICAL MATHEMATICAL SYSTEM

The physico-mathematical philosophers virtually make the whole of existence into a mechanical physico-mathematical system, while a true conception of the Ego and its categories makes the whole into a logical system of thought.　Though Kant failed to establish his idea theoretically, he introduced an entirely new principle into the philosophy of the universe, which in fact made God to be the centre and circumference of all in all, and this he did, in spite of his defective execution when treating the most vital questions involved therein.　If this principle were logically carried out, science and philosophy would be brought into harmony with the true science of logical thought—the science of reason. This principle would harmonize philosophy with the moral and theological doctrines of the Bible, or, in other words, philosophy would be harmonized with the Christian religion ; for man being ' the image and glory of God,' man and God are both Ego. Kant failed to see the Ego in its fullness and transcendent glory, and thus he also failed to harmonize the teaching of the senses with the teaching of pure reason. In an important sense, both teach the truth, and in no real sense does the one exclude the other, but each is rather the complement, the one of the other, and so they are essentially one. Kant was mistaken when he came to think it was impossible to know things in themselves, but only possible to know their external appearance. He failed to recognize that there was a relation of ideas in all things of sense, or in all matters of fact, and that the relations of ideas were as truly there in all sense-objects as they are in the proposition, 'that the three angles of every possible triangle are, without exception, equal to two right angles.' In no case is the relation visible to sense-sight only ; both sense-sight and intellectual insight are necessary to reveal this relation of ideas, since the transitory, however transient, is so far as real as the eternally permanent. Further, if the relation of ideas does not belong essentially to every sense-object, what becomes of the law of gravitation, wherein every material object is believed to attract every other object ? Of course, Kant does not deny these relations, but his empty transcendental system of categories or notions does not furnish the necessary proof of their unity in Nature. If the objects are there, the relations are there, for the relations of ideas constitute the essential nature of every matter of fact.

HUME—MATTERS OF FACT AND RELATIONS OF IDEAS

Hume divides all objects of human reason into two kinds, viz., matters of fact and relations of ideas. An example of what he means by the relations of

ideas is, ' That the square of the hypothenuse is equal
to the squares of two sides,' which Hume says, ' is
discoverable by the mere operation of thought,
without dependence on what is anywhere existent
in the universe.' But with him, matters of fact ' are
not ascertained in the same manner '; 'nor is our
evidence of their truth, however great, of a like
nature with the foregoing.' We have already, in
part, shown the incorrectness of this statement.
He goes on to say, ' The contrary of every matter of
fact is still possible ; because it can never imply a
contradiction, and is conceived by the mind with
equal facility and distinctness, as if ever so conformable to reality.   That the sun will not rise to-morrow,
is no less intelligible a proposition, and implies no
more contradiction than the affirmative that it will
rise. We should in vain, therefore, attempt to
demonstrate its falsehood. Were it demonstratively
false it would imply a contradiction, and would
never be distinctly conceived by the mind. It may,
therefore, be a subject worthy of curiosity to inquire
what is the nature of that evidence which assures us
of any real existence and matter of fact beyond
the present testimony of our senses or the records of
our memory. All reasonings concerning matters of
fact seem to be founded in the relation of Cause and
Effect.' This distinction of Hume's is really absurd,
for the testimony of the senses tells us that Nature
is a matter of fact, and it can be shown by ' the mere
operation of thought ' that the Relations of Ideas are
as truly present in Nature as in any circle or triangle,
or in ' the truths demonstrated by Euclid.' The
' mere operation of thought ' also clearly demonstrates that the non-rising of the sun is impossible.
Hume's ' possibles ' are as impossible as round-
squares or gold-men. Thought itself is always both

within and beyond the testimony of the senses and the records of our memory.

STIRLING ON MATTERS OF FACT AND RELATIONS OF IDEAS

Take the case of the transitory existence of a cabbage; it can be proved that it has no existence apart from ideas. So, as Stirling says, ' Mathematics, quite as much as physics, depends on an element double, matter of fact and Relations of ideas; if on the one hand we see intellectually, on the other we see only sensuously, lines, circles, triangles, squares, oblongs, angles, points, are quite as much in sense and of sense, at bottom, as any amount of bricks and mortar. Hume and Locke say, ' Were there never a circle or a square in existence, its truths would remain '; but I say, were there never an ordinary thing in existence, the whole estate of geometry would be, as it were, blank. Squares and circles are no more à priori and ideal than bricks and paving stones. All at last rest on experience.' Even space is an empirical perception. All facts imply experience and ideas, all of which have their root in the universal Absolute Ego, God. Again, all have their seat and manifestation in the finite spirit of man made in the image of God. First, we have the abstract notion of God. But the abstract notion of God in man is in essential unity and thought with this Concrete notion of God. External Nature is the sensible manifestation of the abstract notion of God, as the sphere of difference; but in reason, in ' eyesight intellectual,' in the identity of differents, we have the concrete notion of God in finite Consciousness. This is necessarily so, seeing that man in his thought is infinite.

No doubt Nature is a realm of sense-contingency,

but it is really a system of necessity quite as much as any triangle. The clove-hitch is, with Dr. Stirling, a favourite example of the unity of sense and reason, contingency and necessity. He says: ' If a triangle is a necessity of the Relations of ideas, so is the clove-hitch. If a triangle is synthetic, so is the clove-hitch. Nay, even say this, If a triangle is *à priori*, so is the clove-hitch ! For if the construction of the clove-hitch is a Matter of Fact, and all the lines existences of sense, it is not one whit less so in either respect with the triangle.'

Stirling's exposition, in *What is Thought ?* of the essential unity of sense and reason, fact and idea, contingency and necessity, is one of his finest achievements. Therein he demonstrates that the Begriff (Notion or Thought) is not only logical, but at the same time existential ; the absolute concrete logical Idea is the body, soul and spirit of all sense Matters of Fact. Consequently he is justified in saying, ' That has been the one error all the time,' viz., ' what was intellectually seen was surely naturally a great deal higher than what was only sensuously seen : the last was contingent and probable only ; but the first might be necessary and apodictic.' ' Buttons with button-holes and hooks with eyes are with truth relations of necessity.' Aristotle and Hegel have always believed that ' experience tells only how objects are, and not how they must be, nor yet how they should be.' Kant says, ' It is just possible that experience is itself a compound.' In a sense, Hegel agrees with this statement of Kant concerning experience, but our point is, that with Dr. Stirling, in all matters of fact in human experience, Thought is the one universal principle of identity in sense and reason, without which existence in any form and content is absolutely impossible ; and that this identity is the principle of the categories in the Absolute Idea.

What is the good of any person saying, ' Though there never were a true circle or triangle in nature, the truths demonstrated by Euclid would for ever retain their certainty and evidence,' for the same can be said with equal truth of all matters of fact, of all experience ? If there were never any true matters of fact, any true men, any true logic, any true syllogism, judgment, notion or idea in Nature, would not the truths demonstrated by logical science for ever retain their certainty and evidence ? No mathematical or logical science is more certainly synthetic and *à priori* than are the physical sciences. So, if thought were extinguished, all would be extinguished ; or conversely, if the physical universe were extinguished, this would involve the extinction of relations of ideas, mathematical or logical. But these are absurd suppositions, and are only on a par with the old saying, ' If " ifs " and " ands " were pots and pans,' etc.

Contingency is an essential category of thought and being, and this implies change and freedom. An inactive processless thought is impossible. An Ego that does not think is not an Ego. Thinking is activity, movement, process, change. This is not only a fact of conscious experience, but is manifest in every department of Nature. Contingency is an infinite crossing in every direction at the same time. It forms a basis for the theory of universal gravitation, since it is admitted, every particle of matter attracts every other particle. Photography makes evident the crossing of light without intermission, in all directions, at every moment. In contingency, then, we have necessity and accident, freedom and possibility.

As Dr. Stirling well observes, ' But for contingency

there would be no freewill; contingency is the possibility, and the condition, and battle-ground of freewill.' ' When a man acts from motive, he is moved by reason : he is free when he is so moved. He is only bound when moved by sense and unreason.' So, ' it is given to man to rise to reason, if he will.' Thus, whether viewed internally or externally, contingency has extraordinary importance. We thus see man is exposed to this infinite contingency, but it is absurd to talk only of a physical necessity, for man is ego, and can act from motive for his pleasure, whereas a stone only moves at the pleasure of another.

Kant made a great blunder in dividing the categories into two classes—one—mathematical, quantity and quality—the other, dynamical, causality and reciprocity : the latter regulative and referring to action. He holds all categories have their source in the Ego. That being so, it is obvious they are all inherently dynamical as well as constitutive of the substantial nature of the Ego, and partake of the Dialectical logical movement of the Absolute Ego. The result with Kant, however, was, that the three proofs for the existence of God lost all their logical theoretical value, and the proofs could only be regulative, not constitutive, elements of being. If this were so, thought has no real permanent being, or it is only a delusive phantasmagoria.

Yet the Kantian philosophy, in spite of its contradictions and illogical form and content matter, recognized consciousness as that which knows itself as totality within itself. This is, indeed, his absolute starting-point. It is true, his infinite was treated only as a subjective abstract universality. But it is not difficult to see that this implies an absolute concrete universality. He speaks of different understandings, especially of a *divine* understanding, an *intuitive* understanding, a *percipient* understanding. With him these three are one—the divine understanding. How did he come to see the need of such ? Because he saw the need of subsuming the particular under a general, and when only a particular is given, the necessity of finding a universal. The one he defines as judgment, the other as judgment of reflection. Here, then, we have at once an intuitive understanding and an infinite reflection. And it is Kant that thinks them. If he had been true to his own thought, he would have seen there is no other understanding than the one that is at once intuitive, reflective and logical, and that human thought in its reality is Divine. The result then, is, gravitation is spiritual.

CHAPTER XIII

THE HISTORICAL RECORD

IN seeking for a thorough and logical knowledge of the truth, the teaching of the Bible may well and consistently be placed in the foreground as the starting-point and basis, for the great themes of the Bible are equally the great themes of philosophy.

The most fundamental of these themes are God, Christ, Man, Creation (Nature) and their necessary relation. Self-consciousness, thought, personality reason, and spirit all belong to the nature of God, Christ and man, and to creation in general. It is a matter of direct or immediate knowledge that they all belong to the nature of man, who is the starting-point of philosophy. The truth of Biblical teaching concerning God and Christ and the other great ideas already mentioned, does not depend entirely for proof on the historical record, but can be demonstrated from the philosophy of man's own nature, providing a knowledge and use of the proper clue be obtained. This is found, as previously stated, in a correct knowledge of the Ego.

Yet to disregard the historical record would be most irrational; what is required is to show that the record is in agreement with true philosophy. If I say the historical record is true, such is only an assertory judgment, which may be either true or false; consequently it is only a problematical judgment, which can only be proved and become an apodictic judgment in and through an absolutely correct, logical process of reasoning. The greater part of our knowledge that pertains to history is not capable of being demonstrated mathematically or logically, and therefore admits of, and depends only or chiefly on, probable evidence'; and because it deals largely with the contingent events of human action and life, whether good or bad, apodictic certainty becomes more wavering the further we go back into the obscurity of the past. Still, we can affirm that all events and deeds recorded of great men and of nations are not mere fiction. In spite of much uncertainty with regard to what is recorded, we are quite sure that such recorded history is not fiction, and that there has been a past history of the world is as certain as that there is a present. Thus a philosophy of history is possible, as certainly as is a philosophy of Being in general. A written revelation from God, wrought out in connection with human history, must necessarily take on a form of externality. A genuine criticism of the Bible demands a sound philosophy, for criticism can never be satisfactory if it is confined to the mere external forms of speech, and treats speculative or logical philosophy with disdain. Perfection of thought can no more be put into the externality of language than a tree can take into itself the conscious rationality of man. The Biblical record is given chiefly in a brief historical form ; even its moral and religious teaching is so interwoven with the narrative that the whole partakes of a historical character.

It is next to impossible to ascertain the genuineness of the historical record given us in the Bible by what the higher critics call the scientific method of investigation, which is simply induction based on analogy often merely superficial. This course we do not propose to pursue.

Where, and under what circumstances the various books were written, may, within certain limits, be interesting matters of inquiry, but certainly are not the most vital and important so far as a knowledge of the truth of the contents is concerned. Necessarily, a detailed account of human history is unwritten, while much that is written is clouded with great uncertainty, even in relation to what are named the facts of history. The method of studying history, named ' Higher Criticism,' which *claims* to be scientific, tends to throw doubt on the best-established facts of human history. The very nature of historical criticism is enveloped at every point with some uncertainty. What man or woman can, or ever could, write a faithful, unerring record of the facts and details of his or her own life ? To write the life of another person is still more difficult. Who can write the life of an average family and show the influence for good or evil each member has had upon the other ? Who can truly write the history of his own particular section of the Christian Church ? The under and side-currents of thought are many and deep. In how different a manner do various persons write and read the history of their own country, the histories of the various Churches, and the lives of great reformers and other eminent men. It is the same in the case of the Bible itself. Critics, from slight superficial resemblances, insignificant events, small points of similarity in language and customs in surrounding nations or tribes, will draw wide, sweeping generalizations. The result is that critical experts are continually contradicting each other, because superficial resemblances give scope, not only for ' bold guessing,' but even for drawing opposite conclusions from the same premises. In this way the fundamental and permanent principles of theology, religion and morality are overlooked and relegated to a subordinate place in human thought and action in religious, political and social life.

Further, to be acquainted with the various readings of the numerous manuscripts of the Scriptures, and to know whether interpolations can be verified, may be useful knowledge, but the substantial truth of the record cannot thereby be refuted or proved. Such an examination could not but be a life-work for any man, and would require every man to go over the same ground to see whether the examination made by others had been carried out honestly and correctly. Even if the correctness of such an examination were ascertained, this could not give a knowledge of the truth and reality of the doctrines taught therein; and a knowledge of the essential doctrines of the Bible is the one vital requirement.

The truth of the Bible doctrines in no way rests on their analogy with doctrines held and taught by nations contiguous to the Hebrew people or nation. Any partial resemblance is no proof of their derivation from surrounding sources, any more than any resemblance of the teaching of the Hebrew prophets to Greek philosophy proves that the prophets derived their teaching from the Greek philosophers, or that the Greeks derived their ideas from the Hebrews. There is certainly a deep and strong resemblance between the NOUS of Anaxagoras and the Logos of the Gospel. The former means mind, understanding, reason, the disposing and arranging principle of the universe; the latter, the Person by whom all things were made, and who became flesh in the *person* of Christ. Plato says (to quote from Dr. Stirling's *Gifford Lectures*), ' God, least of all, should have many parts '; ' God is what is absolutely simple and true.' ' Of this, the All, to find the Maker and Father is difficult, and having found Him, it is impossible to declare Him to all men.' ' When the Father created it, saw it moving and alive, this the created image of the blessed gods, He was well pleased.' Evidently by the ' created image ' he meant the visible universe. ' The blessed gods ' resembles ' the only-begotten ' of St. John, which is also translated as the Son. Yet in spite of their resemblance, they differ widely in meaning.

Much that is very fine in the writings of Plato and Aristotle closely resembles the teaching of the Bible, but we hesitate not to say that there is no sure evidence that the superior clearness and excellence of the Bible teaching was derived in any direct way from either of these writers.

The Bible doctrines, like the principles of science in nature, are not presented to us in logical forms (at least in one sense), yet the Bible is none the less full of rational or logical thought. The grand old Hebrew prophets were excellent reasoners, although, I suppose, they knew nothing about the science of logic or the syllogisms of Aristotle.

True knowledge is the strict demand of the science of logic, and this is also, throughout, the demand of the Bible. ' My people have gone into captivity, because they have no knowledge ; because thou hast rejected knowledge, I will also reject thee.' ' The priest's lips should keep knowledge.' Thus the Bible teaches, not only that God is known by man, but its chief aim is to impart and enforce an ever-growing knowledge. It teaches that the worst state of a people is when there is ' no knowledge of God or truth in the land.' Agnosticism, and even ' Christian ' agnosticism, is in direct and flagrant oppositon to the

teaching of the Bible and Logic. A science which
professes to teach that God can only be believed in,
and not known, is not worthy the name. This
implies that man, a rational being, acts more unreason-
ably than the irrational animal. 'The ox knoweth
his owner, and the ass his master's crib, but Israel
doth not know, My people doth not consider.' ' Yea,
the stork in the heaven knoweth her appointed times;
and the turtle and the crane and the swallow observe
the time of their coming; but My people know not
the judgment of the Lord.'

The Bible from beginning to end is, in its teaching,
in direct opposition to agnosticism. Any theory of
agnosticism (the unknowableness of God) is destruc-
tive to morals, religion, the welfare of the State, and
the true knowledge of man. Hegel and Stirling
belong to the class of men who take their stand on the
ground that God can be known, and not merely
blindly believed in. On this ground stood the
Prophets, Apostles, and Reformers; yea, and the
Lord Jesus Christ Himself; by these, ignorance of God
is strongly denounced and treated as the cause of
all evil. To call worshipping an 'unknown God'
advanced thought is somewhat absurd. Those who
do so, read neither their Bible, logic, science, nor
philosophy aright, but call true logical philosophy,
Pantheism. Socrates, Plato and Aristotle will rise up
in judgment against such and condemn them, for,
in seeking to know God, these three men made a brave
attempt to solve the mystery of existence, and to
acquire a knowledge of the great principles of logical
science. To call the philosophy of Hegel and Stirling
pantheistic because it teaches that God is in Nature,
and Nature is in God and man, is as foolish as it would
be to call the teaching of the Bible pantheistic, for
fundamentally the teaching is the same. ' In that

day,' said Christ, 'ye shall know that I am in My Father, and ye in Me, and I in you.' 'In Him we live and move and have our being.' Hegel and Stirling only present these truths in more logical forms. The study of the *Secret of Hegel* completely reveals the theological and religious position of both these men, and shows that they adhere to the fundamental doctrine of Christianity as taught in the Bible. They hold that philosophy and Christianity are fundamentally one. Hegel was very severe in his criticism of the Kantian form of agnosticism.

It is a curious fact that an unsound philosophy, completely at variance with true Christianity, should be popular with so many Christian ministers in nearly all sections of the Church, and that a sound philosophy, which ' vindicates and harmonizes orthodox Christianity,' should be so unpopular. This is chiefly due, no doubt, to the cry of Pantheism, and to the prevailing ignorance of the Nature of Concrete Logic. The critics rightly draw a distinction between the letter and the spirit ; but there is a way of dealing with what they call the Spirit, which is as defective and erring as is keeping to what is called the literal interpretation of the word. Under what they are pleased to call the guidance of the Spirit, many have used the Bible in support of very dangerous error. In relying on the Spirit, we must be sure it is the Spirit of Truth, for many false spirits have gone into the world.

There is also a mode of dealing with the letter of the word in which it is almost made to take the place of the Spirit, or even of God Himself, as if the word or letter were the supreme source of man's salvation and worthy of a veneration and worship almost equal with that due to God alone. On the other hand, there is a mode of treating the word as if it did not contain any special revelation of God, or of the spiritual nature of man. So far as it is external, merely, it is subject, like Nature, to contingency, accident and perishableness. In its internality, it is truth as thought, which in its spirit is God's revelation in, and to man. Just as it is of the most vital importance to know Christ after the Spirit and not merely after the flesh, though He could only reveal himself in the Spirit through His appearance in the flesh, so in the outward letter of the word there is always an inward revelation of the Spirit of God. Pure love in a pure heart is the first requirement for realizing a clear vision of God in spirit and in truth.

If the ' letter ' or ' literal ' interpretation be rejected, we must first be well assured as to what is meant by ' letter ' and ' literal,' and what is involved in such rejection. Critics may err, and have erred seriously, both in reference to the letter and to the spirit at one and the same time. On this account we need to know what is meant by ' verbal ' and ' plenary ' inspiration. A written revelation from God must be in words and letters. So far as the external form of the letters, words, and sentences of a language are concerned, there has never been a perfect language, and in this respect we may confidently affirm, there never will be one ; yea, we may go further, and say that such a perfect external form is not necessary. A necessary contingency is attached to both ' matter and form ' in a Divine revelation, and this was recognized by Christ when He said, ' For the hardness of your hearts he gave you this precept,' and ' I have many things to say unto you, but ye cannot bear them now.' Here, again, the distinction is recognized between ' verbal ' and ' plenary,' and between ' transitory ' and ' permanent '; for both form and content may be either transitory or permanent.

The very idea of a word implies thought. A word is a word only because of the thought that is in it, and so 'external' and 'internal' are in essential unity; the same is the case with every object, in part and in whole, of this vast universe.

Perfection, as perfection, cannot be found in parts, as parts : nor merely in externals if men try to understand these as being absolutely separated. The value of everything consists in its unity with the whole ; thus a hand ceases to be a hand in reality when separated from the rest of the body. Even the death of Christ only retains its deep significance when seen in its vital relation to His person, life, teaching, resurrection and ascension, and the relation of these to God and man.

The special external form of words amounts, in one sense, to little; so long as a word embodies the thought, we have all that is required, no matter in what language it may be expressed. Nor does it matter much when, where, or by whom the Bible was written in its entirety or in part. Direct evidence of sense-perception is impossible and unnecessary on these points. My belief is, in fact, a matter of pure reason, and substantially rests on the same kind of evidence as my belief that Hegel, Wesley, Newton, Luther, Calvin, or Wyclif lived in the flesh. It seems to me absurd to make so much of little ' bits ' of discrepancies, or of some moral and religious peculiarities to be found here and there in the Book. Contingency, expounded so clearly by Dr. Stirling, in *What is Thought?* and in his *Gifford Lectures*, prevents a perfect, logical, philosophical form and matter, and so renders a Divine revelation absolutely and necessarily transitory, both in its content and its verbal form; but the Revelation is none the less Divine on this account.

The contingency of Nature and of human life must necessarily pervade the Biblical record from beginning to end; and yet there is Divine truth and necessity running through it all as a golden thread, forming its substance and living connective tissue. Thus, events and persons come into contact with Christ in an external, accidental manner, giving occasion to His sublime teaching and miracles: as, for example, when Nicodemus came to Jesus by night, and the woman of Samaria came to the well to draw water. The circumstances which gave rise to His deep and incisive words in reply to the Jews and others, are full of contingency, but this does not detract from their essential truth and force. The secret power of all was in Himself; He was the truth enshrined in living, human form; but the thought could only be given in the language then and there in common use. The same applies to the Old, as to the New Testament. When it is said that the Bible is not infallible, it is necessary to know what is meant by such a statement. We cannot affirm that such and such contingent circumstances occurred through an unavoidable necessity, yet if the particular occurrences had not happened, we may confidently affirm that some other very similar contingencies must have taken their place. Just as, for example, it is largely a matter of chance as to whether a piece of ground is planted with beans, potatoes, or grass, yet the growth of these is not all chance. The living Spirit is the cause of their growth. ' Thou takest away their breath, they die and return to their dust; Thou sendest forth Thy Spirit, they are created, and Thou renewest the face of the earth.' I believe that all the so-called errancy of the Bible can be explained by this principle of contingency. Certainly unity, purpose and spirituality pervade this Book, which infinitely distinguish it from all others. If people persist in looking for what they think ' infallible— ought to be' in the settling of the unessential, essential contingency of mere outward changeable nature, then they will never find it. What is needed is an infallible key to the exposition of the Bible, and this I believe is found in Hegel's Concrete Logic, and especially in its clearer exposition by Dr. Stirling.

No doubt it is not easy to understand this *New* Concrete Logic, but no one can hope to know man, nature and God, as he ought and may, without hard study. The philosophy of Paul is as difficult to comprehend fully as is the system of Hegel. Such knowledge is our body, soul and spirit, without which man is undone. Only cowards shrink from the task. To them we may apply the words of Paul, ' Of whom we have many things to say, hard of interpretation, seeing ye are become dull of hearing. For when by reason of the time ye ought to be teachers, ye have need again that some one teach you the rudiments of the principles of the oracles of God, and are become such as have need of milk, and not solid food. For every one that partaketh of milk is without experience of the word of righteousness, for he is a babe. But solid food is for full-grown men, even those who, by reason of use, have their senses exercised to discern good and evil.' *So* far, milk is good, but many have been willing to be fed with chaff. Words, without thought or Spirit, are worthless chaff.

It is a painful fact that men, through a bias, are unable to read either the Bible, Christ, man, nature or philosophy aright. They chiefly fix on the excrescences of the shell and miss the kernel. Mere opinion rules almost everywhere in Church and State, and even in much of what is named science and philosophy.

In investigation of the somewhat wide fields of Oriental and Biblical literature of the far-distant past, slight shades of general resemblance, both in style and thought, appear, and give great scope for the ' bold guessing ' which has acquired such ascendancy among the ' Higher Critics.' I once heard Professor Budde of Strasburg, a leading higher critic, say that in such studies ' bold guessing ' was required. But ' guessing ' is not science, however ' bold ' it may be ! In the field of philology, especially in connection with the literature of the far-distant past, certainty is impossible. These methods and ideas, together with the theory of Darwinian evolution, have been applied to the criticism of the Biblical record until the Book is almost torn to pieces. Some of the Higher Critics say that they are thus making the Bible more acceptable to educated readers ; and that they are coming to an agreement as to what part may be accepted as reliable. It appears to me that their chief agreement is in doubt, and not in certainty, and that they have not proved that what they doubt is really beyond doubt, for it may still be true, for anything they know to the contrary. This, truly, is a sphere open and favourable to ' bold guessing ' : truth can only be found by another method.

The literary critics, like the evolutionists, profess to proceed in their studies and investigations on strictly scientific principles. The evolutionists admit, however, that their theory is not yet scientifically established. This is acknowledged by Professor H. Drummond in his *Ascent of Man*. It is only based on a superficial plausibility such as would render improbable every fact of history, every principle in physical science and logical philosophy, and would reduce the teaching of the Christian

Religion to a vague, mythical fancy. The best that can be granted these Biblical critics is, that they are guided by plausible guessing as to what they fancy is most likely to be correct, even though it is just as likely to be incorrect.

Induction and analogy are two chief principles in this mode of reasoning. Induction proceeds from particulars to generals, or, it is the principle of generalization. In its perfection it rises from the finite to the infinite; and contains the principle of relativity, both finite and absolute, for the one cannot be without the other. The absolute is relative, and the relative is the absolute; the absolute includes the finite, and the finite stands in absolute essential relation to the infinite and absolute. This is the ultimate induction—the absolute Concrete Notion, the Ego, or I. It is that of which Dr. Stirling says, ' It, and it alone, shall be the ultimate of the universe. It, and it alone, as it is the last of induction, shall be the first of deduction.' And what is this but thought, the absolute rational Notion between God and man, the I-Me, the I as God, the Me as man ; that is, the Ego is always double.

Perfect induction belongs to logical philosophy, and not to any of the finite sciences. The generals in the finite sciences depend for their validity on the complete enumeration of all the particulars, and this, so far as sense-perception extends, can never be completed. In finite spheres of knowledge, certainty chiefly depends on the greater or less extension of a general term, and therefore admits of different degrees of probability only. The same uncertainty does not apply to the extension and intension of the term man, for he is Ego, and this, according to Kant, ' raises man infinitely above the reasonless brutes, or any other living being on earth.' To know man in his individual and universal nature, I need not have a sense-perception of every man : I only need to know myself. To know men in their differences is of little account so far as a sound philosophy is concerned. The ' general ' or extension of a tree or metal is an indefinite finite; in man, it is a definite infinite.

Induction rests on analogy, the principle of similarity or resemblance. This has been defined to be ' a certain relation, likeness, or agreement between two or more things which, in other respects, are entirely different.' Hegel calls analogy ' the instinct of reason anticipating a common principle at the root of things.' It may, however, be either superficial or thorough, which is a distinction of great importance. What is it that makes analogy thorough or perfect, notwithstanding the fact that in many respects the things compared are very different ? It is simply that in the nature of the things, or objects, there is a substantial likeness, or identity of nature, and not a mere superficial or external resemblance. The fundamental nature of man is the same in all men, and so all men are made in the image and likeness of God. Every man is a self-conscious rational being, and so is a moral and religious being. Intellectually, every man in his thought is infinite; conscious infinite thought alone constitutes Self-consciousness; and thus he is one with God in possessing a moral nature. It is this intellectually moral nature that lifts man infinitely in thought above the reasonless brutes. The differences between one man and another in the colour of his skin, or the configuration of his skull, or in the matter of genius and of memory, are of no account in comparison with his infinite, intellectual, substantial nature. The analogy between God and man, or between one man and another, is perfect and thorough, notwithstanding the difference between them in other respects. Superficial analogy or resemblance, of itself, can demonstrate nothing. If the analogy or resemblance belonging to the nature of things is deep, and not superficial, then it is of great utility in the advancement of knowledge, for superficial analogy only gives a probable judgment at best, whereas the substantial and essential nature of things gives a categorical and apodictic judgment. Thus, when Christ likened the operation of His words and Spirit in the human heart, in imbuing it gradually with the graces of the kingdom of heaven, to the working of the leaven in the meal, He did not mean that the two operations were the same, only that they deeply resembled each other. Their logical sequence was different, because their natures in other respects were different. Such analogies are instructive ; but the one is not the logical sequence of the other. Men, however, are very liable to draw false conclusions from superficial analogies ; what is needed is a thorough insight into the nature of thought itself, which constitutes the real nature of the science of logic ; that is, the Dialectic exposition of Self-consciousness.

Kant furnishes two cases which show how great and acute minds can be led astray by, shall we say, imperfect, in contrast with perfect, analogies. One is the comparison of our notion of a hundred dollars with our notion of God; he argues that, as we possess the notion of the dollars, such notion is no proof of the existence of real dollars ; and though men possess the notion of God, such notion is no proof of the real existence of God. This analogy is very defective. A dollar is necessarily a finite, perishable thing; its existence depends on many contingent circumstances. This is not the case with the existence of God ; the existence of God is, and must be, that of a

Being such that His existence cannot rest on any contingent circumstance; He either exists necessarily and eternally, or not at all. The notion and being of a dollar may come to be, or cease to be, but the notion and being of God in man are of such a nature that they cannot either come to be or cease to be. The relation between the notion and being of a dollar is a separable relation, for the dollar may perish and man still retain the notion of a dollar. The relation between the notion and being of God is an inseparable relation; God cannot perish and the notion of God in man remain; if the Being of God is necessarily eternal, the notion of God is also necessarily eternal. God is the only Being possible whose notion and being are inseparable in human thought. If a man says, ' There is no God,' he is only contradicting in speech what he thinks, for if God were not in his thought, he could not say, ' no God.' Thus the kind of analogy Kant uses utterly fails. The resemblance between the nature of a dollar and the nature of God is very superficial, so superficial, indeed, that he thereby proves nothing, in spite of the apparent plausibility of the argument.

Kant next uses the analogy between the abstract principles of succession in time and the necessary sequence in the relation of cause and effect, to explain the nature of the necessary relation of cause and effect. With Kant, objects of sense and notions of the intellect are viewed as independent. The category of cause and effect in its necessity belongs only to the intellect. Cause and effect occur only in the sense-world, but he holds that, so far as objects of sense-perception are concerned, there is no necessary relation between them. He can only regard them as bare matters of fact, and affirm that they are, and not that they must be. The ' must ' can only come from the category as an affair of the intellect, for he holds that cause and effect and succession in time are sequences independent of each other. Seeing there is sequence in the one as well as in the other, he maintains there is an analogy between the two. They are still, however, so far independent, and the imagination alone can give the necessary unity to the two sequences, and only so can the necessary connection between cause and effect become an apodictic judgment or a genuine synthetic judgment, for he holds the imagination contains all that belongs to the unity of Sense and Intellect. His analogy, however, fails, for it alone cannot demonstrate the necessary relation between cause and effect and succession in time. It is a mere illusion to say that abstract time can by the aid of the imagination become the essential connecting link between cause and effect. The analogy, then, is superficial, and in no way explains either the necessary relation of succession in time or the essential relation between cause and effect, for a perfect analogy contains in itself the principle of absolute identity, the absolute Ego of thought's own self, the creative power of the universe—that is, identity requires no analogy.

If so sober, honest and acute an intellect as Kant's could be misled by analogy, how much more easily may honest critics be led astray by analogy and induction in the wide field of literary criticism, Biblical or otherwise.

Kant wished thus to check the spread of the scepticism of Hume, but at the same time he struck a serious blow against the ontological, cosmological and teleological proofs of the existence of God; nevertheless, he laid the foundation for a sound, logical Theology, Christology and Humanology. The honest Biblical critics, while attempting to combat the looser and nore extravagant critics of the external contingent liscrepancies of the Bible, and the miraculous element found therein, often fall into worse errors, so ar as the knowledge of truth is concerned, and do 1ot make the Bible any more acceptable to educated nen. The critics need the steady power of sound ogical philosophy.

Induction and analogy are virtually linked together n the progress of human knowledge, and they are also in essential unity with intuition and reflexion n logical thought. In general, however, induction 1as too much neglected the highest generalization founded on *thorough* analogy, and this has led to the ignoring of the value of religious knowledge in human life. Analogy in the experiential sciences has led to many valuable results, yet on the other hand, in the philosophy of nature there has often been a frivolous play with superficial analogies. In different species of plants, resemblances in colour, shape, or in other respects, give no proof that such plants spring from one original species. The same is the case with regard to the different species of animals; if the existence of one created original species be admitted, then the belief in thousands of created original species is much more rational.

In the material, or inorganic world, matter certainly exists in a variety of forms; so different are some of these forms, that ether itself has been named, like light, 'immaterial and spiritual matter'; so on the same ground, gravitation may be named a kind of matter, but these cannot be named universal facts of sense-experience in the same way that it is a fact of experience that water freezes at a temperature of 32° F., whether we know the why or not. In all this difference, the principle of identity unites and pervades all in one common nature. We are logically

21

certain that this is necessarily so, notwithstanding
the universal play of contingency, chance and freedom.
Indeed, possibility involves contingency, and is as
necessary as necessity itself, is absolute and universal.
We do not attain such knowledge by mere superficial
analogies. It is realized only through the principle
of perfect induction based on thorough analogy, and
this at bottom means identity in infinite difference.

Now the scientific method on which the ' Higher
Critics ' claim to proceed in their Biblical researches
is almost entirely the induction which rests on more
or less superficial analogies—partly in the words,
and partly in the precepts and doctrines found in the
mythical teaching of the peoples with whom the
Jews came in contact from the days of Abraham
until the time of Malachi.

Philologists have met with great success ; a linguist
has come to be regarded as a prodigy of wisdom and
erudition, even though in other respects he may
have only a minimum of knowledge. Such men have
been treated as experts, like the leaders of the evolutionary theory, to whom all non-experts must submit,
or be held up as religious bigots shutting their eyes
to the light of advancing science. Whilst meta-
physicians have been laughed at as dreamers, spinning
subtle cobwebs of empty thoughts, or evolving the
universe out of the depth of their own consciousness,
philologists have had no difficulty, after deciphering
a few words from a discovered tablet, in reconstruct-
ing history and exploring the ocean of the prehistoric
past.

All we have held most sacred must, since their
discoveries, be treated as myths. Our mighty dead
only lived in a vain show ; their very names are
made to fit into purely suppositional meanings ;
Jewish history is a plagiarism from Babylonian

nyths. Professor Winkler makes the words, ' Joseph :ame at noon,' to mean that Joseph stands for the un ; Joshua is also the sun ; Son of Nun-fish ; Caleb Kelb), a dog ; so Abraham, Isaac, Jacob, Simeon, [oseph, Joshua, Saul, are all reduced to myths. >urely here we have analogy ' run mad ' ! Yea, .hese critics strike at greater persons, as Moses and [esus Christ. Yet these great personalities, whom ve must now regard as myths or mere types, have nade a great mark, and left an undoubted influence ipon the thought and history of the world. The ollowing may serve as an illustration to show that ve need to be very careful in accepting all the con- :lusions of these critics, even though they may be experts ' in some special subject.

Dr. Robertson Smith, when assistant Professor of Natural Philosophy in Edinburgh University, wrote a >aper on *Hegel and the Metaphysics of the Fluxional Calculus*, in which he stated that Hegel had made an attempt to establish the calculus on a new and naccurate basis.' This he did at a time when the >hilosophy of Hegel was almost unknown in Britain ind America, and when it would scarcely fail to >lace Hegel and his philosophy under great suspicion is to whether or no it could be worthy of any atten- :ion from serious men. What he attacks is a ' Hege- .ian Calculus,' on which he says: 'To this subject Hegel devotes his second note, professing to point >ut a purely analytical method, whereby without iny application of the doctrine of limits, everything necessary for practice can be deducted.' Nowhere in the writings of Hegel is there the slightest attempt to do what he is here charged with. In the same paper Dr. R. Smith tells us frankly that he is un- acquainted with the principles of Hegel's philosophy, and does not profess to be able to treat this question from the standpoint of Hegel's own philosophy; but he thinks Hegel's position in this matter ' can be fairly examined by one who does not profess to have mastered Hegel's system.' This shows that he thought himself capable of honestly criticizing Hegel without first ascertaining what it was Hegel really meant. One cannot even surmise how Dr. Smith came to put into Hegel's words a meaning so entirely different to what they clearly convey.

We have here, not merely a question of 'a new basis for the Calculus,' but also a question concerning literary criticism. Surely no criticism of any writing, ancient or modern, is justifiable unless the critic is sure of the writer's meaning ! If the meaning is not clear, a critic may say so, but he ought not to put into the words a meaning entirely foreign to the general scope and bearing of the author's writings.

In the sphere of literature, especially such as had a more direct bearing on the Old Testament writings, Dr. Smith was more than an ordinary expert. Our chief excuse for introducing him here is, that if he erred so much in criticizing so modern a work as Hegel's, it behoves us to be very cautious in accepting his conclusions on the Biblical record, where it is more difficult to follow him.

The condition and surroundings of the Bible writers belong to such a dim and distant past, and are withal entangled in such manifold, erroneous reasoning as then prevailed among the surrounding nations, that in dealing with such matter, those who follow this line of research are very liable to yield to even more erroneous conclusions. Indeed, truth cannot be obtained by this method, which only tends to greater and greater confusion of thought on all subjects essential to man's salvation.

In recent times, however, the more sober critics

have chiefly aimed at showing that 'evolution,' applied to the Bible, helped to bring to light a more rational conception of its Divine inspiration. We hold this has not improved the Christian situation, and that a solid foundation must be sought elsewhere. It is not enough, after tearing and rending the Bible from end to end, to say that the process has increased, and not lessened, our confidence in its Divine authority.

Probably the strongest point of attack on the credibility of the Bible record arises from the numerous miracles recorded therein. Some of these are often referred to with the view of bringing the others into discredit, and thus opening a way to a free treatment of the texts of the record. Among the miracles especially selected are : the speaking of Balaam's ass ; the falling of the walls of Jericho ; the flood of Noah ; the standing still of sun and moon ; the passage of the Israelites through the Red Sea ; the plagues of Egypt ; Jonah and the whale ; Daniel in the lion's den ; the three Hebrews in the fiery furnace ; and many others of the like kind in the Old Testament. In the New Testament considerable prominence is given to the miracle of the swine, and the injustice therein done to the owners by their loss. The New Testament, as well as the Old, contains many remarkable miracles, not the least being the resurrection and ascension of Christ. Whether any miracles have been interpolated into the original record it is difficult or impossible to ascertain with certainty, but even if it could be proved that some have been afterwards inserted, this would be no gain to those who argue against the fact of miracles, unless it can be proved that all are false, and that miracles are absolutely in the nature of things impossible ; nor is the possibility of miracles lessened by the fact that men have believed in pretended miracles.

It is of no use talking about the fixed laws of nature, the regularity of nature's law, or the uniformity of nature. We utterly reject the view that the miracles of the Bible imply in any sense the setting aside of the laws and constitution of Nature. Millions of changes are constantly being made through the action of human thought and will that would never have occurred if Nature had been left to its ordinary course. If it is said that miracles are widely different from the ordinary changes brought about by man, we still affirm that the ordinary course of Nature is changed by the power and free exertion of man's thought. The changes wrought in nature by man do not change the constitution of the universe, any more than miracles involve such a change. Even the standing still of the sun and moon does not involve such a change any more than the quick increase or decrease in the speed of our great ocean steamers disturbs the order of nature. The size of our earth in comparison with the magnitude of the starry heavens is not equal to that of all engines, steamers, and other powers used by man daily, when compared with the earth itself, and yet all these motions go on as if nothing were being done by man. Why, a little boy can make his top spin more slowly or quickly according to his pleasure ! yet God must have no freedom, but must be tied to some so-called fixed order that never was fixed except according to His own perfect reason, love and pleasure. The notion of fixed laws and the consequent impossibility of miracles has, by constant repetition and custom, got into the ' blood and bones ' of many men, even through their very educatedness, just as the craving for signs and wonders had got wrought into the very nature of many Jewish minds.

Many write about miracles as if those who believe

in the reality of those recorded in the Bible were obliged for that reason to make its Divine authority depend on miracles. Surely this is a very narrow and unwarrantable way of treating so important a subject. Of course, if it can be proved that some miracles are unreasonable because they are impossible, there would then be a solid reason for rejecting them as real facts. No rational person can think for a moment that even if miracles were wrought by thousands in the sight of men they could have any direct influence on their hearts in renewing their moral nature in righteousness and holiness. This power is not claimed for them either by the prophets, apostles, or by Christ Himself. Such a renewing can only be accomplished by a knowledge of and trust in the saving truth of God in Christ, no matter how or by what means a knowledge of such truth may come to men; though as a rule it can only come by the direct preaching to them of the once-crucified Christ, and through the witness of God's Spirit in man's spirit. Still, it does not follow that miracles were useless in drawing men to a genuine trust in God, and to a saving faith in Christ, just as now, reading about the miracles of Christ unquestionably does some real good.

The divine authority of Christ does not rest on the miracles, but the reality of the miracles rests on the reality of God and His Christ. The reality of miracles cannot be regarded as logically impossible so long as the reality of God and Christ stands logically sure. Whether any spurious miracles have been interpolated, is another matter.

I confess that for upwards of forty years I have been astonished that intelligent men should have stumbled so much at the speaking with man's voice of Balaam's ass, the falling of the walls of Jericho, and the return of the sun ten degrees backwards. So long as God is the centre and circumference of the universe, such return of the sun backwards cannot affect the harmonious movement of the heavenly bodies, the mathematical calculations of Laplace, or Newton's law of gravitation. So long as the miracles of Christ and His resurrection stand firm, there is no logical, philosophical, scientific difficulty respecting the others; they cannot be logically disproved. Thorough disbelievers in the possibility of miracles see clearly that if they accept one miracle as real they may accept all, therefore they endeavour to explain them all away. Those who only go half-way fall into a ditch of their own making.

I cannot explain fully how God revealed the future to His servants the prophets, but such revelation cannot be proved to be impossible. I cannot explain fully how at the Pentecost the disciples were enabled to speak miraculously in divers tongues. These two miracles I consider more difficult of explanation than any other recorded in the Bible. But the known operations of man's thought, and its logical essential relation to the Divine thought is so real and glorious as to render not only possible, but probable, the gifts of tongues and prophecy. However, just as we accept innumerable facts in nature without explanation at present, so we can just as rationally accept the psychological facts recorded in the Bible without explanation at present, if we cannot prove them to be impossible, and only in part probable. Miracles possibly involve one of the least revealed mysteries in the Christian revelation, and their true logical nature may remain unsolved for some time, but this is no solid reason for rejecting their reality. Quite as great, too, is the mystery of the spiritual growth of plants. Hegel's logical exposition of the spirituality of Nature is the most sublime work ever achieved in the history of philosophy.

The question of possibility or impossibility is of great importance, both in relation to philosophy and the Bible record. It certainly is altogether impossible that the creation of the heavens and earth should have taken place in six natural days of twenty-four hours each. Creation in six natural days neither agrees with geology, astronomy, nor logical philosophy. We need not *here* discuss the agreement or disagreement of the record with geology and astronomy on the one hand and with philosophy on the other. Our contention is that the earth, sun, moon and stars must have existed during eternal ages before six or seven thousand years ago. Our point is, does the Bible account agree with logical philosophy ? There ought to be no unnatural forcing of the two into agreement. The facts and explanations of each must stand on its own ground, awaiting further light. Man, however, in his empirical existence is certainly of recent creation. (The week of seven days, we reserve for after consideration.)

It has long been noted that the word day in the first chapters of Genesis has three different meanings. First, the light is called day and the darkness is called night ; then the evening and the morning is a day, thus day includes the unison of light and darkness ; then we read, ' In the day that the Lord God made the earth and the heavens.' The word day here neither stands for light, nor a time of twenty-four hours, including light and darkness, nor for an indefinite geological period of time. The word day in its third meaning is the most important, for it involves no division of time whatever, neither past nor present : it rather signifies an eternal day, and if the word day stands for light, as it undoubtedly does, then it would mean that in the eternal light-day of God's own self, God made the earth and the heavens. Without thought, day and light have no meaning.

Further, it must be noted that in this early account it is not at all definitely stated that God created the heavens and the earth in six ordinary days. Such statement is found in the Decalogue, but not in the first biblical account of creation. Leaving this for the moment, we may note, that it is not even stated that God created anything on any one of the six divisions now called days. It seems permissible to regard these six divisions in creation as six stages only (not six geological periods, for the creation of all in six such periods, however long or short, is as impossible to reconcile to true reason, as in six ordinary natural days), in which they present themselves as a total whole at once to the writer of this account. This panorama of Nature in its external form as presented to sense-perception, is there a matter of fact in a total necessary relation of ideas. So far the external sense-view is, in the form of a rational presentation, absolutely in unity with the rational thought of man, in which he is at one with God in thought and reason.

In the first stage is the recognition of light and darkness, day and night, that is all; in the second stage is the recognition of the sky above, named the firmament, together with the water above and water below, that is all. In the third there is simply the recognition of dry land and seas; in the earth, grass, herbs, and fruit-tree, each having a seed of its own and each yielding seed and fruit after its kind. In the fourth stage, the recognition of lights in the sky (expanse), sun, moon, and stars shedding light upon the earth; the sun by day, and the moon and stars by night. 'For signs and for seasons, for days and for years.' In the fifth stage, the writer recognizes the fish of the sea, and the fowl of the air, each bringing forth abundantly after its kind. In the sixth stage, we have domestic fowls and all kinds of land animals, all bringing forth young after their kind, and then the creation of man and woman ('male and female created He them'), made in the image of the Creator, to have dominion over all. Here are six stages or great striking divisions, standing out openly in absolute relation in all their parts to the Creator, and claiming the contemplation of all as the work of the Creator; for the Bible requires men to study the works of God—the operations of His hands.

It is a simple, artless account as it presents itself to ordinary *sense-perception*, but yet creation is quite rationally presented as the work of God, the infinite, eternal Spirit. Such a descriptive view of creation necessarily partakes of the limitations that belong to a period when the general system of the universe was unknown. It is quite remarkable that the writer of the Epistle to the Hebrews speaks of the seventh day, the Sabbath rest, and of God as the present and final rest into which His people enter by a true and living faith; the Psalmist speaks of God as his true resting-place.

The whole of this early period contains a remarkable natural blending of what is real to sense-perception with the philosophical, making the reader feel that he is not reading fiction but something really true. If each day can be legitimately regarded as a natural division of Nature; and God, the Creator, as man's sabbath rest, then this sense-view would form a not unnatural reason for setting apart one day in seven for the special united worship of God on earth. According to the words of Christ, ' the Sabbath was made for man, and not man for the sabbath.' If this division into different stages is real, they are seen, not as one springing or being evolved out of the other, but there at once, together. We cannot admit that the Mosaic account is a mere myth on its own account ; and further, because a mythical origin is indirect opposition to the teaching of the writers of the New Testament. The account as given is both natural and rational. There is no warrant for saying, as some critics do, that this account was derived from ancient Babylonian sources. It cannot well escape the notice of any person that the methods of the Higher Critics tend to lessen in the end the authority of Jesus Himself, and this lays their methods open to suspicion. The true method for a right understanding is the Ego, or the science of Concrete Logic.

The critical biblical study of the person and teaching of Christ has taken a strange turn in its treatment of the fourth gospel. This is treated as if its teaching were a mixture of the teaching of Christ with some elements of Grecian philosophy, and, therefore, unreliable. The teaching of Christ concerning His own Divine personality is certainly fuller here than in the other three gospels, though to a certain extent they are in perfect agreement. St. John is a little more explicit and full on this subject than are the other three evangelists. Concerning the Divine person of Christ, the teaching of Paul and John is in explicitness in perfect agreement. To a certain extent one explains the other, which is thus a real gain so far as their philosophical foundation is concerned. John has kept well in mind many of the great sayings of Christ about Himself, and we have no difficulty in seeing that what he states in the prologue to his gospel is in perfect accord with Christ's own words. However, though we attach the highest value to the teaching of the New Testament about Christ, our faith in His Divine personality and work does not rest entirely on the wording of the record. It may seem an extreme view, but we venture to say that the Ego of reason is in perfect accord with the God-man the record claims Him to have been. The record does not make Him to be what He was, rather He makes the record; both His claim and record rest on a genuine logical philosophy. We base our belief in the genuineness of both on this fact, and further say that anyone refusing to acknowledge the record as truth must show that it is absolutely contrary to reason.

A sound philosophy and divinity of Christ through a knowledge of the Ego reveals Christianity as the Religion of Reason. What it does in helping to a right conception of the personality of Christ, it also does in setting before us the sacred volume in a light that makes it worthy of our highest admiration, love, and confidence. It is not, however, the book that saves us; God and Christ are our salvation. But, as Christ says, ' The words that I speak unto you, they are *spirit* and they are *life* '; also, ' Man shall not live by bread alone, but by every *word* that proceedeth out of the mouth of God.'

Whittle away the authority of the word, and thereby you whittle away the divinity of the Spirit, the reality of the miracles, the divinity and authority of Christ, and then comes chaos. But the Spirit of God, the Spirit of Christ, is so interwoven into the very letter of the word, so constituting its web, warp and woof, that its living eternal power cannot be diminished. So, in spite of the human composition of the Bible and its finite limitation in the *external* form of the *letter*, God and His Christ are in the word just as certainly as they are in every finite object in Nature.

CHAPTER XIV

THE PHILOSOPHICAL CHARACTER OF THE BIBLICAL RECORD

IN the second sentence of the first chapter of Genesis we have the apparently senseless statement that 'the earth was without form, and void.' The literal form of the words, ' without form, and void,' does not express the whole truth. It is impossible that the earth in the full sense of the words could have been ' without form, and void.' The literal without the spiritual import would be devoid of meaning. The true substantial meaning of the words expresses the beginning of the philosophy of spirit, which meaning is identical with that of the first words of Hegel's *Logic*, in which he expresses the starting-point of the demonstrated science of the philosophy of spirit: ' Being is the indefinite immediate,' ' Pure Being without any further definition,' ' Being, the indefinite immediate, is, in fact, Nothing, and neither more nor less than Nothing.' The complete specification and development of the spirit rises in its logical evolution to the full conception or notion of the absolute spiritual nature of the universe. In like manner the words, ' without form, and void,' form the starting-point of the six days' creation as the six stages of the revelation and manifestation in man of the absolute spiritual nature of the universe. As a matter of fact, ' without form, and void,' expresses precisely the starting-point of the infant consciousness, that is, of its spirit.   With man, all demonstrated science begins with the dim, indefinite, immediate consciousness of the infant.

Light is day and darkness is night, but without thought, light and day, darkness and night have no meaning.   Without thought all would be a blank nothing.   Nothing, however, is more evident than that thought is consciousness, reason and spirit, and that spirit is the self-active, self-creative power, the source of all natural and spiritual life.   Darwin said, ' We are profoundly ignorant of the cause of variation.'   The self-activity of spirit is the logical development of the categories, which Hegel says, ' is alone demonstrated science.'   If Darwin had seen this he would have known the cause of variation and have been a true scientist.   Merely to say, ' natural selection,' is no science at all, for all science is spiritual in its nature, and in its dialectical development is alone true science.

If, as already stated, the teaching of the Bible is in perfect harmony with the teaching of logical philosophy, the further development and fuller exposition of true philosophy will only tend to confirm the fundamental truths set forth in the Biblical record.

Man as a philosopher is the only being who can perceive the true nature of things, and even in the earliest chapters of the Bible there is evidence of a deep insight into the nature of God, man, and creation. When the record is closely examined, it will be seen that the writer of the account of creation as given in the Book of Genesis was somewhat of a philosopher. He was at least a monotheist, and therefore a genuine philosopher, and with him God was the Creator of the universe ; he speaks of God as a spirit, ' eternal,' the great 'I am that I am,' and therefore, in a real sense, the beginning and foundation of all things.   The writer of the first three chapters of Genesis was by no means an ordinary man, but one possessed of true and vital thoughts concerning the nature of God and the unity of all things in Him. He possessed a deeply religious spirit and a very high moral tone and character. He was not carried away by pictures of a vain imagination, but thought in a style only possible to a great man living under a deep sense of the presence and glory of the infinite God. There is nothing in the record to indicate that the writer did not realize the truth and importance of what he wrote. The honour of the great God who ' made heaven and earth, the sea, and all that in them is,' dominates his mind. All that is made is in his eyes very good, but God and ' man in the image of God ' are seen to be in value infinitely above all things else. Such a man could never bring his mind to be a writer of mere myths, nor even a reproducer or improver of myths concerning God, man, and creation. Our estimate of the writer agrees well with what Stephen declares concerning Moses : ' Moses was learned in all the wisdom of the Egyptians, and was mighty in words and in deeds ' ; and also with the writer of the Epistle to the Hebrews when he says, ' he endured, as seeing Him who is invisible.' Just as the great Apostle Paul received both a Grecian and a Hebrew training, so Moses received an Egyptian and a Hebrew training. While Moses had all the advantages in education connected with the palace of Egypt, his mother, as his nurse, was instilling into his young mind the great ideas of the God of his fathers, Abraham, Isaac and Jacob. His mother and his mother's God became more to him than the honour of being called ' the son of Pharaoh's daughter.' The invisible God was not to him an unknown God. Moses, like Paul, was not an agnostic ; they both clearly saw the invisible things of God. To see the invisible is to know the invisible. In man, as a rational self-conscious being, sight and insight exist in absolute identity in reason-vision. While we have no wish to make Moses into an Aristotle, a Kant, a Hegel or a Stirling, yet in the depth of his religious apprehension of God he was in an important sense their superior. It is declared of him in a special sense that he saw God face to face. If the old pagan philosopher, Aristotle, could see in the νοῦς of Anaxagoras τὸ Θεῖον, why should it be thought incredible that the more highly-favoured Moses should see, as Dr. Stirling puts it, ' Die grosse Anschauung des Juden—the mighty intuition of the Jew—I am that I am.' Thus with Moses, God was All in All, at once both thought and being. With him, God was not a mere architect, but the Creator of the universe, for, as Hegel says, ' The production of form is utterly impossible without the production of matter.' True, Moses did not make known the rationale of how God created the universe and man in his empirical existence ; he only names the fact, stating especially that ' God made man in His own image,' on the side of earth, earthy ; on the other a living soul. If we really take the trouble to look into the question of what it is truly to think, and not merely vainly to imagine, as man is prone to do, we shall see that to think truly is to determine, to determine to act, to act, to do something, and with God this is to create. Consequently, the man who does not endeavour to understand, and to do something substantially rational, misses his vocation and destiny. He loses his life, and in this way mars his divine image. Man only comes to his true self when he rises to think God, to think I, to think I as I. I, then, is self-consciousness, I thinking itself, self-acting and self-productive, and that is Ego, that is God, that is man in God and God in man. This unity is creation as the self-activity of the Ego, for a beginning can only denote unity in progression and creation, and that which is created is always in essential relation with the Creator. With Moses, the earth, sun, moon and stars, the universe with all its content, were not regarded as a vast machine that God had created and set going as something independent and in some inexplicable manner outside and alongside of Himself. Such a supposition only came into vogue in consequence of the alienation of man from the life of God through practical moral evil, so through sin and guilt entailing a darkened understanding; or by man seeking to understand existence from mere hypotheses, and especially in consequence of him regarding the existence of God as a mere hypothesis. Hegel says: ' It is not to man's credit that he finds it easier to doubt the existence of God than to doubt the existence of the world.' Surely thought, self-consciousness, is more vital, precious and permanent than the outward changing objects of sense. All the value of the outward is derived from, and rests on the inward, on that which to sense is invisible, though to thought ' the invisible appears in sight ' in visible objects. It was with this sight that the grand old Hebrew prophets and the more spiritually-minded priests saw God, and in this they ' lived, moved and had their being.' It is worthy of note that the writer of Genesis begins with the Light called Day, God's Light, the daylight of God, and that he declares that all else is derived from and has its being in the invisible God, and is reflected into the invisible man, for that which constitutes the substantial nature of man is invisible to sense-perception, just as God is invisible. But no man will ever see man or the world properly who does not see, or who refuses to see, God, the God which, as Paul says, is 'manifest in man.' So of all needs, the greatest is a sound philosophy.

No linguist can be a true critic of the texts of the Bible who is not a genuine student of philosophy. Only this can save the linguistic critic from disfiguring, torturing and distorting the biblical account of our first parents, their temptation, their sin, and the simple, natural, brief description of creation in general. As we have already noticed, this confessed lack caused Dr. Robertson Smith to fall into many errors in his criticism of Hegel, and afterwards led to his erroneous criticism of the Mosaic forms of religion. An eminent biblical scholar, Professor T. K. Cheyne, has recently ventured to write: ' I am myself one of those who hold the historical personage called Moses to be unproved and improbable.' In this he agrees with Professor Winkeler of Berlin; yet the Bible is saturated with Moses from beginning to end. Such a mode of criticism eliminates from history every great historical character that has ever lived; yet these critics are especially lauded for their great learning. Professor Cheyne is one of the experts whose findings, or supposed findings, in his department, the general reader is expected to accept without demur. Although of necessity words embody thought and serve as a means for imparting knowledge, yet they must for the most part be of a figurative, metaphorical, allegorical or symbolical character, and must be subject to the analytical and synthetical forms of thought in its dialectic movement in judgment, reason, and understanding as exhibited in sense-forms of existence. ' The serpent of eternity ' belongs essentially to self-consciousness, in which there is a knowledge of ' an invisible dividing line ' between good and evil, right and wrong, knowledge and ignorance, wisdom and folly, happiness and pain. This tempter confronts the Lord Jesus, as it does every man, and as it confronted our first parents. This is the dividing line between the broad and narrow way, the wide and the straight gate, the way of life and the way of death. Every man has within him the tree of life and the tree of knowledge of good and evil, for ' in God we live, move and have our being.' Sin only bars the way to the tree of life, and converted the world from a garden of Eden into a region of briars and thorns. Sin only—especially sin in the form of pride—makes men intellectually blind to moral and spiritual realities, and prevents them from hearing the voice of God externally in Nature and internally in the rational action of self-consciousness. ' Holy men of old spake as they were moved by the Holy Ghost.' There is nothing more true than that ' there is a spirit in man, and the inspiration of the Almighty giveth him understanding.' But true inspiration is not something independent of the activity of human reason, nor is human reason something independent of divine inspiration. The true development of man consists in the united activity of these. Christ censured His disciples for their slowness in comprehending His person and work, thus recognizing that they were not devoid of the power of knowing His divine personality. In modern times our greatest men, such as Wyclif, Luther, Knox, Wesley, and Bourne, were especially distinguished as deep Christian philosophers. They were imbued with an intense spirit of inquiry for a true knowledge of God, so they were epoch-making men like Moses and Paul. It is remarkable how little notice is taken of their philosophical studies, yet these formed a strong element in their character and even, in a sense, made them to be what they were. This it was that led Wesley into the full assurance of faith and the conscious witness of the Spirit. It is very important to notice that the breadth and fullness of an assured knowledge of truth may be of very varying degrees. Our illustration as to a knowledge of the certainty of an eclipse of the sun or moon may be here used. With many, their faith in the certainty of a coming eclipse rests merely on a statement seen in the almanack. Because such an event has always occurred exactly as predicted, the majority of people, though knowing nothing of the process by which such a fact is ascertained, infer that such an event will again occur. Such reasoning is logically sound so far as it goes, though it seems to rest on a very narrow and slender basis.

Similarly, in religion, many excellent Christian characters have been formed on as slender a basis of intelligent faith ; that which they knew and believed, however, was true, and thus gave a firm though, in a sense, narrow foundation. On the other hand, with many the path of logical certainty is left and mere hypothesis takes its place. This is the case both in science and religion ; false reason takes the place of true reason, and even educated men become ' in wandering mazes lost.' Still, in all ages not a few educated men have kept firmly to the fundamental doctrines of ' the faith once delivered to the saints,' though their teaching or writings may have shown some small deviation from the Truth. This has an important bearing on the origin and evolution of philosophy. There is a philosophy in the development of truth all through the Bible, though it differs widely from the process of the Grecian philosophy and the modern theory of evolution. With the Hebrews, God is always the supreme ruling idea. With the Greeks, their beginning is from external nature—earth, water, fire, and air—to νοῦς, logic and God ; their philosophy reached its highest expression in Aristotle. To me it appears very evident that logic was the life and soul of Aristotle's philosophy of nature, morals, and of God as the eternal life of All. As the Greeks, in order to find the *universal* all-common principle of all existence, began to philosophize from one or other of the above-mentioned forms of nature, so Moses began with God as the *universal* principle and Creator of all, and then presented the general forms of creation in a real sense-panorama of the various stages or natural divisions thereof, as they presented themselves to his reflection in sense-perception. It can scarcely be said that the Hebrews had a philosophy of nature, except so far as God was held by them to be the creator, sustainer and controller of all, though certainly they in a rational manner recognized Him as Spirit, all-knowing, omnipresent, all-good, eternal. Logic as the science of the nature of thought was unknown to them, so far as we know, but since all men are rational beings, the science of thought was implicitly in them. To this extent, in spite of much error, they could, and did, in many important matters, reason correctly. So there is a divine philosophy in the Hebrew Scriptures, though not in the explicit form of logical philosophy, just as there are the sciences of astronomy, geology and chemistry discoverable in nature by a rational investigation. Hebrew philosophy began and ended with God : man's duty was to love, fear and obey the laws of God, which also embraced the duty of each man to love his neighbour as himself. Christianity, in the person of Christ, came to them with a new and surprising light respecting the indwelling of the Spirit of God in man, and man's essential unity thereby with the Spirit of God. Higher than this neither philosophy nor science can rise. The Religion of the Greeks was chiefly polytheism ; that of the Hebrew writers, monotheism; to this extent the beginning of rational thought with the Hebrews was much superior to that of the Greeks. After the NOUS had entered vitally into Greek philosophy as its dominating principle, it culminated in an inquiry into the fundamental principles of the science of logic (logos) as the science of reason-thought. This was an immense permanent step in advance in philosophy, because now, for the first time, did reason receive its more exact form in the Aristotelian syllogism.

Eighteen centuries after the introduction of the Christian principle, Hegel came to see that, when the science of logical thought was properly understood, it was essentially one with the Spirit and Truth of God as revealed to man by Christ in His person and teaching. He all but perfected a concrete system of the logical nature of thought from the concrete Notion of Kant. Stirling, through a thorough study of the history of philosophy, especially that of Hegel, has by a fuller and clearer insight into the philosophy of the Ego, contained in Hegel's Begriff (Notion), made the philosophy of Hegel shine with a clearer and brighter light; and so has made possible a philosophy of the Christian Religion in its depth, fullness and detail, in such a manner as was never possible before. In his *Pathway to Reality*, Lord Haldane considers that Hegel has opened the way to a correct reading and understanding of the long-neglected metaphysical philosophy of Aristotle. Our best philosophical thinkers seem to be following the lead of Hegel and Dr. Stirling, and probably at no distant date the shallow Aufklärung-philosophy of the eighteenth century will come to an end.

Men have been slow in realizing clearly the distinction between the true and false in reason, wisdom, faith, religion, science, logic, and philosophy; between

true and false theory, true and false principles, or
the distinction between true and false supernatural
and human inspiration, so that what is really divine
has been entirely eliminated from the Bible, or is
regarded as having a purely mythical origin. Through
a failure to realize the ground of these distinctions,
truth comes to be looked upon as no more than a
mere matter of opinion, or it is said that truth or
God is unknowable, or what is worse, that absolute
truth as distinct from error does not exist. It is no
wonder that when such estimates of what truth is
have become general, men as a last resource take
refuge in the barren and comfortless doctrine of
agnosticism and evolution from unconscious matter.
Indeed, if God is not, truth is not; and if God is
unknowable—for God is the truth of all that is—then
truth is unknowable. Further, if there may not be
differences in the degree of man's knowledge of the
truth, then truth to him is unknowable, for man cannot
be omniscient. Again, if man's knowledge is not at
once finite and infinite, absolute and relative, then
neither a knowledge of God, nor truth, nor the world,
nor man, exists, and that which man thinks he knows
is nothing but a baseless phantasmagoria, and so no
person can be sure that two and two are four; but
as a matter of fact, such suppositions are unsupposable,
just as is the idea that man can cease to think God.
As there is a sound reason for belief in an eclipse
foretold by an almanack, or a sound reason why
thousands of so-called uneducated men become
spiritually renewed by faith in Christ, or as there is a
sound element of philosophy in the Ionic, Pythago-
rean, and Eleatic philosophers, however deficient
in knowledge these various persons might be otherwise, so there is a sound philosophy in the Mosaic
account of creation, in spite of its partial and limited

nature. Strictly, no man is totally ignorant. Its purpose and scope are entirely religious and moral; in this it is one with the teaching and mission of Christ and the whole doctrine of the apostles. It dealt only with the deepest need of man—his restoration to the life of God—and left general science and civil government almost entirely alone. It, like Moses, kept to the bare statement of God as Creator of all and to the fact that God was supreme King and Father of all spirits in heaven and earth. In all its teaching the Bible proceeds on the ground that the real permanent well-being of man can only be secured by truly knowing, loving, fearing and obeying the will and mind of God. To know God and His Christ in spirit and in truth is to know the source, spring and fountain of all spiritual life, and also to possess the key which opens ' all the treasures of wisdom and knowledge.' Touching the question of moral obligation so generally discussed by modern writers, we may notice that the Bible nowhere attempts to formulate a system of moral philosophy any more than it attempts to teach any merely physical science. A knowledge of the Spirit of God and Christ contains all; on this tree of life grew all the fruits of the Spirit. This is the secret of all true science and philosophy, for apart from the knowledge of the eternal Spirit in its truth, science and philosophy are only ' the wisdom of this world,' which ' is foolishness with God,' or it is ' the wisdom that knows not God.' It is the wisdom that still ' crucifies the Lord of Glory '; the same wisdom that is now named agnosticism and evolution by natural selection. Nevertheless, the revelation of the mystery of God is still ' Christ the power of God, and the wisdom of God.' The secret of true science or of true philosophy can only be found in the words of Christ, ' This is life eternal, to *know* Thee the only true God, and Jesus Christ whom Thou hast sent.' All must be looked at through the light of God, ' which lighteth every man that cometh into the world.' The solemn warning is still needed, ' Take heed that the light that is in thee be not darkness, for if the light that is in thee be darkness, how great is that darkness,' even if that light be named advanced science, or popular philosophy, and however plausible may be the reasoning with which it is presented.

In the Mosaic record of Creation there is no mention of the week or month. These two divisions of time seem to have had a religious origin. The day, month and year are definitely marked periods of time, but the week of seven days as a fourth part of a moon period is not so definite. Still, it was sufficiently definite to mark off four weeks of seven days, with every seventh as a day to be devoted to congregated worship of God by men, women and children. Man is not only a religious but also a social being. Indeed, in religion there is a social element, and therefore provision for united worship is necessary. Hence the need of both a sanctuary and a sabbath; a sanctuary wherein to meet and a day of general cessation from labour, so that all may have an opportunity of coming together. This is all recognized in the words, ' Ye shall keep My sabbaths and reverence My sanctuary, I am the Lord.' There is no special sanctity in any particular twenty-four hours, hence the command respecting the sabbath is so far arbitrary or positive; so the moral element in connection with the sabbath only arises because of the moral nature, the moral needs, and the moral and spiritual culture of man ; as Christ said, ' The sabbath was made for man, and not man for the sabbath.' The periods of the moon afforded opportunity for arranging special religious occasions.

The Bible, then, is specially a religious book, and all other matters are only introduced as they bear directly on this divine principle of man's nature. Hegel regards approvingly the ' Mosaic description of creation, when it quite naïvely reports : To-day arose the plants, to-day the animals, to-day man. Man has not developed out of animal, nor the animals out of the plant. Each is at once completely what it is.' He does not regard such an account as discordant with his philosophy. The only evolution he allows is the development or growth of the germ to the maturity of the individual, whether of plant, animal or man. Evidently here the life is God's life, and the day is God's day, wherein is the essence of every particular form of existence in external manifestation. The external form is the divine element of thought, and has its thorough, eternal, analogical reality in the internality of Thought, and of the Spirit in the divine image of man. This internal vision of the divine substantiality in man and Nature was first brought into human consciousness in the fullness of time by Christ, and was first given a logical philosophical form by Hegel and Stirling. The biblical record of creation, whether named fable, parable, allegory, sense-image, similitude, or however named, is a faithful and true presentation of the internal, eternal power of thought as the almighty creator of all things visible and invisible, so far as the external can represent the internal power of the universe, without entering into a thorough detailed logical explanation of the universal Being of the Ego in its spiritual particularity ; for nature in all its forms is none other than the work and manifestation of spirit, the Spirit of God, as the absolute personal self-consciousness of the universe. The kind of contemplation brought to the consideration of this record will show here, as in other matters, that wisdom is justified of her children. The eternal reality is in the depth of the divine and human, which reality was long shadowed forth by means of blood and sacrifice. It can be truly said that the law of animal sacrifice and blood was given because of spiritual blindness. The real vital element in blood is love and truth, as revealed to men in ' the agony and bloody sweat ' of Christ when He poured out His soul ' in strong crying and tears.' Christ ' came with water and blood,' so when the soldier with a spear pierced His side, 'forthwith there came out blood and water '—the outward symbol of His love. Dying love is the most intense, so ' the death of our Redeemer is the most intense event in history.' This reveals the core of Christianity. Unrequited love gives the greatest pain to the bestower, and this broke our Redeemer's heart. Paul comprehended the love of Christ most deeply. He says, ' I will very gladly spend and be spent for your souls, though the more abundantly I love you the less I be loved.' The external form of the words which declare Christ to be Creator are, like nature itself, perishable and subject to manifold contingency, while their spirit and truth are permanent and eternal. As in Judaism, so there is in the Christian religion an external transitory and an internal permanent reality. Their external forms however, must not on this account be trifled away. for therein the unessential is essential, just as the eternal Spirit must have an external manifestation, so it is written, ' By the word (thought) of the Lord were the heavens made, and all the host of them by the breath (Spirit) of His mouth.'

This enables us to see how what is named the ' mythus ' of creation in the Mosaic record may be viewed in a manner utterly false, as if it had no external objective reality, or may be regarded as a mere created fancy, falsely named a mere subjective idea of the intellect. In a certain respect, even the wildest freaks of fancy have an objective as well as a subjective existence. Thus a gold-man, as such, can have no real existence either objectively or subjectively, for, like so many other so-called ideas, it is only a foolish freak of fancy; yet both gold and man are at once real objective and subjective existences. A gold-man, however, is an illogical absurd putting together of two notions, which in the nature of things can never have a real actual existence as an object, for man cannot become gold, nor gold a man. ' A gold-man ' is not, then, a false statement because it is only subjective and not objective, but it is untrue simply because it is illogical, an absurd judgment, similar to the expression, ' a round-square.' The error has a still deeper source, and that is the supposition that an idea can be in the intellect without having an objective existence, whereas an idea is only such because in its true essential nature it is at once both objective and subjective. This is substantially Kant's ' Synthetic Judgment à priori,' and every category is a synthetic judgment, thought and matter, subject and object, internal and external, for one is impossible without the other. In a manner, Kant resuscitated the Idea of Plato and Aristotle, for with Aristotle an idea is an ' entelechy,' a principle of life, a something which as internal realizes itself in an external form. With Kant there were three unconditioned Ideas, the Soul, the World and God. Hegel saw that these three Ideas could be reduced to the one eternal logical ideal, and as such, in its completion, would form a complete system of the categories, ' a logic of pure reason as the realm of pure Thought.' The Mosaic account of creation, then, when properly understood, is not a mere subjective creation, but has its genuine philosophical and objective import and truth in the eternal form of the self-consciousness of God and man. Idea being an eternal living reality, to name any other conception an Idea is a misnomer. The Mosaic record of creation, then, is not necessarily an illogical subjective fancy, but may, and does, embody a true idea of the divine work of creation in its various forms. It is in no sense a legendary fabrication derived from Babylonian records, but a divinely-inspired account, and in harmony with sense-perception, and also with all the other Scripture. In any mode of speech the principal thing to notice is whether the idea embodied therein is true or false. The true idea is the logical thought, whether that thought is the absolute universal or is in the form of particular thoughts in the one universal thought. Particular thoughts are finite, as manifested in the particular forms of the existent world in their universal necessary relation, and consequently are in essential relation in the infinite Whole. Ideas are false when objects are presented in an illogical relation to each other without regard to their rational relation in pure reason in the Infinite Ego. Man can in his thought combine things in an irrational conception, for unreason stands in relation to reason in thought, just as lying and fraud stand in relation to truth and honesty. The illogical, the irrational, the immoral acts of thought always disorganize, disrupt, and produce confusion and pain in human society; if these were out of all relation to thought, they could do no harm and cause no pain. The true and false can be expressed in all modes of speech, fable, parable, allegory, irony, poetry and prose. Truth is perfect correspondence of thought in its particularity with absolute thought in its universality, as manifested in Christ. In philosophy it is the logical system of pure reason; but it cannot be expressed in its absolute fullness in any finite external mode of speech, for such external form is necessarily perishable, while truth is imperishable and absolute. Then what is the bearing of all this on the divine inspiration of the Bible and what is called the Higher Criticism? Verbal inspiration is denied, plenary inspiration is denied, the literal meaning of the word is set aside, it (the Bible) is not free from errancy, it is not infallible, it is not scientific, and it is even said that Christ and His apostles accommodated their teaching to the erroneous traditions from the past, and to the vague and erroneous opinions of their times. What does all this amount to? Is there any truth left? Surely there is something sadly wrong in this method of dealing with the Bible. The critics, however, allow that all recorded in the Bible is not utterly false, but they cannot agree as to what is trustworthy and what is not; they cannot say where error ends and truth begins. Even when the fullest authority is allowed to the teaching of Christ, they are still at a loss to say which is Christ's own and which is the evangelist's contribution to the record. Why these differences? The reason is, that their whole method of criticism is at fault. The written divine revelation must be verbal; take away the words and the revelation is destroyed. Plenary inspiration it must be, otherwise it is not God's revelation. Does divine, plenary and verbal inspiration, then, mean that every word and sentence must be perfect, that the thought can, under no circumstances, be more fully and clearly expressed? If so, we aver, no such inspiration is possible, nor is it necessary. Such an assumption is absolutely unwarrantable; neither the infallibility, nor the exact scientific quality of the teaching of the

Bible requires such assumptions. Exactly when, where, and by whom the various portions of the Bible were written ; when, where and how the canon was completed into its present form, are matters of very subsidiary importance. Such demands for a perfectly infallible and detailed record are unreasonable and cannot be answered. Even discrepancies in dates and other matters of fact do not weaken its divine authority, especially when we consider the numerous, various, manifold, contingent, accidental and chance circumstances it had unavoidably to pass through. Its substantial worth and reality are independent of these things. Even its scientific quality cannot be summarily set aside, for all knowledge is scientific that is true, and all untrue knowledge is unscientific. The scientific character of the Mosaic account of creation did not demand a full detailed description of the structure of all the various plants and animals, the chemical composition of rocks, nor the laws of motion of the heavenly bodies, nor does it require an explanation of how God made the entire universe and all its manifold parts. To have done all this would have required hundreds of volumes and would have been practically of no service, as far as we can see. The utility of a book does not depend on its extrinsic form, but on the use men are willing to make of it, as witness the almost universal neglect of the study of Aristotle's philosophy and of the teaching of the Lord Jesus Christ. With many sceptics and critics the want of enlightenment in the world is not due to the sinful intellectual indifference and moral perversity of man, but to the obscurity of the writings of the great departed, of our great divines, theologians and philosophers, such as Aristotle and Hegel, and especially to the defects of the Bible ! They study the Bible in a hopelessly wrong manner.

There is order and symmetry in the old traditional form, but the arrangement of the critics is confusion confounded. The mode by which they would lead us to the foundation and truth of the Bible resembles the analysing and dissecting of the hair, skin, flesh, blood and bones of a dog in order to know what a dog is. Such a process helps not in the least to a clearer knowledge of God, man, and the world, and this is what we most need to know. Knowledge is not untrue because it is in one sense small in degree, or superficial, just as a boy's knowledge of arithmetic is correct as far as it goes when he knows how to add, though he may not understand fractions. In the same way, we hold that the philosophy of creation as given by Moses is sound; since creation has its foundation and being in God, we have all at first required; a more perfect philosophic form could well afford to wait.

We have noticed that all men are born philosophers because they are rational beings. All men, however, do not fulfil their vocation. Hegel holds that philosophy in its fundamental principle is one, and that the different systems are only stages in the true evolution of logical philosophy. It would be a mistake, then, to regard the writers of the Bible, its commentators, and our theologians and scientists as in no sense philosophers. Their aim in the main has been to explain what might appear difficult for the general reader to understand, and so far as they reasoned correctly, their labours have been attended with much profit. But to the extent that their philosophy was defective, their exposition would be faulty in consequence of their attempts to make every part harmonize, both with every other part and *with* whatever untrue general conception they began. The theologian, on the other hand, aimed

23

CHAPTER XV

MOSES AND THE PENTATEUCH

NOTWITHSTANDING all that the critics have written to the contrary, we are firmly convinced that Moses was the real author of the Pentateuch. He may not have written all with his own hand. He may have had other writings and used them in a manner suitable to the divine purpose he had in hand. Our modern critics talk a great deal of scientific methods, but when we examine the results of more than a century's work, we see great disagreement. As Dr. Orr says : ' The critical school is rent within itself,' and it seems possessed with a ' mania for disintegration.' Such general chaos and uncertainty remain to us that Dr. Orr remarks, ' We are happy to allow them (the critics) to answer each other.' It is of no use appealing to the verdict of the majority of critics, or telling us that certain theories are now accepted by all scholars, for we find that the conclusions of these experts are continually changing. This they argue is necessary, as the present age is one of transition, but surely some definite result is to be expected after the work of more than a century ; we find, however, that what at one time is regarded as settled beyond doubt, is a few years later held to be quite unworthy of serious consideration. Until the time of Graf, the unity of the main part of Deuteronomy was generally regarded as firmly established.

Thus we find that Bleek, De Wette, Colenso and Driver all speak of the marks of unity to be found in this work. Now, however, it is broken up into fragments, each being the work, not of a single writer, but of a ' school.' With the later critics the main idea is to make the Pentateuch and the Bible as a whole ' fit in ' with the theory of evolution.

The Graf-Wellhausen theory is supposed now to have established firmly the ' date ' of the production or compilation of Deuteronomy as the reign of Josiah, about 622 B.C. It is stated that the parallelism, which they find to exist between the history of Israel and the gradual development of the religion and ritual, proves the late date of this book. Moses is entirely set aside as its author; by many he is not even held to be a historical character. The book is a pseudograph, produced or ' invented ' by either the priests or the prophets of the eighth or seventh century B.C. Space forbids us to enter fully into the question of the finding of the Book of the Law in the temple just prior to the Reformation of Josiah's reign. Dr. Orr deals with the whole of the critical theories and their results very thoroughly and convincingly in his *Problem of the Old Testament*, and to this book we would refer all serious students of Biblical criticism. We are convinced that a careful study of the Book of Deuteronomy from the point of view of a product of the time of Josiah shows such a position to be utterly untenable. These scientific critics show great readiness in accepting as ' probable,' hypotheses which, to an unbiassed mind, seem to be mere conjectures or ' bold guesses,' lacking any mark of truth. In this direction their faith is indeed great and can with little compunction even ' swallow whales,' though nothing can exceed their contempt towards the simple, ungrounded beliefs of the traditionalists. By the Graf-Wellhausen theory the whole History of the Jewish nation, as handed down through many centuries, is 'wiped out,' nothing certain being, however, substituted. Moses, David, Solomon, etc., are non-existent or unrecognizable ; then, why believe in Josiah or Ezekiel ?

Another essential discovery of this theory is the post-exilian origin of the Priestly Code, as given in part of Exodus, Leviticus, and Numbers. The critics declare that no trace of these ritual and ceremonial laws can be seen in Jewish History previous to the exile, while this history presents to the scientific student abundant evidence of the late origin of these laws. The Priestly Code is said to be based on Ezekiel's vision, though the two by no means coincide in their details. It is the work of a school of priests, who produced it during their exile in Babylon. About 444 B.C., Ezra presented this code to the assembled Israelites as the work of Moses. Strange to say, as Dr. Orr shows, no one demurs in the slightest to this new set of laws, but everything is taken for granted by the whole assembly, including priests, etc. This strikes us as very remarkable if the Code is quite new, and if, as some critics declare, nothing was previously known of the ark, the tabernacle, the great feasts, incense and other great institutions. On the other hand, those critics who hold that the scribes and Ezra simply codified old existing laws or ' praxis,' must admit that if we have no evidence of the existence of a previous code, neither have we evidence of an existing ' praxis.' Thus the argument from silence breaks down for them by proving too much, while certainly it must be allowed that a record would more likely speak of a custom rather than a code. Besides, though we may not be able to find many definite references in the historical record to the feasts and other details of the code, yet the whole record is saturated with priestly influence. Ezekiel's vision, above all, implies both for himself and his audience a thorough knowledge of the very code he is supposed to be instituting or introducing, and for which he claims Divine sanction as given by God to Moses. Incidental references in the record are regarded by Dr. Orr as very valuable evidence of the early existence of this Mosaic ritual. Another powerful point against the new dating for this code is the manner in which the historical atmosphere tells against the critics' argument. The ' wilderness ' or archaic surroundings are everywhere too evident to be a mere invention of post-exilian times, and the whole code is thoroughly unsuitable for the period in which the critics claim it to have been produced. Though Dr. Peake in his recent book, *The Bible*, repudiates the assumption that the critical (Graf-Wellhausen) theory is largely based on these two grounds, e.g. silence and historical parallelism, yet he devotes a whole chapter to the discussion of ' History as a Channel of Revelation.' We agree that history must be a channel of revelation, but much of what the higher critics present to us as history has very little foundation except in their own imagination. Read through one of their books, and before long you will be struck with the number of ' probables ' and ' mays,' etc., you will encounter. Their discoveries are paraded as science, yet nothing is certain. The Biblical Account is generally straightforward and clear, though often naïve to our modern ideas; thus the account of the reading of the law by Ezra is quite coherent and trustworthy as given, yet many critics now doubt the existence of Ezra as a person; to these he has become the mythical or ' ideal ' scribe. If there is no proof of the existence of Moses, or even of Ezra, what proof have we of the numerous redactors, compilers, ' schools,' etc., who are never referred to in the records. How could a school of writers possibly produce a work showing such marks of unity of thought as does this code ? As for the new dating of the books of the Pentateuch by the critics, a careful examination of their arguments shows that they are largely based on suppositions and require great credibility on our part.

In reality they claim that the ritual and ceremonies, so long imagined by Jews and Christians alike to be of special Divine origin, are due to the pagan influences surrounding the Jewish nation on all sides. This by no means explains why one nation has exercised the tremendous influence it undoubtedly has on the history of the world and on the development of Christianity, while the other nations have left little trace of their existence on the modern world. Since the critics have proved to their own satisfaction that Moses is not, and indeed could not have been in any sense the author of the Pentateuch, they now generally turn to the Babylonian and Egyptian records *as the ultimate sources*, not only of the ritual, etc., but also of the chief accounts, *e.g.* The Creation, The Fall, The Flood, etc., as given in Genesis.

It is impossible to attempt to follow all the intricacies of the whole critical system as now exhibited in their latest achievements, with their D^1, D^2, D^3, etc.; P^1, P^2, P^3, etc., their Elohist and Jehovist writers, different schools existing or continuing through many centuries, and the many fragments into which the books have been torn, not to mention numerous interpolations, etc. ; we must therefore confine ourselves to general broad philosophic principles.

Had not the critics for the most part been

honest men, and their work for that reason all the more misleading and evil in tendency, their arguments against the Mosaic authorship of the Pentateuch would not be worth considering. Rightly viewed, the evidence that Moses was the author is overwhelming. The best evidence is what the Bible tells us about Moses himself. Like Christ, he is a character at once ideal and real, not fancied. Considering the age and circumstances in which he lived, he was probably the grandest character, excepting Christ, that has ever appeared in human history. No man manifests more highly and divinely true inspired thought. In the light of his recorded character and work it is justly said of him, ' And there hath not arisen a prophet since in Israel like unto Moses, whom the Lord knew face to face ; in all the signs and wonders which the Lord sent him to do in the land of Egypt to Pharaoh, and to all his servants, and to all his land, and in all that mighty hand, and in all the great terror which Moses shewed in the sight of all Israel '

Moses is more intimately associated with Christ than any other prophet. He is the head of the old, as Christ is of the new and better covenant. ' The law was given by Moses, grace and truth came by Jesus Christ.' Moses is honoured by being present with Jesus on the Mount of Transfiguration. The saints are said to sing the Song of Moses, the servant of God, and the Song of the Lamb. It is also said, ' Moses verily was faithful in all his house, as a servant,' as ' Christ was faithful in His house as a son,' and he was inspired to declare, ' The Lord thy God will raise up unto thee a prophet from the midst of thee, of thy brethren like unto me ; unto him ye shall hearken.' ' I will raise them up a prophet from among their brethren like unto thee, and will put my words into his mouth ; and he shall speak unto them, all that I shall command him. And it shall come to pass that whosoever will not hearken unto my words which he shall speak in my name, I will require it of him.' These words, as quoted by Peter and Stephen, are so very important in their bearing on the Mosaic authorship of the Pentateuch, and especially of Deuteronomy, that we must quote them in full. ' For Moses truly said unto the fathers, A prophet shall the Lord your God raise up unto you of your brethren, like unto me ; him shall ye hear in all things whatsoever he shall say unto you. And it shall come to pass, that every soul, which will not hear that prophet, shall be destroyed from among the people' (Acts, chap. iii. verses 22, 23). ' This is that Moses, which said unto the children of Israel, A prophet shall the Lord raise up unto you of your brethren, like unto me ; him shall ye hear' (Acts chap. vii. ver. 37). The critics are not consistent when dealing with the terms ' letter,' ' spirit,' or literal, verbal and plenary inspiration. They disparage or uphold the letter and spirit, etc., according as they imagine them to be favourable or unfavourable to their own theories. Christ and His apostles only cared for the true meaning of the words. Luke, Peter and Stephen knew that the above words referred directly to Christ. To them the slight change in the phraseology was nothing, yet to the critics these direct references to Christ imply an impossible divine vision on the part of Moses. So the meaning given by Peter and Stephen must somehow be annulled. Either God could not have given such prophetic sight to Moses, or Peter and Stephen must have made too free a use of the real meaning of the words as understood by Moses ; or rather, such words were neither used nor written by Moses, even though Christ said of him, ' he wrote of Me,' for at any rate John, who wrote the fourth Gospel, says, ' Christ said, Moses wrote of Me.' The critics are hard pressed to reconcile to evolution either the fourth Gospel or the New Testament generally without belittling them. In their eyes all must bend, or give way to Darwinianism, or some other form of evolution by natural selection, or to some form of Agnosticism, however arbitrary.

As already shown in a previous chapter, the logical is the ideal principle of realism and is the only true method of interpreting either the Bible or Nature.

The logical principle of realism has its basis in man as the image of God. In this connection we may quote here what relates directly to the creation of man : ' And God said, Let us make man in our own image, after our likeness ; and let them have dominion over the fish of the sea, and over the fowl of the air, and over the cattle, and over all the earth, and over every creeping thing that creepeth upon the earth. So God created man in His own image, in the image of God created He him ; male and female created He them ' (Gen. chap. i. 26, 27). It is evident that man is only capable of dominion because he is in the image of God. The following words contain a fuller account of man's creation : ' And the Lord God formed man of the dust of the ground, and breathed into his nostrils the breath of life ; and man became a living soul.' Here we see that the body as the visible part of man is of the same material as the earth, while his soul is in essential relation with the Spirit of God, so that it can be said (slightly altering Thomson's words), ' Whose body nature is, and the Spirit of God and of man the soul.'

We know as a matter of fact that man on his divine side as the image of God is Ego, and therefore eternal, that his bodily structure is one with the dust of the ground, and therefore a creation in time, consequently not eternal. There is, however, a wide difference between an organized body as flesh, and matter in the form of dust. This difference involves a great transformation in the quality of matter. According to the Biblical narrative, the Lord God made man in full stature directly from the dust of the ground, and breathed into him the ' breath of lives,' and he became a living soul. Then the Lord God made woman in full stature from the rib of man, and Adam said, ' This is now bone of my bones, and flesh of my flesh; and he called his wife's name Eve, because she was the mother of all living.' They each;possessed the soul and spirit of lives, and bare children after their kind in the image of God. We see also a spiritual principle in the earth, for God said, ' Let the earth bring forth grass, the herb yielding seed, and the fruit tree yielding fruit after his kind, whose seed is in itself. Let the waters bring forth abundantly the moving creature that hath life.' The creation of man and woman alike was miraculous in that they began life in full bodily stature. Since then, men and women begin life as babes and sucklings; at the beginning it could not be so. The nature of marriage is based on the fact that the first woman was taken out of man : ' therefore shall a man leave his father and mother and shall cleave unto his wife; and they shall be one flesh.' The bond is spiritual; so even in the flesh there is a spiritual bond, and as such it is Christian. The bond of love between husband and wife is the same as that between Christ and His Church. It is the Church of Christ in Eden. So we are members of His body, of His flesh, and of His bones. ' This,' says Paul, ' is a great mystery,' now revealed to the world in Christ and His Church, God in man ; man in the image of God and in the image of Christ. Herein is seen the true realism of the true idealism.

We see the same real idealism in the words, ' We see Jesus, who was made a little lower than the angels for the suffering of death ' ; ' as children are partakers of flesh and blood,' ' also Himself likewise took part of the same,' ' for both He that sanctifieth and they who are sanctified are all of one, for which cause He is not ashamed to call them brethren.'

Some may object to the miracle of God making woman from the rib of Adam as being unscientific, but we hold that the denial of miracles is unscientific, while much more certainly can what Darwin claims as the origin of man be named unscientific. He says, ' Our ancestor was an animal which breathed water, had a swim bladder, a great swimming tail, an imperfect skull, and *undoubtedly* was a hermaphrodite '; then afterwards, ' the early progenitor of man was a catarhine monkey, covered with hair, its ears pointed and capable of movement, its foot prehensile, its body provided with a tail, and its habits arboreal.' And this is called science ! Surely it is more in harmony with true science to say that miracles are but a very special work of the Spirit of God.

Since the doctrine of evolution by natural selection has come into vogue it has become the fashion to insist on interpreting the content of every book of the Bible separately, so as to discover the degree of moral and theological truth contained in each without reference to the real content of earlier or later books. This is done to show that the teaching of the Bible harmonizes with the hypothesis of a natural gradual evolution in inorganic and organic nature in its infinite variety of forms. In this way it is attempted to prove that the fuller teaching of the New Testament is but a natural development from the Old

selves, What is earth ? What is air ? What are
water, life, soul and spirit ? What is the nature of
the power in the earth, plants and animals enabling
them to yield their kind ? (The term ' yielding,'
with the author of Genesis, is idealistic in its import.)
With these questions science and philosophy begin.

To the modern mind the theory of science is chiefly
confined to physics, and is based on what is named
universal gravitation and mathematics. It sees no
science in these three chapters (yet the science of
numbers is implied even in the words ' every,' ' all,'
and ' seven '). The spiritual or real idealism is dis-
carded. If logic is spoken of, it is only Inductive,
and empty, abstract, formal logic ; there is no recognition of Concrete Logic. The result is that the
nature of Thought and Reason is, in one sense, unknown ; in another, there is nothing more immediately
present to thought's own self. God, also, by the
modern mind is relegated to a region beyond experience. If God is believed in, it is a belief devoid of
real knowledge—a belief in an unknown God. This
is not the God of Abraham, of Moses, or of Christ, who
saw God face to face, and talked with Him as man
to man.

With Moses, the one universal life in all life was
spirit. With God, word and act were identical.
Moses saw the spiritual side of all sense-objects, and
he endured as seeing therein the invisible God. From
the time the angel of the Lord appeared to Moses
in a flame of fire in the bush and said, ' I am that
I am,' he saw God face to face in all things. God
appeared in sense-form, i.e. human form, as an angel,
just as He afterwards appeared as Christ born of a
woman. As an angel He, ' the God of Glory ' appeared
to Abraham, Isaac and Jacob, and also to Noah and
Enoch. It was evidently in this manner He showed

Himself to Adam and Eve when He talked to them in the garden. In both cases sense-sight was an aid to reason-sight.

It is often said, the three first chapters of Genesis cannot be understood literally, but the literal meaning of every word, whether written or spoken, is always spiritual. The true meaning can only be apprehended in and by the spirit. The spirit of things is only known by spirit. Face to face always means reason-vision, or intellectual insight, though it is always in some form associated with sense-perception. The words, soul, sight, sound, taste, smell, and touch, are spiritual in their meaning. Take away their deep meaning in thought and spirit, and they are nothing. True science properly means true insight into the meaning of anything. The visible and the invisible are always in essential unity ; the visible is immediate sense-sight, the invisible is always a matter of intellectual insight, and therefore spiritual. Again, mere sense-sight is always superficial knowledge, though it is true as far as it goes : or we may name it superficial science. The deeper the spiritual or intellectual insight into anything, the more truly can the knowledge be called scientific, that is, as distinguished from the knowledge of animals, which is mere sense-knowledge, for animal knowledge is not properly scientific. In man, sense-knowledge and understanding (spiritual insight) are always present in a greater or less degree.

For special forms of rational inspiration and work, a special providential means was required for the discipline and training of the men, to fit them for their difficult calling. This is very evident in the case of Moses, for no man was ever called to undertake a more difficult work than he. We have already noted the two main factors in his early education,

24

viz. his Egyptian education combined with the religious Hebrew instruction of his mother. His chief instructor afterwards was the Angel of the Lord. In both, sense lent aid to Reason.

To be a leader and law-giver to his people, was a mighty task imposed upon him, but to give in writing a real and ideal account of creation (the ideal is the spiritual and real), that is, of a real and ideal day, a real and ideal light, a real and ideal Sabbath, a real and ideal creation of man and woman, a real and ideal garden of Eden, a real and ideal tree of life in the midst of Eden, a real and ideal tree of knowledge of good and evil (for knowledge has both a good and an evil side), a real and ideal ' serpent of eternity' in self-consciousness wherein there is ' an invisible dividing line ' between truth and error, good and evil, right and wrong, sin and holiness, wisdom and folly, innocence and guilt, demanded a much higher divine inspiration. The line between educated pride and educated humility is very subtle and invisible to mere sense-perception, just as is the case with the line between thought with and thought without love, since the essence of true thought is love, for with God and man thought and love are one. It is only in the invisible line between the divine and human that the veil of guilt and sin can enter and dim man's intellect. Shame, and the need of clothing is the natural, that is, the spiritual outcome of guilt and sin, as also of the spiritual pride of intellect. An educated intellect which is full of pride is the darkest and most perverted. It prides itself that it is ' rich and increased in goods, and hath need of nothing,' whereas it is wretched, miserable, poor and blind and naked. Christ counsels men of such disposition to seek the true wisdom, not the wisdom of the world, which is foolishness with God. He says:

'Buy of Me gold tried in the fire that thou mayest
be rich, and white raiment (of righteousness) that
thou mayest be clothed, that the shame of thy naked-
ness do not appear, and anoint thine eyes with eye-
salve (of love) that thou mayest see.'   Here we have
a very striking blending of sense and reason-vision
like that which we see in Moses in the record of the
first three chapters concerning God, man, and the
universe.

The garden of Eden is no true Paradise without
the presence of God in the human soul.   God in
Nature, then, is the tree of life.   Further, there could
be no true garden of Eden without the tree of knowledge of good and evil.   Without the presence of
these two trees in the garden, man could not be man.
There cannot be a tree of life without a tree of knowledge.   The tree of knowledge is at once the tree of
life and death.   The fruit of knowledge may be truth
or error, virtue or vice, good or evil, holiness or sin,
nourishment or poison.   There is good in everything
because there is a divine side to everything, for every
creature of God is good.   Things are only evil to
man when he regards their real value as having no
essential relation to the Spirit of God ; this is so
when ' knowledge puffeth up.'   All knowledge has
its common root in thought, or the Ego, wherein
all things have their identity.   Kant suggested
that sense-knowledge, understanding and reason
have one common root.   In this he was right.
Sense-knowledge consists in a boundless variety of
sights, sounds, tastes, smells, and touches.   These
have, however, their unity in man's infinite thought,
the image of the invisible God.   In thought we see
the finite spirit in immediate unity with Nature and
the Absolute Spirit of God.   Dr. Stirling says: 'It
is in this perfect generality of views that we should

wish that the serpent of Eternity, which self-consciousness is, should be seen as the underlying prescriptive and determinative form of all.' Ego in all this dividedness of self-consciousness ' is fabled ' in the common serpent in its subtle, wriggling movements. Paul said : ' I fear lest by any means, as the serpent beguiled Eve through his subtility, so your minds should be corrupted from the simplicity that is in Christ.' Pride is a subtle feeling, it may pass almost imperceptibly from a noble self-esteem to a vain self-conceit ; just as truth and error, good and bad thoughts have their seat and source in thought itself : there is a subtle line between them, nevertheless. ' Woe to them that call evil good and good evil, that put darkness for light and light for darkness.' Man in his search for knowledge and wisdom is apt to be led astray by the pride of intellect. Love and the harmlessness of the dove alone can keep him from the paths of error and sin. Adam and Eve were led astray by false pride of knowledge, and pleasure in mere sense-objects. They became possessed of shame, then of the feeling of guilt. Their guilty conscience dispossessed them of Eden, and became a flaming sword turning every way, preventing them from realizing and retaining the true knowledge of the tree of life. The mere subtle wisdom of the serpent causes men to eat the dust and grovel therein, notwithstanding their knowledge, for apart from a true knowledge of God, though they are ever learning, they never come to *a knowledge of the Truth.* Isaiah says of such, ' Thy knowledge and thy wisdom hath perverted thee.'

The critics seem to regard the progressiveness of the divine revelation as only consistent or in harmony with the hypothesis of evolution, but not at all consistent with the traditional view of the Biblical historical record. Having accepted evolution as if it were something more than a mere hypothesis, they think the progressive unfolding of revelation confirms the theory of evolution, and removes what they consider the more serious moral difficulties of the Bible. But admit the existence of God, and the moral difficulties remain in full force. On the other hand, the traditional view never held that the later books did not contain a fuller divine revelation than the earlier concerning moral and religious truth, or that there was not a continual unfolding of doctrine bearing on the way of human salvation. The unfolding of the great law of spiritual sacrifice was slow and difficult to bring into man's consciousness. No law is so difficult to reveal to the spiritually blind. To men blinded by sin and guilt, it appears foolishness. Such blindness can only be overcome, for the most part, by the individual passing through a long process of severe painful discipline. It is an utterly mistaken view of the progressiveness of revelation to regard it as one with any of the modern theories of evolution, or to confound personal choice with ' natural selection,' the ' struggle for existence ' with the conflict between right and wrong, truth and error, good and evil, or ' the survival of the fittest ' with the final triumph of righteousness in the world. Though these partial resemblances are made to have a plausible appearance, they are illusory, and an example of how Satan appears as an angel of light, deluding the unwary from the path of truth, deceiving the very elect. The later critical theories are almost entirely based on the theory of evolution by natural selection ; they, in the main, stand or fall together. Then they are made to rest on the belief that the Priestly Code did not in any way depend on a divine sanction or command. This may be admitted respecting the pre-Mosaic altars and sacrifices without denying that the Levitical ritual was such as God commanded Moses. But having accepted evolution, it became quite natural for the critics to suppose the Priestly Code to be an invention of the priests, and this, together with evolution, is why they (the critics) have proposed a later date than the time of Moses for the entire production of the Pentateuch. The central principle of the Levitical ritual is sacrifice (the core of which is blood, life, spirit, love and truth), the altar, the priesthood, and all other ceremonial laws being subsidiary to this main idea, Holiness to the Lord.

The origin of animal sacrifice is a little obscure; still, it is not difficult to see that it has an intimate relation to man's sense of guilt and sin (for to have a sense of sin is not the same in the sight of God as to have a knowledge of good and evil,) and the need of doing something to please God and to obtain His favour and forgiveness. The choice of evil is the fall. Animal sacrifice evidently arose spontaneously from this felt need, for we find no direct evidence in Scripture that the offerings of Cain and Abel were commanded by God, or that Noah, Abraham, and the rest of the patriarchs built their altars to God in obedience to His commands. Sacrifice had become a general custom to which they conformed, and God accepted their offerings when presented in sincere faith. As the offerings meant the giving up to God of something valuable on the part of the offerer, they became a symbol of true worship. We have full evidence, however, that, in the wilderness, sacrifices were reduced to a complete system by Moses at the command of God, and purified from everything base and unholy that was associated with the iolatrous worship of other nations; hence every offering was required to be clean, without blemish, and of the best. It is evident that the whole system of animal sacrifice was only provisional and, at best, intended to indicate the true law of spiritual sacrifice.

If Abraham was to be the father of the faithful, it was necessary that his faith should be tried in the severest manner. The only way at that time in which this could be done was by the sacrifice of his only son, and to test his obedience, God commanded him to do this. Abraham's faith in God was so clear that he believed He would raise Isaac from the dead. It was not as an atonement for sin that God commanded him to do this, but to test his faith, for it is impossible for the blood of animals or the blood of children to take away sin. The sacrifice of Abraham, and indeed the whole system of the Mosaic sacrifice, was only intended to shadow forth the true meaning of spiritual sacrifice. So it is written, ' Sacrifice and offering Thou wouldst not, but a body hast Thou prepared me,' ' In burnt offerings and sacrifices for sin Thou hadst no pleasure. Then, said He, lo, I come to do Thy will, O God.' ' He taketh away the first, that He may establish the second.' ' This Man, after He had offered one sacrifice for sins for ever, sat down on the right hand of God.' ' For by one offering He hath perfected for ever them that are sanctified,' which is the putting of His laws into their hearts and minds. The real reason why God, by the hand of Moses, sanctioned and commanded animal sacrifices, is the same as that given by Christ in relation to divorce—' the hardness of their hearts.' The Mosaic law was intended as a schoolmaster, to bring them to Christ, to fit them to offer themselves a spiritual sacrifice to God, to write His laws in their minds and hearts.

It has always been most difficult to teach men the

need of true repentance and the true nature of spiritual self-sacrifice. At the best animal sacrifice was a poor substitute, and by itself necessarily weak, although in connection therewith the necessity of being holy, as God was holy, and likewise of having just balances and measures, was impressed upon the Jewish nation. They were forbidden to imitate in any way the idolatrous practices of other nations, and were required to hearken to, and to keep all the commandments of, the moral law. If they refused, God said, ' I will break the pride of your power, and will punish you '; if they obeyed, He would ' bless them in their substance.' Thus the moral or spiritual law and the law of animal sacrifice were never separated, yet through unbelief their minds were blinded, and comparatively few repented and followed the Lord fully. In one sense, this is not to be wondered at, for even under the clear light of the Gospel of Christ, few truly repent. Yea, even the Christian Church has for the most part failed to see the true spiritual cross of Christ ; instead of being spiritualized, it has been materialized and sensualized. Its essence is to suffer with Christ, in the same spirit, for the same purpose and end—not only in the manner of His death, but of His life, while we live, for His cross reached from birth to death. Paul says, ' I am crucified with Christ.' He does not mean here the death of the body, for he adds, ' nevertheless, I live '; then he feels as if he had said too much, for he adds, ' yet not I, but Christ liveth in me.' His I is Christ's I, Christ and he are one, so he adds again, ' The life I now live in the flesh I live by the faith (Christ in me is my true self) of the Son of God, who loved me, and gave Himself for me.' The cross, then, is ' the law of the spirit of life in Christ Jesus,' that ' hath made me free from the law of sin and death.' The ' law of sin and death ' is, ' whosoever will save his life shall lose it,' and ' the law of the spirit of life in Christ Jesus ' is, ' whosoever will lose his life for My sake shall find it.'   This, again, is the law of spiritual sacrifice, and consists in the knowledge of the truth (for to know God is to know the Truth) as it is in Jesus. ' This is life eternal, to know Thee the only true God, and Jesus Christ whom Thou hast sent.'   The real cross, the real sacrifice, is to-day little known even in what are called the Free Churches, and much less in the Anglican, Roman and Greek Churches.   The teaching of Christianity is that the entire virtue of the blood of Christ lies in His Spirit and life.   It is written, ' For if the blood of bulls and of goats, and the ashes of an heifer sprinkling the unclean, sanctifieth to the purifying of the flesh ; how much more shall the blood of Christ, who through the *eternal Spirit* offereth Himself without spot to God, purge your conscience from dead works to serve the living God.'   ' It is the spirit that quickeneth ; the flesh profiteth nothing ; the words that I speak unto you, they are spirit, and they are life.'

The Mosaic law and the Levitical ritual were evidently intended to be only provisional.   The critics, in order to make evolution fit in with the history, doctrine and morality of the Old Testament, have made a complete mass of confusion of the teaching of the Bible.   They have endeavoured to prove an evolution of religious thought through ancestor worship, human sacrifices, and the worship of images, to monotheism.   With all deference to the honesty of the critics, we say that to call this mode of reasoning scientific is absurd.   To anyone free from the evolution bias, nothing is more evident than that the Bible teaches that man was at first a monotheist, and not a polytheist, much less that he was a totemist or animist. It only proves how prone educated men are to imagine a vain thing, just as many of the learned Greeks wrote ' swelling words of vanity.' The same applies to the learned Rabbis of whom Christ said, ' In vain do they worship Me, teaching for doctrines the commandments of men ' and ' reject the commandment of God,' thus by their interpretation ' making the word of God of non-effect.'

The statement that ' the fall of man is the birth of conscience ' is equally absurd. The term ' fall ' naturally implies a descent from a higher to a lower state of moral excellence. Only a being with a conscience can fall into sin, and such is a higher form of being than one without a conscience. Animals have no conscience, and so can have no sense of guilt and sin. Guilt implies a knowledge of good and evil and an evil choice. Shame is caused by choosing evil rather than good. No being who does not think the infinite, that is, who does not think God, has a conscience knowing good and evil. The thought of God in man is the universal and essentially necessary basis of all theologies and christologies, whether such be true or untrue. Nay, the thought of God, as infinite, is the basis of polytheism and all mythologies. With the Greeks Zeus was recognized as ' the father of gods and men,' thus man as infinite-thought was, with the great philosophers of Greece, the measure of all things. Thus Aristotle says, ' God is a living being, perfect and eternal. Life eternal and enduring being belong to God. And God is that.'

The idea of God is at once truth and goodness. What is theoretically true is good, is love, for what is not good is not true, either in theory or in practice. What is evil in practice is false in theory. Man as finite, though in thought infinite, knowing moral good and moral evil, can in thought choose to do evil, which, as a matter of fact, he does. In such choice we have the fall of man and the origin of polytheism and of every form of sin that arises therefrom. The foundation of all morality and true religion is in the *love of God,* who is at once both truth and love, which unity is thus expressed in the words, ' Thou shalt love the Lord thy God.' Man only truly loves himself and his brother when he truly loves God with all his heart. Only so does he realize his true manhood. In the highest and fullest sense this is only attained by the witness of God's Spirit in truth and love in theoretical experience. Man can have the same assurance of his oneness with God as he has that twice two are four, or that every effect has a cause ; this is the absolute goal of logical philosophy. Such philosophy is possible because man's thought is infinite. Herein is the Christian religion, the religion and morality of reason.

Illogical philosophy is what Paul calls ' the wisdom of this world and of the princes of this world, that comes to nought,' ' for the wisdom of this world is foolishness with God.' It is also what he names, ' science falsely so called.' On the other hand, logical philosophy is what he calls ' the wisdom of God ' as distinguished from ' the wisdom of men,' or worldly wisdom as distinct from divine wisdom. No one can dispute that there is a false wisdom and a true, just as there is a false and a true knowledge, for the knowledge of truth is not the same as the knowledge of error. Logical philosophy, then, is the same as a knowledge of wisdom. So with Paul, ' Christ is the power of God and the wisdom of God,' ' the wisdom which God ordained before the world unto our glory.' Christ is the wisdom ' by whom He made the worlds.' ' He that is joined to the Lord is one Spirit,' is the

THE PHILOSOPHY OF SPIRIT

principle of Paul's philosophy. Logical philosophy
alone is true science. The seat and basis of all
science is the manifestation of God in the Finite
Spirit of man, wherein man as spirit is in thought
infinite. Apart from the infinite thought in man, no
conscious wisdom, no true philosophy, no real knowledge of God, Christ or Man, no particular science
of any department of nature or any branch of mathematics, is possible. If man's thought were not
infinite he would not be a person—only an animal.
(See chapters on The Ego, and Concrete Logic.) It
is one of the most absurd freaks of human thought
for any man professing to be a scientific philosopher
to speak of 'an Infinite and Eternal Energy from
which all things proceed,' and then to declare that
'personality implies limitation,' and consequently
that 'man, as person, in his thought is not Infinite.'
Was there ever a more glaring logical contradiction?
Yet the same would-be philosophers can talk loudly
of universal gravitation, and of an infinite and eternal
energy, whereas the Universal has no true meaning
if it is not infinite. Infinite thought is alone the true
concrete universal. It is utterly illogical to say
'we possess personality imperfectly.' This is the
latest outcome of the so-called advanced scientific
agnosticism and evolution by natural selection.
Human thought, as already stated, is at once Infinite
and Finite, at once all, many and One. As One, it
is absolute Monotheism. In all nations and tribes,
ancient or modern, in every form of polytheism there
is a recognition, more or less dim or clear, of one
universal supreme spirit ruling over all. It is the
universal presence of this thought, however dim,
that renders the darkest tribes accessible to the
teaching of Christian missionaries.

A theoretical experience of God is, as we have said,

the absolute goal of logical philosophy. The Fall of Man, then, is the moral perversion of conscience, the real cause of his fall from monotheism to polytheism. It is the moral aberration of human thought which has led men to call error truth, ' to love darkness rather than light,' since ' every one that doeth evil hateth the light.' This moral aberration is the condemnation of the world. The moral-perverted conscience does ' not like to retain God in its knowledge.' It could not wholly rid itself of such knowledge, so it changed the truth of God into a lie. Having lost the clear vision of the real nature of universal reason-thought, man changed the image of the incorruptible God into images of corruptible sense-objects. Paul, the great monotheistic Christian philosopher, gives the true logical philosophy of the origin of polytheism. ' When they knew God,' their morally defiled conscience led them into vain reasoning, and so ' they glorified Him not as God.' Reason-thought is the Infinite and Eternal Divine principle in man which constitutes him a person in the image of God. The body of man, though exquisitely organized, is only a corruptible image, and is in no real sense an image of the infinite and eternal God. It is in man's intellect alone that the true image of God is found. Man's thought is infinite because it includes and overlaps all limits, all finites; only so is man Ego, person, the real Image of God. The thought of man as a person contains the three essential moments of the Godhead—he is at once a singular self-consciousness, a particular self-consciousness, and a universal self-consciousness; or, person stands for one single man, for all men, and then it stands for the Lord Jesus, who ' is the express image of His person, the image of the invisible God,' and for God, the universal supreme personality. Since man in his thought overlaps all personalities, that is, his thought includes all that is, or thought is all (universal), many, one, man as a person, as an Ego, is a perfect image of God, and God is the perfect image of the personality of man. Man cannot but think God is infinite, because his own thought is infinite. Nothing but a sinful conscience has blurred the mind to this great fact. The science of logic is the scientific exposition of the threefold unity ' of man and nature with the Spirit that is God.' The philosophies of Hegel and Stirling are thus fundamentally one with the monotheism of Paul and Moses, as revealed in the Pentateuch.

If philosophy is the science of Divine Wisdom, as I believe it is, then I believe Moses and Paul are the two most divinely inspired philosophers that ever lived. They had each a specially unique providential training for their great work, Moses for the establishment of the Law of the old covenant which made the Hebrews a nation ; and Paul for laying the foundation of the new covenant of grace and truth in Christ Jesus on a logical basis. But in what does logical inspiration consist ?

First, there is in man the threefold unity of the light of intuitive infinite thought, intuitive reflection and intuitive logical Reason. Second, the mind must be honestly open to receive the bright shining light of the everlasting God. There is no Reflection without intuition, and no Logical Reason without intuition and Reflection. Moses and Paul possessed these three functions of the intellect essential to divine inspiration in a pre-eminent degree. In inspiration the mind is both active and passive. In reference to the Bible as a divine revelation, we may notice that attention is constantly called to its anthropomorphisms as evidence of its human origin and its consequent liability to error in dealing with the nature of God as the Infinite and Absolute. We may ask, Why is the anthropomorphic character of books on the various sciences, such as Algebra, Geometry, Astronomy, Chemistry or Arithmetic never mentioned ? Are they not of human origin ? Is it not because they are recognized as exact sciences, while the science of logic, or rather, logical philosophy, is not so recognized, although it is just as much so as any of the others ? In the true sense all science is anthropomorphic as the outcome of the human discovery of the so-called laws of nature or of the exact sciences. But Concrete Logic or the science of concrete thought as the science of reason, is as yet almost entirely unknown or is believed to be impossible. Although philosophy as a demonstrated science of concrete thought or reason was completed nearly a century ago by Hegel, yet even now it is maintained that the special problems of the Bible may be discussed without regard to questions of philosophy. All criticism of either the Old or the New Testament that discards philosophy as the science of absolute truth must end in failure. If human personality is held to be limitation, then man can in no sense ever know God, and if the doctrine of evolution is true science, then there is no true standard of morality. To say that human personality implies limitation is to ignore the obvious fact that man is absolutely sure, that is, sure beyond doubt, that the infinite thought he thinks did not begin at his birth and will not cease with the death of his body. It is the thought that never was not and never will not be, but always was and always will be ; yet ' the mystery of personality ' is absurdly said to be revealed in the ' subconscious mind.' (The term ' subconscious ' is utterly misleading.) Simply realize what infinite or self-consciousness means, and the mystery of personality, both of God and man, is at once revealed. If the personality of man meant limitation only, the term infinite would have no rational meaning, but be only a senseless name. Even a stone in its essential unity with universal gravitation unconsciously transcends all limitation, but man in his thought consciously transcends all limitation even in his idea of universal gravitation, for he knows that it means universal attraction and universal repulsion. Thus the idea of personality is identical with the idea of the absolute infinity of God. The idea of God as the everlasting God, the Creator and Righteous Judge of all the earth, and of man in the image of God, possessed by Abraham, Isaac, Jacob, and Moses, as given in Genesis and the other four books of the Pentateuch, is more moral and spiritual than the idea of God and man held by the evolutionists and agnostics. With them it is evidently right and proper for the strong and best to crush the weak; yet the weakest may be the fittest to survive, and those which do survive may be the worst. Their theory justifies all the cruel persecutions of all the true and good by the multitudinous, undeveloped, morally bad. It justifies our cruel treatment of the natives in South Africa, from the Cape to the Zambesi, and our late war with the Boers. Cecil Rhodes professed to be helping God, according to the doctrine of evolution. Many advocated the Boer war on the same principle. Indeed, if evolution by blind natural selection were true, all the crimes and sins of this and every other country could not be condemned, for the simple reason that the people were not sufficiently evolved to see the evil of their doings, and that the God of some evolutionists was too helpless to prevent them, whilst the God of another class is no God at all but pure naturalism. The Bible account of sin fixes the responsibility of the practice of evil on man, who has a knowledge of good and evil. Even if sin has blinded the minds of men to much that is evil, if they would only do the good they know and abstain from the evil, the whole condition of things would soon be changed for the better.

Contrary to the teaching of the Bible, the dominant teaching of the agnostics and evolutionists throws the blame of moral evil, sin and crime on men's social environment instead of on man's moral choice, and overlooks the fact that all environment is made by man. What higher motive can be presented to man than that of using the means God has given him to reform himself and to do his best in helping to reform others; in other words, for man ' to love God with all his heart, soul, mind and strength, and his neighbour as himself.' It is not possible in the nature of things to avoid condemning and punishing wrong-doing. If wrong-doing were not condemned and punished by men, we should soon have hell upon earth. To condemn is in complete harmony with the will of God as revealed in the Old and New Testaments, and is at the same time the dictate of reason. Although punishment of itself is no remedy for an evil heart of unbelief, it is in part a great protection of the upright and of the weak citizens. ' Is God unrighteous who taketh vengeance ? ' If so, how can God judge the world ? or how otherwise can society protect itself from reprobate evil doers ? Righteous laws are liberties; thus good civil government is necessarily based on righteousness, and man's power of choice.

As already intimated, the God of the Pentateuch is more moral and spiritual, and more accordant with sound logical philosophy, than the God of the Agnostic

25

evolutionist. One of the latest exponents of the God of agnosticism and evolution gives his idea of God in the following words : ' When I say God, I mean the mysterious power which is finding its expression in the universe and is present in the tiniest atom of the wondrous whole.' Who can suppose this to be a more satisfactory view of God than that given by Moses ?

CHAPTER XVI

EGO—ONTOLOGY AND IMMORTALITY

IT is necessary to explain a little more fully some of the more important points in connection with our main theme, but before doing so we must call attention to the generally recognized proofs for the existence of God : the teleological, cosmological, and the ontological. All three ' proofs ' depend on, and centre in, a right understanding of the Ego in the triplicity of Thought as the Absolute Ratio of the totality of Being; they form a triple unity in Thought, while in a special and fundamental sense the ontological includes the two former proofs.

Ontology is substantially one with Thought as Absolute Ratio of all existence, for the absolute ratio is the universal ratio that contains all ratios, just as the absolute, universal, concrete notion contains all particular notions, and the universal reason contains all particular reasons. The Absolute Ego contains all Egos, the absolute Idea all ideas, the absolute self-consciousness all self-conscious beings, the universal Personality all personalities, while thought, as thought, is the universal ' all in all,' containing all that is. Thought, then, is the Absolute and Infinite. It is the Absolute because it contains all relativity. An absolute that is not relative is a mere empty name—nothing at all. Thought is Infinite because it contains all finites. An Infinite that contains no finite is like an absolute without relativity, a mere empty name. Thought, then, as self-consciousness, as personality, is essentially Being, and is the only form of Being that is intelligibly conscious of itself as at once both Absolute and Infinite. In the highest sense, it is the only absolute Ratio, because it and it alone knows itself as both Subject and Object, as at once I and Me; I as subject, me as object, including all that is, for without a created universe, thought as Ratio, I as subject, me as object, would be mere empty names. There is, and can be, only one Infinite, just as there is only one Absolute, and though the two terms express different thoughts, they have their unity and identity in Thought as the Absolute Ratio. This being so, it follows that absolute notion, absolute idea, absolute reason, absolute spirit, and absolute personality have each and all their perfect and absolute identity in Thought as the all-embracing middle term of the entire universe. It is impossible that there ever was, or ever can be, anything better, greater, or more perfect than Thought. It is the absolutely perfect Being—the all-knowing, perfect love, truth and righteousness. There is nothing more tender and more powerful than Thought. Thought is the absolute Creator, Preserver and Governor of the universe, and that is God, with man ' in the image of God.' As man in his substantial and essential nature is thought, reason, self-consciousness, spirit, and a person, so God is thought, reason, self-consciousness, Spirit, the absolute personality of all personalities, the First and the Last, and that is the Ego of all Egos. Thought is the infinite and absolute being of man, therefore it is at the same time the infinite and absolute Being of God. It is the Being present in man than which he cannot think a greater and more perfect to exist, and which he cannot but think to be a present and eternal actual existence ; for to think otherwise would be the same absurdity as to think that man himself does not exist, since he cannot imagine himself to be non-existent. Thought as a matter of fact is real actual Being which no man can think not to exist ; it is that which never was non-existent.

Thinking-reason, conscious rational thought, then, is the ontological argument for and proof of the existence and being of God. It is that thought or idea, which is at once both subjective and objective, and of which man, in spite of all his vain imagination, cannot rid himself, any more than he can rid himself of the idea of an external, visible world of sense. Nay, the latter is finite, changeable, perishable, while the former is infinite, unchangeable, imperishable, eternal ; to which we may apply the words of Paul, while ' the outward man perishes, the inward man is renewed day by day.' The outward is the created ; the inward, the uncreated. The outward ' waxeth old as doth a garment ' ; the inward is ' the same yesterday, to-day, and for ever.' They, however, are so linked together, that the former has its subsistence and consistence entirely in the latter. The world, in its ceaseless coming to be and ceasing to be, is in its whole and in all its parts totally dependent on the necessary activity and free creative power of thought. Thus the science of the world or universe may be named cosmology, which proves that not only is one part dependent on every other, but also that design and purpose pervade the whole, down to the smallest cognizable particle.

In design, everywhere manifest, we are brought face to face with the teleological argument for the proof of the existence of God. When closely examined, it is soon seen that teleology, cosmology, and ontology, as sciences, are mutually dependent, or as Dr. Stirling says, ' The three proofs are but the single wave in the rise of the soul, through the Trinity of the Universe up to the unity of God,' and that is, ' the triple unity of Man and Nature with the Spirit of God.' Therefore God is Thought, and Thought is man in whom all being is : the Ego, the identity of the divine and human nature. This identity may be illustrated by light as the universal medium of sense-sight. As every person in sense-vision sees through the medium of the same identical light, so each apprehends and reasons in and through the medium of the same identical thought. There is not a special and particular different kind of light for every particular person, neither is there a special individual kind of thought and reason for every individual person. Light in an important sense is universal, pervading even the most dense and solid bodies, though it does not appear so to ordinary sense-sight. The fact of this universality is corroborated by the action of the so-called ' X ' rays and of radium. Sense-sight varies in fullness according to the greater or less perfection of the eye, but the universality of thought and reason is a matter of certainty in man's immediate reflective consciousness. Observation tells us that light, like thought, has its centre everywhere, and is everywhere active in every direction at the same time, just as universal gravitation is admitted to have its centre of attraction and repulsion in every direction, everywhere, at the same time. Further, just as speculative philosophy assures us of the infinite activity of thought and reason, crossing harmoniously in every direction, everywhere, at the same time, so wireless telegraphy in connection with experimental science confirms the great spiritual fact of existence : that Thought is the Absolute Ratio and middle term of the entire universe. There seems to be no doubt that, if in a great city a generator and receiver were placed in each house, different messages could be sent to, and received from, every house at one and the same time. However valuable the conception of universal ether, gravitation and electricity may be, they cannot bring into the light of consciousness the hidden secret of the universe. This secret can only be found in a Being whose absolute nature is conscious, thinking reason. This is not ' natural law in the spiritual world,' but spiritual law in the natural world, therefore the mode of contemplation must not be, ' look through Nature to Nature's God,' but rather, look through God to Nature. Then Nature will be seen in all its glory as the external manifestation of the thought, reason and mind of God.

Since Thought is the absolute Being of God and man, it is, when properly understood, what the Bible calls the direct witness of the Spirit of God in the spirit of man. When so understood, the ontological contains both the teleological and cosmological proofs, implicitly and explicitly the fullness of design in a rationally created world ; and such a world is ours, though necessarily subject to manifold contingency. As Christ controlled and overcame all contingency, so men, when brought ' into the unity of the faith, and knowledge of the Son of God, unto the perfect man, unto the measure of the stature of the fullness of Christ,' are able to control and overcome all contingency, even as Paul, who said, ' I can do all things through Christ which strengtheneth me.' Man, however, can only attain to his perfect stature by realizing in himself the love of God as manifested in the Lord Jesus Christ. That is the love which ' makes itself of no reputation, takes upon itself the form of a servant, and humbles itself and becomes obedient unto death, even the death of the cross.' There is no other way of obtaining redemption from sin and ignorance, for it is only through the knowledge and experience of the love of God in Christ that man can have within himself a knowledge of the clear conscious fellowship with the Father, and with His Son Jesus Christ. As a matter of fact, love is as much a matter of thought, reason, or logical philosophy as any other subject can be, for God is at once the unity of love and thought.

Before leaving the consideration of Absolute Being, we must call attention to an erroneous criticism of Mansel's thereon. He quotes the following from Hegel: ' What kind of an Absolute is that which does not contain all that is actual, even evil included?' On this he remarks: ' We repudiate the conclusion with indignation; but the reasoning is unassailable.' We ask, why repudiate the conclusion if the reasoning is unassailable? Is not evil a fact of present existence? Where else can it be if not in Absolute Being? Mansel's repudiation of Hegel's statement and reasoning arises from two misconceptions: first, he misunderstands the real nature of the Absolute; second, he failed to grasp the real nature of Hegel's Concrete Logic as the Science of Thought. After what we have said on Mansel elsewhere, we need only remark here, that as the concrete logic begins from the Concrete Notion or Ego, so we repeat, the Notion is Absolute Thought and Being, and must contain a *knowledge* of good and evil, and it is therefore impossible to know good without knowing that *evil* is the absolute opposite of good; but it is not necessary for God as the Absolute to be or do evil in order to *know* what is evil. Absolute thought can necessarily only be good and rational;

evil is unreason; and the practice of evil can only exist as a possibility in the finite contingency of created, finite, moral beings; yet even so, evil, as well as unreason, can have no existence without having some relation to Absolute Thought and Being, just as all forms of transitory being are in necessary relation to Absolute Eternal Thought. This does not imply that evil actions are an absolute necessity in rational beings, but only that evil, whether as a fact of knowledge, or as a fact of practice, is included in Absolute Being. This is evidently the reason why Hegel names evil as the absolute *Schein* of negativity. Sin is real evil, but it can be abolished, while evil, as the negative of good, cannot. Evil is a mere contingency which may or may not be sin as a voluntary act, in a finite, rational, moral being. A moral being is only such in and through his knowledge of good and evil, whether he maintains his moral uprightness or not, and he does not cease to be a moral being because he yields to the practice of moral evil, for which he cannot but, according to his light, condemn himself. Hegel says, ' Circumstances and motives master a man only as far as he yields to them. He who appeals for excuse to such influences, only degrades himself into a thing of nature; his act is his own, not that of somebody else, not the effect of something external to him.'

We have said, there is only one infinite, which as such includes all that is. We speak rightly of infinite space, infinite time, of the Absolute as infinite, of infinite quality and quantity, and of many other infinites; still the real Concrete Infinite includes all such infinites, and as such the Absolute is Infinite because it includes all relativity, and therefore Thought, in the highest and most perfect sense, is Infinite, because it alone knows itself as such. The Absolute as Thought, then, knowing itself in its relativity, alone furnishes the true conception of Reason, because it is essentially, absolutely relative ; man without this conception could not be a rational being. Thus the conception, in a self-conscious being, of the Concrete Infinite, is the fundamental basis of all personalities, whether of God, men or angels. The Absolute is thinking-reason ; or as Milton says, ' Reason is man's being.'

How has the true conception of Reason, and with it of Personality, been missed ! We quote two examples used by Dr. Stirling illustrating this : ' Hume says, " We never find two persons who think exactly alike, nor does the same person think exactly alike at any two different periods of time." ' ' Grote says, " Can it really be necessary to repeat that the reason of one man differs most materially from that of another ? " ' To which Stirling replies : ' Can it really be necessary to repeat that the reason of one man does not differ most materially from that of another ; but on the contrary, the reason of one man is essentially identical with that of another.' To which we need only add, men differ chiefly in what they at times falsely call reason, viz. in their fancies, conjectures, whims, imaginings, hypotheses, illogical theorizings and false inferences. Yet, notwithstanding these aberrations, it is worthy of note, how much men of all nations and ages agree in thought, thus indicating that there is but one reason. Probably, such a vast variety of false reasoning was never so rampant among educated people as at present, when much that is named reason is not reason, and much named religion is not religion. Even idolatry, so strongly repudiated and condemned in the Bible, is named religion. Evolution sets aside the teaching of Paul, which recognizes distinctly that man's religious knowledge began in a knowledge of the one true, eternal, living God, but *afterwards declined* into polytheism, and teaches that the original form of man's religious experience was fetishism (or mere animalism), passing through polytheism to monotheism, or rather, only to agnosticism. Paul teaches that men at first knew God, but afterwards ' changed the truth and glory of the incorruptible God into a lie, and worshipped and served the creature more than the Creator.' If the teaching of the evolutionists be true, the teaching of Paul and of the Bible generally must be false. To put the writings of Paul into competition with the best and greatest writers on evolution, or with the work of philologists, would be simply monstrous. It is difficult to understand how educated men—professed Christian believers—can so easily set aside Paul's express statements concerning man's original knowledge of God, in favour of the now generally accepted theory of the evolution of religion. The two views are utterly irreconcilable, or, at least any theory of reconciliation implies the rejection of whatever in the Bible does not appear to coincide with evolutionary theories. Nay, it implies that the doctrine of evolution is scientifically established, and that the doctrines of creation and miracle, and of monotheism as the original religious condition of man, as taught in the Bible, may be quietly ignored. Yet all these assumptions have no better foundation than what is called a good working hypothesis, and it is even assumed that no other explanation is possible.

We are obliged to go further and say, that what is implied *is*, there must be an entire reconstruction of the Bible, with the abrogation of much that, according to the goodwill and pleasure of a false view of The Right of Private Judgment, is considered superfluous. This term was first used principally in opposition to public, which at that time represented the judgment of the Church, to which all individual judgment was required without demur to submit. It was clearly seen that the judgment of the Church could not be relied on : that very many vital doctrines of the Christian Faith, the Faith as preached by Christ and His apostles, had by the Church been perverted and changed into gross errors : and that such erroneous doctrines necessarily tended to subvert rather than establish and promote the righteousness of God, and that a false faith had taken the place of true faith. But the individual or private judgment is often as full of gross error as the judgment of the Church. It is no sure proof that the judgment is either true or untrue, merely because it is the judgment of a majority or a minority, for in either it may be true, or it may be false. In the history of men, Churches and nations, it will not be doubted that there have been many true, and many false, judgments. It is in true logical reason itself that we must look for the sure criterion or principle of *right* judgment.

For confirmation of the fact that there is a true judgment, we first appeal to the teaching of Christ. He said, ' Judge not according to the appearance, but judge righteous judgment.' ' For judgment I am come into this world, that they which see not, might see, and that they which see might be made blind.' He boldly claimed that His judgment was always according to Truth : ' If I judge, My judgment is true ; for I am not alone, but I and My Father that sent Me.' This phrase is grounded on His oneness with the Father, for He said, ' I and My Father are one,' and, ' for I do always those things that please Him.' He claimed to be free from all error, as well as from all sin. We are aware that His appeal is not directly founded on what is now named the science of logical philosophy, but on what He Himself claimed to know with certainty; *nevertheless, it has an important bearing on the* PHILOSOPHY *of the Christian Religion and the divine authority of the Bible, and also on the possibility of all men being able to know with absolute certainty and to judge truly.* In this connection it is not unimportant to add the following words of Christ, as recorded by the Apostle John : ' Had ye believed Moses, ye would have believed Me ; for he wrote of Me. But if ye believe not his writings, how shall ye believe My words ? In the *light of these words* it is not difficult to see why the higher critics *do not know what to make of the fourth Gospel,* for when men begin their criticism with false principles of science and philosophy, it is no wonder that in endeavouring to harmonize the general teaching of the Bible with the principles from which they started, they find it necessary to treat teaching of the highest value as clever fiction merely because it does not fit in with their theory. The canons or rules of the Higher Criticism, as we have proved, are based on false science or logic. Criticism, to be worthy of confidence, must start from *sure* principles. ' The grounds,' says Wesley, ' must be true and right from which we draw conclusions ; for it is impossible to deduce truth from false premises.' To discard Moses as a person, is quite as difficult as to discard miracles, for in doing so, tremendous havoc is made both of the Old and New Testaments, and also of the belief in Christ, as the perfect God-man. Of what use is it to post-date the Pentateuch or to attribute the authorship to any other person than Moses so long as he is so often referred to in the Gospels and Epistles, and so long as Christ

is the predicted Prophet, the Just One, of whom the
Jews were the betrayers and murderers ? Apart
from the fourth Gospel, Luke tells us of Christ, that,
' beginning at Moses and all the Prophets, He expounded unto them in all the Scriptures, the things
concerning Himself.'

To expunge these references to Moses, or to treat
them as unreliable, because their teaching conflicts
with the ideas of the critics is contrary to all the
principles of true reason. The reasons for so dealing with the Bible cannot stand when the true principles of reason and of private judgment are properly
understood, for the theories of the Critics, as Hegel
says, ' contravene the best established facts of
history, and on scanty particulars put subjective
fancies in place of historical data.'

All true judgment contains the principle of true
or logical reason, which is the science of infinite
eternal Thought, and consists of infinite particularity
in essential, universal relation. Particularity is the
sphere of creation, and therefore of contingency and
chance—the battle-ground of free-will—wherein the
true and untrue exist. Reason, however, as the
ground-basis of true judgment is that which only
primarily concerns philosophy, for the untrue is
only the accidental, and not the necessary side of
existence. Lies, fraud, deceit, hypocrisy, envy and
injustice are not necessarily unavoidable forms of
existence (as, for example, men cannot be prevented
from lying and stealing) : indeed, they are untrue
to the core. To call such truths or truth merely
because they exist would be an untrue mode of
speech. It would also be untrue to say they had
no relation to truth and thought; and yet to call
injustice and error truth, would be false judgment,
while to declare them untrue would be true judg-

ment, because truth and reason are identical, and constitute in thought the eternal unchangeable foundation of all true judgment, in which the one and the many can alone find perfect agreement. The one absolute reason is alone the universal element of truth with which every particular judgment must be in essential harmony.

Material nature is, in general, identical with the body of man, which is so far changeable and transitory, or as Paul names it, 'temporal.' Thus, the body being one with nature, nature externally is the body of the Ego, of Thought, of the Concrete Notion, and so the body of God. But that which is externality merely, does not express the totality of Nature, for Nature has also an internal side. It is the same with God and man. Both externality and internality are essential to the existence of God, man, and Nature, as they each exist in a triple unity. This unity of the internal and external in man and God, has a vital bearing on the immortality of man. Paul teaches that both God and man are immortal, and yet he speaks of God as 'He who only hath immortality,' plainly recognizing that the immortality of man is essentially one with the immortality of God. As the body is the external, visible, mortal side of man, so Nature is the external, visible, mortal side of God : then, as Spirit is the internal, invisible, immortal side of man, so it is the internal, invisible, immortal side of God, because the self-consciousness and Infinite Thought of God is substantially the self-consciousness and infinite thought of man, who in this world is the only being made in the intellectual and moral image of God. What a vision of the greatness of man had Shakespeare when he said: 'What a piece of work is man! How noble in reason! How infinite in faculty!' It is only so

that man is in the image of God, and only so is the
immortality of man one with the immortality of
God. As the mortality of Nature does not render
impossible, or destroy the immortality of God, so the
mortality of man's body does not render impossible,
or destroy the immortality of man. When Paul said,
' We know that when this earthly house of our tabernacle is dissolved, we have a building of God, a
house not made with hands, eternal in the heavens,'
his knowledge was based on reason and revelation :
in part on the fact of the resurrection of Christ, and
in part on the great visions of God that were vouchsafed to him. He had no doubt of the bodily resurrection of Christ from the grave. ' The building in
the heavens ' is evidently that which he calls the
spiritual body, the same as the etherealized body of
Christ that ascended to heaven at the right hand of
God. Certainly the evidence for this is as valid as
that for the existence of what the physicist calls
universal ether. The unity of thought, spirit and
matter is a matter of everyday consciousness, and
reason tells us that in the highest sense it can never
be otherwise. Even though at present our relation
to the flesh is at times felt to be a burden, in which
we now and then groan a little, there is no evidence
that this will continue for ever, but rather the time
is coming when ' all tears shall be wiped from our
eyes.'

Bearing on this question of the unity of matter
and thought, and man's immortality, there is an
expression of Hegel's which, when properly understood, for clearness and simplicity cannot be well
surpassed. He says : ' God is therefore *for* Himself,
so far as He is Himself that that is *for* Him.' Now
what is it that is for God ? It is simply what the
Apostle means when he says, ' *for* all things are yours,

and ye are Christ's, and Christ is God's ' ; or, ' *for* whom are all things, and by whom are all things ' ; or ' by Him all things consist.' So we can say, equally with Hegel and Paul, Man is therefore *for* himself, so far as he is himself that that is *for* him—for without God and Nature, man is not man : and Nature is therefore *for* itself, so far as it is itself that that is *for* it—for without God and man, Nature is not Nature : each is only what it is in and through the threefold unity of all existence, in and through the internal and external unity of the categories of thought, con- stituting as they do the entire web, warp and woof of all existence, yet they are all different in themselves. So far as man and nature are one in their externality, they are perishable, but thought, in personality and self-consciousness, constitutes the unity of God, man and Nature. Thought, Spirit, God, is that that never was not. The perishableness of the manifold forms of material nature do not, in the least, derogate from the eternal necessity of the immateriality and immor- tality of absolute self-consciousness as the essence of the universe—for thought alone is intelligibly the First.

How Paul came to his knowledge of the immor- tality of the spiritual nature of man, whether by intuition, by revelation, or by a rational process of reflection, or by these three modes of thought com- bined, the philosophical logical process of Hegel is the real valid science of God and His universe, and the essential truth of the Christian Religion, for the Ego is the Absolute Ratio of Thought, and is the First and the Last. In its immanent Dialectic it is the dialectic, active and creative power in man and nature, in and through which nature in its external perishing is always renewed, so that even in its perishing it does not perish, but is eternal.

26

It is the manifestation of the free, eternal creation of Thought—the negation of the negation. The Ego in its inner pure negativity is the eternal self-create of All-in-All. In the Ego are the immaterial material forms of Nature, or the etherealized forms of matter. Thus simple negation is the dissolution of our earthly tabernacle, while the negation of the negation is expressed in the words, 'this corruptible shall put on incorruption, and this mortal shall put on immortality, and death shall be swallowed up in victory.' Death is simple negation, the first negation, while God, the Eternal tree of life, is the Eternal negation of the negation, the affirmative in all negation. In this unity we have the rational, essential, logical movement of thought, the Ego, the divine eternal Logos. Thus in every form of perishable matter there is an indestructible form and matter, unseparated and inseparable from the essential triplicity of thought, the Ego as the eternal personality of Being. The mere physicist, in his doctrine of Naturalism, proceeds in the various sciences in the belief that matter, energy and motion are indestructible, but overlooks the fact that Thought is even more palpably indestructible than any forms of matter, for the indestructibility of matter rests on the indestructibility of thought.

To assume that thought only begins with every new-born infant is monstrous, for it is in direct opposition to the most ordinary exercise of human reason. No, thought does not start into existence with the birth of the infant, for there is a divine as well as a human father; besides, the infant soon becomes aware of an infinite past and an infinite future. This is an infinite thought belonging only to God, and is sufficient proof that the Son of Man is the Son of God. As already stated, this thought of an infinite past is not a question of mere memory, for memory at best could only carry us back to our birth. Many animals possess memory, but they can never have a knowledge of the past prior to their birth. Reason-thought, not mere memory, assures us of an infinite past or of an infinite future, therefore thought does not begin with man as man in his temporal existence, or with infant as infant. Its original is in God with His external Son, the philosophy of which is in the science of the Ego, in which is found the unity of divine and human thought. Man, in his thought, does not merely rise to the infinite, he *is* infinite; or as the late Dr. Parker once said, ' Man has not a soul, he is a soul, but he has a body.' When fully examined, this furnishes the answer to the question, ' What is man and the Son of Man ? '

Christianity is essentially and emphatically, first of all, a revelation of the infinite nature of man. Thinking-reason is his real permanent quality; the other in man is Physical Nature, which is the other of himself, of Spirit. Spirit as thinking is man's true self. In his physical nature he is alterable ; in spirit, in thought, he continues the same identical self. In man there is a multiplicity of thoughts, subject to manifold variation, but in thought as his true being he is always one and the same. To know himself in spirit and in truth is the key to the knowledge of himself in his externality ; this applies equally to the internality and externality of God and Nature. Man is immediately at home with himself, and in thought he is immediately at home with God and Nature ; hence he has not to go out of himself to find a knowledge of God and Nature. Indeed, he cannot go outside his own thought ; all his thinking is within it; all that is relatively without is relatively within. When the question, ' What is man ? ' is properly

THE PHILOSOPHY OF SPIRIT

answered, the questions, ' What is God ? ' and ' What
is Nature ? ' will also be properly answered. This
does not imply an absolutely complete knowledge of
the infinitude of God, man and Nature, any more
than a true and exact knowledge of any branch of
mathematics means that, on the part of man, a further
knowledge thereof is impossible. Yet no science
has a more sure, fixed and definitely clear starting-
point than logical philosophy. Its original beginning
is thought, self-consciousness, personality, Ego, which
is man himself. But the question here is, how shall
philosophy begin from man himself ? or rather, how
or where in thought must it begin ? in and from
thought or the Ego, which is thought's own self?
There can be no doubt that Ego is thought, and the
real beginning of philosophy, but that is a very indefinite statement. A philosophy worthy of the name
must be logical and must furnish an exposition of the
Ego ; and since the Ego is thought, logic must be
the science of thought, and since thought is concrete,
it must be a logical system of the categories, because
they are at once both the matter and thought of the
Ego ; a complete system of which will constitute
the absolute logical Idea.

As we have said, Ego is the real beginning, but
logic must have another beginning, which is essentially one with the Ego itself, another, that is not
another. If this other beginning, the beginning of
logic, is not one with the Ego, then Ego could not
be the original beginning of the science of logic.
The Ego in its intuitive reflection within its own self,
sees at once there are many qualities that belong
essentially to its own activity, to its own nature.
Each of these is another in itself, that is not another,
for without these qualities named others, Ego would
only be an empty name, that is, the Ego is only real

and concrete through its categories.   The Ego, thinking its own self, finds itself face to face with thought ;
thus thought as thought itself is found to be both
subject and object in and unto itself ; but further, it
finds that thought is the middle term between the
subject-thought and the object-thought, and this
is the absolute triplicity that constitutes the essential
nature of thought, which is nothing else than the Ego,
or the I think.   As *think* is the activity of the I itself, it may be dropped, for the I is itself the absolute
Ego ; but if thought is required to give an exposition
of itself, the least it can say is, that it *is*.   Is, is the
same, then, as pure Being, and pure indefinite Being
is neither more nor less than pure Nothing.   In this
sense, Being is only an empty abstraction ; but
again, it is absolutely concrete, for the term stands
for *all that is ;* everything is Being.   As such, it
includes thought, for since thought is, it is being.   If
we abstract Being from thought, then nothing that
can be named thought is left.   In spite of all this
abstracting, Absolute Concrete Thought and Absolute
Concrete Being are still matters of fact in absolute
relation, and they are identity in difference.   The
process of logical development is the process of logical
thought, and since thought is being, it is at the same
time the process of Being.   We must carefully note
that, while Hegel is explaining becoming, being, and
nothing, he is explaining the nature and process of
thought, notion, idea, Ego.   So Becoming is the
logical dialectic development of the Ego, and consequently the dialectic evolution of Being and Notion
in their unity in human knowledge.   The Ego as
thought, as the logic of thought, in the forms of
notion, judgment, syllogism, is never absent from his
mind ; the process is always his dialectic, or what he
otherwise names the pure negativity, which is at

once both 'the negation,' and 'the negation of the negation,' the absolute affirmative. If negation, ceasing to be, or perishing were the ultimate or end of all action in the being of thought, then existence in its totality would cease to be, or rather existence could never have been, or have come to be. Thought in its activity is negation, and essentially the negation of the negation, the pure negativity as the dialectic movement of thought's own self, which means that the Ego as Thought, self-consciousness, spirit, personality, or whatever named, is in itself a 'Self-create.' Then, if whatever is, is in its purest abstraction Being, it is nothing, and Nothing is Being, for it certainly is a thought. Nothing is a name or noun found in all dictionaries ; it is not a mere fancy ; it is used in all sciences, and is therefore not a mere metaphysical freak ; it is closely allied in use to ' No ' and ' Not.' Without such words no subject could in speech be made intelligible ; so it is that all affirmation is negation. A point is properly defined as that which is without magnitude, or without dimension. If so, then it is nothing—a definite nothing. Yet it is, and is so sure and definite that it is treated as the starting-point in the science of geometry. Before men laugh at Hegel, then, for making Nothing, Abstract Being, and Abstract Thought identical, they would do well to examine and see how far their own special science rests on this same 'ridiculed beginning' for its security. What we may name the point, wherein water becomes ice, is the same as nothing, and is an example of what ' nothing ' means. To say there is nothing between water and ice is correct, but such nothing is Being between the two. It is a limit, and as such, is universal, for everything is only what it is through its limit, that is, through what it is not. Therefore, as Being is universal, Nothing

as limit is everywhere, separating and uniting everything ; it is also the same universal in and through
the inner negativity of thought, wherein All is One and
All Many, in absolute unity.   On the surface, Hegel's
becoming has too much the appearance of having
been derived from a transition of the pure abstractions of Being into Nothing, and of Nothing into Being,
but reflection shows that he derived it from his dialectic, and his dialectic from the essential activity of
thought as the creative power of the Ego, especially
when we see that Being, with him, was the Being of
the Notion, the Concrete Notion, or Ego.   Dialectic
with Hegel, as given by Stirling, ' was the living
internality of an Ego ' as the ' self-moving soul, the
principle of all natural and spiritual life,' the soul of
all ' becoming.'   It was Hegel's new view of dialectic
that made his logic living, and no longer the formal,
mechanical, external affair it had been in the hands of
Kant, Fichte and Schelling.   The value of Hegel's
philosophy, however, must not be estimated only
by his exposition of Being, Nothing, and Becoming,
though this is deep and good and cannot be ignored
in its vital bearing on his system of logical philosophy,
and on science in general.   Material things are Being
and are in a perpetual state of transition, in which
their limit is the Nothing of Being, at once uniting
and dividing the totality of . Being both internally
and externally.   Nothing, then, is not only a negative movement and determination of particular
definite things, but the universal negative determination of the absolute whole.   Limit is as universal as
Being itself, because without a real limit, neither
change, Being nor Thought are in any sense possible.
Hegel's philosophy of Being is not a mere exposition
of something external, or even of his Notion, but of
the Ego ; that is, it is the exposition of God as abso-

lute personality. Neither the philosophy of Kant nor Fichte had come to that.

Hegel names logic ' the pure essence as the system of pure reason and so the expression or exposition of God as He is in His eternal essence before the creation of nature or a single finite spirit.' Thought is self-conscious Notion. Hegel says, ' thoughts are three-fold : categories, reflexions, notions. The first two constitute objective logic, the third, subjective logic.' In their truth, they are at once objective and subjective, since in their unity they constitute the living substance of the Ego ; and what is this but the living. dialectic, creating power of the Ego's self ? If so, is not logic more properly defined as the Ego, as the Eternal Spirit in its dialectic process, creating nature and finite spirits ; not merely as ' the expression of God, as He is in His eternal essence before the creation,' etc., but rather as He is the present and eternal Creator of nature and finite spirits ? The word ' before ' seems to imply that God was once not a Creator, and therefore not God. Hegel here seems to contradict his own words, ' Without a world, God is not God,' that is, without a world, God is not Creator, and therefore is not God, for the Dialectic of Hegel is the logical fullness of the love, life and thought of God as the eternal creative power mani-festing itself in the universe—thus the contradiction is only apparent. It may be said, Hegel's system of philosophy began in and from the Ego when he discovered that logic was nothing else than the living thought of the Ego's own self as revealed in man's consciousness. Whilst logic was regarded as a kind of dead, intellectual, mechanical invention devised by the wit of man, into which the objects of Nature had somehow to fit themselves, it could only be viewed in general as a barren theory. Indeed, so long as logic is regarded as a dead thing and not as the living Spirit and principle of the universe, no progress, in the best sense, can be made in the knowledge of God, man and nature.

In order to develop this all-embracing living principle which he had discovered, Hegel evidently found it no easy task to reduce all the categories of the Being of Thought into a rational, organic, co-articulated system. We owe to Stirling the discovery of the true meaning of Hegel's Dialectic. He also makes it clear that Hegel had two beginnings. His first is in his Phenomenology of Spirit, in which he starts from ' sense-certainty,' ' the conviction of knowledge which is given by sense.' In man the certainty of sense-consciousness is in self-consciousness and reason. There is, however, associated with it an element of illusion, and yet a real knowledge of innumerable matters of fact is thus gained. The ground of certainty in knowledge has a vital relation to consciousness. So far as the bare fact of ' sense-certainty ' goes, Hegel was on sure ground. But the animal possesses the certainty of sense-consciousness. The dog knows with certainty by sight the difference between a man and a sheep, and a sheep, by hearing, knows the difference between the bleating of lambs and the barking of a dog. So far as sense-certainty goes, the man and the animal are on the same level. On this level alone, science is impossible. On this level, there is no Infinite, no Ego, no I, and without the I thinking itself, and thinking its Being, no beginning and progress in science can be made. Hegel tells us that sense-certainty, so far as truth is concerned, is the most abstract and poorest knowledge, yet, it is knowledge, because it is, or exists, and is pure being of the pure I. With Hegel it is the most abstract being of the most abstract I, because this

sense-certainty is in the I, and the I is in it. Because
I is in consciousness, there is more in it than the sense-
certainty of the animal. The difference between
the two certainties is that the animal is sure, but man
knows he is sure, because in man's consciousness
there is a self-consciousness. In Hegel's dialectic of
sense, into which all must be resolved, there is certainty, being, I, now, here, one, many, All, unessential, essential consciousness, self-consciousness, reason,
show or Schein of reality, spirit, religion, and Das
absolute Wissen (knowing), with much else. It appears
a bundle of entangled, mixed threads from whence he
is endeavouring to unwind the scientific thread of
truth. He has endeavoured to prove that everything
finds its centre and basis in ' sense-certainty,' it
being the point where object and subject, being and
thought, are at one in absolute and essential unity
and identity, and also because all activity has its
ultimate source in the immanent dialectic movement
of the Notion or Ego. ' Certainty is truth and object
in consciousness, and as such is knowledge in the Ego,
which knowledge is not only for us, but corresponds
to the Notion, or its Notion.' Our aim here is not
to give Hegel's process of thought from bare sense-
certainty to absolute knowledge; there are, however, in the process a great number of invaluable
statements, helpful in the search for a knowledge of
the Truth. His Phenomenology was a marvellous
production for a man only thirty-seven years old,
but it is evident that before long he was *not* satisfied
either with his beginning from sense, or with his
process therefrom, for in 1812, five years after its
issue, appeared the first volume of his logic, and in
1816, the third volume. In his Logic he entirely
remodelled his system. To reduce his work to a
system of logic involved a great change in form.

From the Propädeutik we learn (1808–12) he was evolving his Logic. His empirical beginning and, in a sense, his empirical process, is entirely set aside. It is now a science of pure thought, which he names the Begriff (Notion); as a science of Logic he names it Idee (Idea), though in the background of his mind he always means the Ego, for strictly speaking, by Logic he meant the science of God, Nature, and Spirit. His Logic begins from pure Being, Absolute Being, in which form and matter are identical, and at once both mediate and immediate; so the dialectic movement (Becoming) is present from the first, becoming at every step more concrete until the absolute concrete Spirit is attained. The Notion of Being is the Notion of God, who is at once both Thought and Being, since neither God nor Thought can be without Being. A Beingless God and a Beingless Thought are absurdities, and since a processless thinker or thought is absurd, so also is a processless Being; this process is the logical dialectic of Hegel. It is the dialectic of the Ego, of God, of Man, of Nature, of Thought, and of Spirit, for more than one logical dialectic in the entire universe is not possible. It is fundamentally what is generally recognized as the reign of universal law, reduced to, and presented as a logical system. There is no object in which this process is absent : it is present in the movements of the heavenly bodies, in every man, animal and plant, in every form of inorganic matter, in every germ, molecule or atom. It is the life and soul of Thought and Spirit, in and through which alone Logic is a living system of thought and reason, and without which Ego is not Ego, and ' I ' is not ' I.' The dialectic is the deepest secret of Hegel's system of philosophy ; it is the true, inner, pure negativität, for without negativity, neither change nor movement is possible. It is the secret living power that can alone intelligibly explain the transformation and conservation of energy. But it is in reality not a secret, for it is consciously present as an intuitive fact in the thought of every man; he knows of no power greater and better than thought-power. In thought there is knowledge, and knowledge is power or energy; yet only so because it is thought, which includes, pervades and overlaps All in a higher sense than does time, space, or anything else. Since man is thought, spirit, he only needs to know himself to be assured of this truth and fact: he is Ego, which is the beginning and end of all that is. It is Kant's Ego that 'raises man infinitely above the reasonless brutes,' notwithstanding his imperfect apprehension and account of its real nature. Kant's Ego is Hegel's Notion or Ego, and the real original beginning of his philosophy. It is also absolutely concrete, in spite of all he says about sense-certainty, abstract being, abstract Notion or the Abstract I; for in their truth, none of these are abstract. Indeed, he constantly speaks of them as concrete. The abstract with him is always the untrue; so whether he begins from sense-certainty, or from pure abstract Being, or the Concrete Ego, he needlessly involves himself in unnecessary mystification. The abstract forms of Being are only modes or aspects in which the absolute concrete Ego is viewed, or in which it thinks itself. It is only in this sense that either sense-certainty or pure Being is abstract. He really begins and ends (at least in his mind) with the Concrete Ego, or as he preferred to call it, the Concrete Notion, or only, the Notion. He may have said to himself, if I say plainly that when I say Notion, Being, I mean the Ego, or God, I shall only shock and repulse my readers; they may say it can never amount to more than a hair-brained product; so if I begin, like Locke and Kant, from sense, and show that sense-certainty is essentially thought and reason-certainty, that will answer the question, ' How are synthetic judgments *á priori* possible ? ' and at the same time prove that there is no need for a supposed non-ego. He failed, however, to make himself understood. He next began his Logic from pure Being, the abstract ' I ': but his system, whatever its beginning might be, involved the principle of the absolute unity of Nature and Thought, but since the general persuasion was that such unity was impossible, he yet failed to be understood. At this we need not wonder, since it necessitated a complete change of view from the generally-accepted rationalized system of the nature of logical science. The substantial forms of nature and thought could not be altered, nor did Hegel's system require such a change. The system of philosophy then in vogue resembled a great, irregularly-built city in partial ruin, on which a new city, according to a new and well-arranged plan, had to be built. To reduce the universe to a consistent system of thought, as was done by Hegel, is probably the greatest feat ever accomplished by man. In the words of Stirling : ' Hegel saw that in actual fact, Self-consciousness was the greatest thing in existence ; accordingly he made it the principle of his philosophy, and explained the world to be a continuous chain of attempts to realize the form and rhythm of Self-consciousness up from the most distant circumferential crassitude into the central life of the Absolute Spirit—God.' This could not be on mere mathematical reason ; a universe without self-consciousness would mean no more than a blank or dead thing. ' Hegel regards a thinking being as the ultimate essential drop of the vast crass universe.' ' Properly looked at, this crassitude will be seen to rise in circles, ever less and less crass, towards this drop—Ego. In effect he says, this circumferential crassitude involves the idea of externality, while an Ego involves the idea of internality as boundless intussusception.' ' Externality is an infinite out and out of infinite difference under irrational necessity (physical contingency, etc.) : internality is an infinite in and in of infinite identity under rational necessity (Freedom, true Freewill).' This out and in of thought, at once subject and object, then, is the infinite Quality of Infinite Being.

In spite of the apparent pure abstractness of the beginning of his Logic, it is thoroughly concrete, and his aim is to show, when his system is completed, that it is the Absolute Concrete Spirit of the totality of Being which he names the Notion (Begriff) but ought to have named the Ego. Thought as the Absolute is both finite and infinite ; as finite it is measure, as infinite it is measureless; on one side ' transient,' on the other permanent. Everything has its measure, the identity of quality and quantity, which within certain limits may be increased or decreased. Measure, like the other stages of Being, is a definition of the Absolute, in which God is the measure of all things, He having appointed to everything its bound. The measureless infinite is itself the unity of quantity and quality. In the process and dialectic of measure, these two pass into each other (for each is implicitly the other) and become explicit as positive and negative. Being in the form of positive and negative is expressly relative, and therefore essence, for the relation is permanent, since the one has no meaning without the other ; thus essence is the result of the dialectic of quality, quantity, measure. Essence is an important stage in the dialectic of Concrete Logic. This is not the mere lialectic of abstract Being or of abstract Ego, but the lialectic of the concrete unity of the being of the Ego n the absolute ratio of Thought. It is the relative, ind implies identity; without identity all notion of relation is abrogated, therefore identity is such only n its difference, apart from which it would be a word itterly devoid of meaning. Thus there is no such thing as ' an excluded middle term ' either in existence or in thought, for this would imply the destruction of the unity of existence as contained in the notion of universal gravitation, and would render impossible any system of logic, inductive or deductive : while neither existence nor thought could be possible. The ground of all existence is in the unity of identity and difference, and the only intelligible ground of this unity is in Thought itself, which when properly looked into is the sufficient Ground of Everything, and that is God. In beginning an explanation of existence from Thought, we are not beginning from a hypothesis, but from an absolutely indisputable fact. The Being of Thought is the only fact that is immediately present in man as universal identity in infinite difference. Essence as thought is the absolute, that is, Absolute Being; as identity in difference, it is infinite reflection of itself in its other. As difference, it is existence in general wherein every fact stands in relation to every other fact. A fact is something done, and so Hegel says, ' Existence is Being which issues from the ground, and Being is existence.' Yes, but he means that being and existence are thought in its difference—the Thing in its properties, which in thought is the true thing in itself, and therefore not unknown, for thought is self-knowing in its differences as reflected into itself. Thus everything has its essential matter and form in Thought.

This brings us to the question of actuality of

appearance in thought. Thought is actuality, and apart from it as the all-seeing eye, appearance is an empty name. The world is an appearance, but it is the appearance or external manifestation of thought in consciousness, just as self-consciousness is the internal manifestation of thought in the Ego's own self. The appearance is at once both matter and form, content and form, in essential relation, for a matterless form or a formless matter is impossible. In this there is a distinction between philosophy and other sciences. The latter are viewed as finite, and derive their content from without, therefore the content is not recognized as formed from within. This distinction disappears in philosophy because philosophy deals directly with the infinite, even though it includes the finite. If content is limited to sense-perception, then logic and philosophy are devoid of content; just as a book without content is without thought, or as the content of a book is the thought it contains, so the matter and form of existence is the matter and form of thought. Thus when the essentiality of appearance is explicitly stated, it appears in immediate relation in the bond of thought as the Whole and its parts, for the content is the whole and consists of its parts. Externally it appears in parts, internally it appears as an actual infinite Whole; or, in other words, in human thought God reveals Himself in the fullness of His glory both internally and externally as one infinite Whole. When Nature is looked at as a whole through God in human thought, it is seen to be full of glorious Ideas in an absolute unity. Viewed otherwise, a ' macula ' here and there may obscure the mental vision, as was the case with Darwin when he wrote to Hooker, ' What a book a devil's chaplain might write on the clumsy, wasteful, blundering, low and horrible works of Nature.' Like

Laplace, Darwin had no need of God in his system of thought. The latter fancied he could explain by Natural Selection all this so-called ' waste ' and ' blundering.' The former accounted for all by pure mathematical reasoning. Hegel refused both'modes, and held that quantity was both discrete and continuous : and in a further developed form it is the whole and parts ; to it belongs possibility as the unessential essentiality, contingency, accident or chance, in which the process of necessity is so far blind. But this does not mean that design is not an all-pervading factor in existence, and that its ultimate aim is not a realized fact. Even men realize their aims in life, in spite of accidents—much more does God in Nature realize His purpose, which only perverted minds fail to see, notwithstanding the apparent lavish waste ; indeed, the ' waste ' is rather superabundant provision. Possibility in part explains how the unessential is essential ; thus it is unessential whether a particular field be planted with turnips or potatoes, but it is essential that it should be possible, in certain circumstances, to plant it with some kind of vegetation that will be useful as food. As a matter of fact, men often revel, in their imagination, in all manner of absurd ' possibilities ' which in the nature of things are impossible : but the constitution of Nature must not be blamed for such vagaries. Christian men and philosophers have, and have had, their vagaries, and even our scientists have not been behind in contributing to the sum of human vagaries. ' Nevertheless, the foundation of God standeth sure,' in His unceasing activity manifesting His infinite power, wisdom, justice and grace throughout the great whole and in every part. The man who in thought banishes God from Nature, who thinks God is unknowable, or who views Nature as a huge ' hotch-

potch,' is much to be pitied for his intellectual blindness ; such blindness is his own creation and choice
however much he is tempted to cast the blame on
others, on Nature or God. Man must choose, for
that is his nature, but choice is only possible because
possibility belongs to the very essence of the existence
of thought. That is so because, as Hegel says,
freedom is the truth of necessity, because man is a
spirit, and the essence of spirit is freedom. It is the
necessity of man's being to be choosing every moment,
and his choice determines his character : this is
rational freedom. To choose the impossible is wil-
ful stubbornness, and to choose wilfully another
man's property is crime. Thus necessity, possibility
and freedom are in essential relation ; in the con-
formity of the particular to the universal will, lies
the true freewill. Hence it would be folly for every
man in a nation to choose to be its king, or president,
since it is only possible for one person to occupy that
position. If a man conceives the possibility of the
sun not rising to-morrow morning, he is only deluding
himself by a vain possibility ; but there are before
every man great possibilities, if he will only choose
in a rational manner to make himself worthy of them.
He must not, however, repine over what he fancies
he has not, but must make a good and proper use of
what he has and is, especially remembering that he
is a person made ' in the image of God.' To do
otherwise is to act like a child crying for the moon.
Possibility must not be fanciful, but real, actual,
rational. It is therefore most important to grasp
clearly what are the true conditions of genuine possibility, which is impossible apart from actuality,
necessity, and free activity ; but the most blessed and
certain condition is that freedom rules at the centre
and circumference of the universe.

What, then, is substance ?   What is causality ?
What is reciprocity ?   Each exists in and through
relation.   Substance is that which constitutes a thing
what it is, and therefore is its essence.   It is that
which is permanent in the midst of all change.   It is
the absolute essential principle of the universe in all
its infinite diversity, and consequently is of the most
superlative value—the content of all the riches of
the universe.   It is that which cannot not be.   In
its accidentality it is that which in Nature is alterable and transitory ; as that which is permanent, it
is the absolute self-consciousness of the universe, which
is God, Thought, Personality, Ego, I-Me.   As Ego,
God is certainly that which is most worthy to be
named substance ; but God is more than the Idea of
substance, he is Subject, Personality, or according
to Hegel, ' the absolute Person.'   Substance, then,
is not some dead, inactive, unconscious power, but
the living, active, creative intelligence of the universe.
Creation, as seen in Nature, constitutes the externality of the substance as the sum-total of its accidents, in which substance and accident stand in
necessary relation.   In this relation of substance and
accident, substance is the cause, and the accident
an effect—an actual something, but only a created
actuality.   So far, the cause has passed into the
effect ; they are different and yet identical, for the
same substance is in the effect that is in the cause.
If the substance as cause is not in the effect, then there
is no necessary relation between the two.   This
identity is evident in finite substances ; thus rain
(the cause) is the self-same existing water as the
moisture (effect).   Water as a finite substance may
pass into another finite substance, as ice or vapour,
and so on, ad infinitum.   In the merging of one finite
substance, or accidental, into another, there arises

not only the sequence of cause and effect, but also of action and reaction, or Reciprocity. The link here is the principle of identity, which reveals the secret necessity and infinite connection in the circulation of the finite qualities of substance through all kinds of causality and reciprocity. Here, says Hegel, ' We are on the threshold of the Notion,' or what is more properly named the Ego, or, to use the still more light-giving expression of Stirling, the ' I-Me,' which is the Spirit and Thought of the universe revealed in the finite spirit of man.

Hegel says, ' This truth of necessity is freedom ; and the truth of substance is the Notion.' Also, ' The Notion has, therefore, Substance as its immediate presupposition ; or substance, is that in itself which the Notion is as in manifestation. The dialectic movement of Substance through causality and reciprocity outwards, is therefore the immediate genesis of the Notion, and by this genesis its Becoming is represented.' By manifestation of the Notion, he means the light of Thought's own self, which is the essence of freedom. Abstract necessity is not freedom, but freedom implies necessity. A crime may be called a free act, but it is an action in which the principle of true freedom is violated. A good man does not feel that this is necessary in order to retain his true freedom. ' Where the Spirit of the Lord is, there is liberty.' Thus the most perfect principle of causality, reciprocity and freedom is in the infinite thought of God as manifested in the spirit of man, for thought, as thought, is infinite, whether in God or in man. With Hegel the Notion was understood to express this unity of the divine and human nature. It is a term, however, that only obscurely expresses the infinite thought of the Ego ; or what is the same, the infinite Personality of God.

As the exposition of the Ego is the exposition of Personality, the philosophy of Spirit may be thus summed up—

In its essential nature personality is the Spirit of infinite Thought : man is only a Person because he possesses this thought, in and by which he is in conscious reciprocal relation in universal self-consciousness, that is, in its own self infinite thought. The unity expressed by the I-Me is the unity of the divine and human nature in the infinite thought of man. I is me, and me is I ; I is Ego, and Ego is me ; therefore I and Me are one in the Absolute of Thought. I is Subject, me is Object, and Thought is ratio as middle term embracing absolutely both I and Me. This, then, is the absolute categorical triplicity that constitutes thought in its eternal, essential, infinite nature. So far as man is a product of nature, he is not so in the same sense as finite perishing objects, for man in himself is conscious that he is in thought an infinite self-consciousness. Cause, effect and reciprocity, in finite objects, have their place in thought, but in thought thinking itself, it meets its own other in itself, and thus realizes its perfect freedom in the reciprocal consciousness of the Ego, or I-Me, for I is always double, which is not the case with anything else. The hardness of necessity is dissolved in thought, in the perfect unity of God and man in love ; in the unity of loving-thought as in husband and wife, wherein the two are one flesh ; in the unity of the Spirit in the Church, wherein all the members are one body in Christ ; and in the unity of a Christianized State.

The Mission of Christianity is the Christianizing of all States, or in the words of Paul, ' To make all men see what is the fellowship of the mystery, which from the beginning of the world hath been hid in God, who created all things by Jesus Christ.'

Lightning Source UK Ltd.
Milton Keynes UK
UKOW041334110313

207455UK00001B/119/P